THE
MID-CAREER
SUCCESS
GUIDE

THE MID-CAREER SUCCESS GUIDE

Planning for
the Second Half
of Your
Working Life

Sally J. Power

PRAEGER

Westport, Connecticut
London

Library of Congress Cataloging-in-Publication Data

Power, Sally J., 1947–
  The mid-career success guide : planning for the second half of
your working life / Sally J. Power.
     p.   cm.
  Includes bibliographical references and index.
  ISBN 0-275-98801-5 (alk. paper)
  1. Career changes—United States—Management. 2. White collar workers—
United States. 3. Mid-career—United States. I. Title.
  HF5384.P69 2006
  650.1084'40973—dc22   2006022461

British Library Cataloguing in Publication Data is available.

Library of Congress Catalog Card Number: 2006022461
ISBN: 0-275-98801-5

First published in 2006

Praeger Publishers, 88 Post Road West, Westport, CT 06881
An imprint of Greenwood Publishing Group, Inc.
www.praeger.com

Printed in the United States of America

The paper used in this book complies with the
Permanent Paper Standard issued by the National
Information Standards Organization (Z39.48–1984).

10   9   8   7   6   5   4   3   2   1

Contents

Preface   vii

Key Terms   xi

1   Introduction: How the Career Landscape Has Changed   1

2   Four New Strategies for Career Management:
    The "Employability Plus" Model   13

3   Success Strategy #1: Articulating a Personalized
    Work Focus   29

4   Success Strategy #2: Learning about the Near Future
    of Your Work in the Multiple-Employer Environment   53

5   Success Strategy #3: Taking Action to Shape Your Career   83

6   Success Strategy #4: Managing Your Career Cycle   117

7   Epilogue: Changing the Deal   145

Appendix: Career Management Resources by Janice Kragness   153

Suggested Reading   175

Notes   181

Index   195

Preface

This book arises out of my own decision to redirect my career. I had spent the majority of my earning life focused on teaching and helping to build a successful, part-time MBA program at my university. I had always thought I wanted to eventually be an administrator, but a two-year administrative assignment showed me that, although I was a successful manager, I did not get the emotional payoffs from it that I had expected. I wanted to find something I really enjoyed doing, and I wanted more employment options during the last twenty-plus years of my career.

After much thought and reflection I decided I wanted to build on my current experience but become a content expert in some specialty. The next task was to decide where to focus, so I began to read broadly using interest as my guide. What my reading eventually began to center around were the major shifts occurring in employment dynamics and their effects on individuals. These changes were already having wide-ranging, negative impacts on many people. Real incomes (i.e., after adjusting the figures for inflation) had been stagnant or declining for the majority of Americans beginning in the 1970s, and the numbers of individuals affected by this trend was growing significantly. Fewer and fewer workers were getting benefit packages. Downsizing was becoming a routine management tactic. And increasing numbers of workers—not just unskilled and blue-collar workers but white-collar professionals and managers as well—were having trouble getting new jobs comparable to the ones they had lost.

Through my study of management, I could see why these changes were occurring, but I was very concerned about their long-term ramifications for our society. For this reason I began to think about what would need to happen to reverse some of these trends. The result of that focus and of much reading and thinking, talking and experimenting is this book.

The book is focused on white-collar workers who are in mid-career. Defining "mid" anything is quite difficult.[1] What we consider middle age is changing as the average lifetime extends. Middle class has been defined on the basis of many things—for example, income or home ownership.[2] And mid-career has similar difficulties.[3] Here is how I define mid-career: It is the period in an earning career that begins *after* an individual has moved through those first years of orientation into the full-time, adult workforce—after the individual's first round of experimentation with different types of jobs and employers. The period starts when the person has settled into a type of work in which that person believes she will be happy for the foreseeable future. For those who have studied Super's theory of career stages,[4] it is after his "establishment" stage. For me, mid-career lasts until the individual has either made the psychological decision to "coast" into retirement or leaves the earning workforce.

I decided to focus this book on white-collar earners. It is true that those with fewer skills and less formal education are also suffering as a result of the changes in our economic system, but there are many people already focused on their situation. Many people believe that white-collar workers can take care of themselves. After all, they are some of the most educated individuals in our society, and they tend to have more resources than most. Yet, I think that national statistics, articles in the popular press, and many of the academic studies that have been done show that many in this group are struggling. Furthermore, the number of white-collar workers negatively affected seems to be growing with each economic recession. As you will read, I do not think that the way to deal most successfully with the impacts of the changes in employment dynamics is obvious to most.

The second reason for focusing on white-collar workers is that my proposed model for proactive response to the changes in the earning world is still fairly abstract, and it relies on the ability of individuals to move into new activities or to give old activities a new twist. I think that white-collar workers as a group are the most able to understand the model in its present form and use it to their benefit. If this approach helps a significant group of these individuals, then I expect that a number of individuals and organizations will move to provide a more formalized infrastructure that will make the needed information and this model more accessible to more individuals.

This is a book focused on a new kind of career and on a new kind of career management. While this model can accommodate those interested in learning what is needed to "move up" at their current employer or one very similar—that is, the traditional organizational career model—it is more focused on how individuals can manage their careers to build them in many different directions, not just up. And while I do include some thoughts on preparing to own your own business because there are so many individuals who say that that is what they want to do in the second half of their earning careers, this book is not focused primarily on how to become an independent professional or free agent.

This book is primarily aimed at employees in the middle and upper-middle levels of medium and large organizations. It is likely these employees will need to seek employment with new employers repeatedly in the future. Furthermore, greater competition for jobs and the accelerated pace of change in the earning world means that the way people should manage their careers for these transitions needs to change as well.

I have received a lot of help in writing this book, not only from people who have known that they were being helpful, but also from many who have not. I have read and pondered many more books and articles on this subject than appear in the endnotes and the Suggested Reading essay, even though I have tried to wedge direct references to many of the most important books and articles into them. Without the work of all of these scholars, I could not have written this book. Also, from 1986 to 2004 I taught an MBA course that had as its major assignment the writing of a personal growth statement. The statement's purpose was for each student to describe what he or she wanted to accomplish in his or her career and life and draft a plan for moving forward toward those goals. The students in this course were virtually all working adults, and a significant number of them could be classified as being in mid-career. Teaching that course gave me the chance to watch over 1,000 individuals grapple with many of the same types of career challenges that are the focus of this book.

I am sure that many of my ideas came as a result of reading and thinking about the creative solutions some of these students developed, although I may not be able to say exactly who showed me what. I have worked with a number of other working adults in recent years, and they have taught me a lot as well. The vast majority of stories that I tell in this book to illustrate various points come from these experiences, although the names have been changed, and any identifying details have been disguised to maintain confidentiality.

I want to thank some people in particular. Mark Savickas wrote a letter urging me to work on a book early in my transition to becoming an expert on mid-career development. That letter is still under the glass on my writing desk. I have been an active participant in the National Career Development Association's (NCDA) national conferences since 2000, and I have learned a great deal about the challenges of working with people in mid-career from my many colleagues at those conferences. In particular, Ray Palmer, Associate Dean and Director of Business Placement and Career Services, has been an important colleague who has helped me develop my ideas over our years of presenting programs at NCDA conferences. Janice Kragness, who has written the appendix for this book, has also been an important partner in developing some of my ideas. In addition, I want to thank all the librarians and staff at Keffer Library and the interlibrary loan librarians for their help.

Craig Cox was the person who first taught me how to write for a general audience, and he has been an incredibly important coach and mentor in the production of this book. I also want to thank my friends who listened and supported me when I was frustrated at various points in the process. A few people have actually gone the extra mile and read drafts of the book and deserve special recognition. They are: Ray Palmer, Sherry Sullivan, Barbara Nelson, and Nathan Dell. Finally, thanks to Steve Piersante for connecting me up with Nick Philipson, my editor. He and the others at Greenwood Publishing Group have been a major help during the publication process. While I have received a lot of help, I take full responsibility for the final product and for any shortcomings you may find.

This book argues that people with earning careers need to adjust how they manage them in mid-career because of how our global economy has developed. Rather than describing in general terms how career management should look now, I have provided pragmatic detail about how daily behaviors and beliefs need to change. I think that readers will find that these changes are feasible. Further, I hope they also find that the arguments for why these ideas work motivate them and lead them toward happier lives and more fulfilling earning careers.

Key Terms

Because this book describes a new approach to mid-career management, I want to highlight some of the terms and phrases I will be using and give readers a basic grasp of the ideas behind them.

Career: The series of jobs individuals have and their perceptions and meanings of their experiences. This definition is very similar to definitions put forth by major career researchers including Schein in 1991 and Hall in 2002 (see note 5 in chapter 3 for exact citations).

Mid-Career: Mid-career is more a state of mind than a phase of life that begins and ends at certain ages. In this book, I will consider individuals in mid-career when they have finished that first period of experimentation with different kinds of work and have also been through an initial learning period about how the earning world works. Mid-career is often marked by individuals committing themselves to a particular type of work for the foreseeable future. Of course, their commitment to the work may evolve or change completely as time passes—it is the nurturing of that evolution or the management of that change that is the focus of this book.

Career Success: This book uses an individualized definition of success that asks each individual to determine what combination of intrinsic and extrinsic rewards are most important at various times while moving through his or her earning career. Rewards from a career are more than just monetary. They include fulfilling interests, making contributions, creating positive personal meaning, and having positive lifestyle impacts. The blend of these types of rewards, including the weight of each, would be different for different individuals. This is more highly individualized than many definitions used in the past, which focus on societal cues for success such as hierarchical position, income, or status in society. Also, it is broader and recognizes that your earning career cannot be easily divided from the rest of your life, particularly as you get older. This newer definition seems fitting in an increasingly diverse society, where types of employment opportunities and mobility among employers are becoming more frequent. This definition also allows people a greater potential for self-actualization.

Employability: The ability to get another job based on employment you have had. This ability to get another job does not include the assurance that your skills and knowledge will be in demand at other employers or that you will be offered comparable salary or benefits.

Employability Plus: The ability to repeatedly get other jobs that you will enjoy at the same level or at a level of greater rewards.

Personalized Work Focus (PWF): An individual's work is the primary contribution the individual can make or wants to develop herself to make, to potential or actual employers. The concept of "work" is broader than a job; it identifies a theme, either among a series of jobs that the individual has had and wants to continue to pursue, or that the individual wants to pursue going forward in her career. Your work is made possible by the knowledge, skills, and experience you take with you from employer to employer. You own these things.

Work Arena: The work arena is the larger context in which an individual's work exists and includes the major ways that the content of the work is shaped so that it fits into the larger flow of providing products and services to society. Because there are significant overlaps in the knowledge needed for various roles within a work arena, it provides a way of generating options for employment. See Figure 3.1 for a graphic presentation of the abstract components of the work arena.

Bridging: Using your current knowledge, skills, and experience to help you change work units and/or employers so you can get access to new learning opportunities as your career interests evolve. This is a prime way that people in mid-career can begin to make a major career change while maintaining their income.

Career-Management Intensity: This is a rough categorization of how involved an individual is in his independent career management for any particular period of time. It is determined by comparing an individual's current job with the personalized work focus he has articulated. Individuals in mid-career have many competing life interests and responsibilities. Furthermore, many have found work that they enjoy and are satisfied with the rewards they receive. Also, their work and employer may be relatively stable. These factors should be prime considerations when individuals determine their career-management intensity. There are three major intensity categories:

Maintainers: These are people who enjoy their current work focus and are satisfied with the rewards provided by their earning careers. Their level of career-management intensity is the lowest, but in today's turbulent economy they still need to pay attention to how the work is changing and/or to what is happening to employers in their preferred location so that their worth as employees is maintained.

Builders: These are people in a phase of their career who want to build on their current knowledge, skills, and experience to get more and/or different rewards from their earning careers. Their level of career-management intensity is more than a Maintainer's but not as much as a Changer's.

Changers: These are people who want to change their personal work focus in a radical way. This often involves changing the sector of the earning world in which they work and the role they play with the employer. Their level of career-management intensity is highest because they have much more to learn to manage their transition. Often they can take a major step toward the new type of work they want by "bridging" into their new sector. Once they have moved into their new sector, they can then become Builders.

Hot Topics: These are the changes, challenges, and controversies that are currently under discussion by those concerned with a given type of work. Studying them will help identify the skills, knowledge, and experience that are likely to be most attractive to particular types of employers in the next three to five years. They also help you see your current job and its activities in a larger, multiple-employer environment so you make good decisions about the skills, knowledge, and experience you focus on developing as you continue your career.

Skills, Knowledge, and Experience: The components of an individual's capabilities that allow him or her to do a particular type of work. Skills have to do with being able to accomplish certain activities, for example the ability to use Excel spreadsheet software or engage in conflict resolution. Knowledge involves task-specific knowledge as well as knowledge of the larger human context and of how various other environmental factors work together to influence how you do your work effectively. Experience is included in this list because it is the prime way in which mid-career workers both learn about particular situations and show prospective employers that they can apply their knowledge and skill.

Chunking: A tool to help individuals manage their ongoing career learning. It is based on the idea that dividing an ongoing task into short-term subunits will help individuals recognize that the activities are feasible, see their progress, build on what they are learning, and make midcourse corrections if their approach is not producing clear results or if the larger environment changes.

Critical Path: A set of functions or goals that managers inside an employer see as the priority functions or goals that must be achieved for the organization's current and future success. This is a concept that combines the organization's strategy with its current method for making profit in the for-profit world or for obtaining operating funds in the non-profit world. It is often connected to what the organization sees as the particular characteristics of its product or service that make it successful in the marketplace in comparison to other similar products or services. It identifies what the organization's priorities are, who is directly responsible for the work that generates the funds for running the organization, and who contributes to the organization by providing support and information for that priority work. Understanding an organization's critical path helps individuals to recognize what skills, knowledge, and experience are likely to be most valued by an organization. Also, understanding your current employer's critical path can help you identify which of your job responsibilities are likely to be most important to your managers. This can help you better manage your time on the job.

CHAPTER ONE

Introduction: How the Career Landscape Has Changed

There are no longer career paths. Twenty years ago, you could fairly easily plot a career. It might have had a few twists and turns, but you would progress through a hierarchy of positions that were more or less predetermined. Career paths are gone. They're not even trails. They're not even horse paths.

—Secretary of Labor Robert Reich[1]

This book is directed primarily toward white-collar employees in mid-career who want to reenergize their earning careers. They may be uneasy about the downsizing and restructuring so common today and seeking a way to hedge against the possibility of becoming displaced. They may be frustrated and bored because they feel they have hit a "career plateau" at work. They may want their work to have more personal meaning in the second half of their lives. What they are all looking for is a way to take more control of their earning careers.

The book is of equal value to professionals assisting those who are managing established careers. Although the desires that many have in mid-career are the result of normal developmental changes in adults, the activities required to achieve these goals have changed substantially in recent years. By the late 1990s, the changes in the earning world had reached a point where most large organizations in the United States had made it very clear in their policies that employees could no longer routinely expect long-term, stable employment.[2] As Robert Reich's statement which opens this chapter contends, the career paths that had long been templates for success have deteriorated greatly. These and other related changes mean that more mid-career individuals need help in achieving their goals. So the people providing that help also need to understand these changes.

The large companies that have led the way into this new era of employment dynamics have habitually spent a good deal of time and money trying to interpret the trends and changes within the larger business environment as well as trying to adjust to them effectively so that their enterprises can prosper. Their new employment polices, which formalize the change in the psychological contract between employers and employees, were a part of that response to emerging business conditions.

Unlike these large companies, individual employees usually don't have the time and resources to explore the big picture and develop a proactive response to the changing business environment for themselves. They are busy working—scrambling to keep the job they have or to find another one if they have been downsized—and busy with living the rest of their lives.

The purpose of this book is to describe how individuals can develop their own individualized, proactive response to the changes in employment dynamics. The first chapter will describe the major trends and changes in the workplace during the last 30 years, recognition of which, I think, is crucial to developing such a proactive response. Then, in the second chapter, I will provide an overview of the four success strategies I believe people need to include in their career management activities in order to take a more proactive role in the development of their careers.

How Employment Dynamics Used to Work, and Why

The period after World War II has been called the "golden age" or the "wonder years" of the U.S. economy.[3] American companies wielded immense economic power in the world. They competed among themselves to meet the pent-up domestic demand after the war and to rebuild the world economy as well. At the same time, our industrialized economy was maturing. Employees at all income levels saw their incomes rising at about the same rates—partially due to their employers' economic health and influence, and perhaps partially due to the egalitarian feelings among Americans engendered by the war experience.

Doing business in this era was much different than it is today. Many of the variables that affect corporate strategy now (e.g., infrastructure, labor costs, political environment) were held constant then, because most corporate competitors were based in the United States. Efficient internal processes were more important to a company's competitive success, because of the lack of variability in external factors among major competitors. Employee retention was in an employer's best interest because it was the primary way of maintaining knowledge of the company's unique systems.[4]

Finally, the pace of change was slower, so there was plenty of time for developing and retraining employees as the company evolved.[5]

The desire to maintain a stable workforce led to a number of familiar career norms in large organizations. First, leading companies developed internal labor markets. Career paths were laid out in order to provide incentives for employees and to reward them for their loyalty through internal promotion.[6] Thus, promotions became a standard indicator of career success. In fact, the primary, popular definition of "career" became the progression up through such a sequence of jobs.[7] And because these organizations were so vital and pervasive during this era, their norms influenced how people thought about their careers, whether they were employed in big organizations or not.

A second career norm was that the jobs that employees were asked to take on, while sometimes influenced by an individual's pre-entry career preparation, were primarily the choice of the organization's management, and reflected what management believed needed to be done and who they believed could do it.[8]

A third career norm was that the psychological contract between employers and employees essentially demanded that the company provide long-term employment as long as their employees performed their jobs adequately, were loyal to their employer, and did the jobs they were asked to do.[9]

While such a contract seems appealing—particularly when compared to the instability of recent years—it also had its dark side. For example, scholars have pointed out that the contract in this period caused a shift away from "self sufficiency, independence, and humility."[10] Charles Handy, the British business guru who now writes about the challenges and rewards of what he calls "portfolio careers," spent the first ten years of his career as an employee of Royal Dutch Shell in these post-WWII years (1956–65). He recounts the story of his new wife telling him, "You must be out of your mind, handing your life over to these people. They own you." He realized that in many ways she was right and exited the company to regain his freedom. That was the start of a very successful and fascinating career that he directed personally, rather than relying on his employers.[11] For those seeking the freedom to choose more variety in work settings and challenges, these organization-bound careers could be very limiting.

The Economic Changes of the Last 30 Years and Their Impact on Employers

Beginning in the early '70s the world economy began to change in ways that profoundly altered management practices.[12] Eventually, these changes would affect employment dynamics, even among white-collar middle-earners, and lead to the need for the model presented in this book.

U.S. businesses during this period began to experience more competitive pressure as the more advanced economies destroyed during World War II began to participate more actively in the global marketplace (e.g., France and Germany, and later Japan). Technical innovations such as container ships, widespread commercial air travel, and fax machines began to change not only *how* things could be done, but also *where* they could be done. This greatly increased the number of strategic options available to companies because they could move operations to many more strategically attractive locales and this increased competition as well.[13]

Our industrially based consumer economy matured and services became much more important. This also increased the competition and complexity of business. Companies increasingly moved to develop new product+service combinations that would reap increased profits.[14]

Upper management has also had to contend with more powerful and aggressive professional investors. As the financial services industry has developed, the majority of stocks and bonds have come to be controlled by institutions and professional money managers rather than by individuals. Institutions owned only 16 percent of U.S. equities in 1965, but owned 61 percent in 2001.[15] The constant monitoring and push for short-term profits by professional money managers has added to the pressure on the managements of large, publicly-traded firms to produce steadily increasing profits.[16]

As part of this drive for consistently improving profits, and to pay for new strategic initiatives to become more competitive, companies have increasingly focused on cost cutting. And since the U.S. labor force is one of the best paid in the world and must increasingly compete with equally well-trained labor pools elsewhere in the world, [17] it has been a prime cost-cutting target.[18]

Many business activities have been moved offshore to obtain cost savings and other strategic advantages. And, even in the United States, companies are cutting salaries and other costs by changing locations. A *New York Times* article in July 2000 reported that the number of corporate migrations annually had doubled in the late 1990s from what it had been between 1980 and 1994. A primary reason driving site selection was the cost and quality of local labor. For example, the article reports that when the Rayonier Inc. headquarters moved from Connecticut to Florida, the company's corporate staff was downsized from 85 to 72 people. Of those remaining, only 44 chose to relocate and the 28 new executives who were hired took salaries at least ten percent lower than what had been paid in Connecticut even though they were equally skilled and knowledgeable. In addition, salaries in Florida were expected to rise more slowly.[19]

Competitive pressures have forced companies to implement changes more and more quickly. Downsizing and flattening their internal hierarchies have helped organizations to increase flexibility and speed.[20] And when organizations change their strategic focus, they often try to hire people who already have the needed knowledge and skills rather than train current employees.[21] Companies still rely on internal efficiencies as they did in the go-go years after WW II, but the means for achieving that efficiency has changed substantially. Generic systems for quality and process improvement now exist (e.g., Total Quality Management and Six Sigma) that can be applied to a wide range of jobs and work processes. Furthermore, rather than relying on unique software systems for running the business, most companies now rely on software packages that are commonly in use by many other companies (e.g., Microsoft Word, Oracle, Unix, etc.). Unique systems are saved for the company's core competitive processes which change more often than in the past because of heightened competition and the increased pace of change.

Because these managerial responses have proven successful for industry leaders, they have encouraged similar cost-cutting measures in other U.S. employment sectors, including government, education, and non-profit organizations.

There is no indication that these trends are receding. In fact, a 2003 study by Forrester Research highlighted a growing trend of employers toward shifting white-collar jobs, many of them professional-level positions, offshore, due to the growing educational levels of people elsewhere in the world, the more sophisticated and reliable communication capabilities now available, and the much lower overseas labor costs. "We estimate that of the 700 service job categories in the United States, about 550 will be impacted by offshore outsourcing in some way over the next 15 years," the study noted.[22] Since that report, Thomas Friedman has studied the impact of the economic development of countries such as India on the U.S. labor force and reported his findings in his bestselling book, *The World Is Flat*.[23]

In summary, from an employer's perspective, the pressure to produce profits in this more competitive, complex, and fast-paced environment means that they need to change their organizations' capabilities more often and implement changes as quickly as possible. And for companies in the United States and other developed countries with high salary levels, they need to reduce costs where they can by relying on generic infrastructure and quality-improvement systems to a larger extent, as well as outsourcing and offshoring when they can. One of the mechanisms companies have used for this is downsizing and restructuring, and this is one of the main causes underlying the end of the traditional psychological contract between employers and employees.

What this means for workers in developed countries and how they can respond proactively to these changes is the focus of this book. The new employment dynamics mean that employees will change jobs more often in mid-career, that the "bar"—that is, the criteria employers use to decide whom to hire—will be raised each time they go into the job market. And it also means that proactive employees will devise ways to build their own career paths based on work that is done by multiple employers, gather information about how that work is changing in the near future, and constantly add to their skills and abilities to maintain or increase their worth as employees. But before I get into any detail about all this, let's look briefly at how employees have faired in the short term as a result of the changes in employment dynamics.

Impacts on Employees

In March, 1993, *Fortune* published "The New Unemployed," which described the plight of a number of white-collar workers. The article's main contention was very similar to the point of this chapter: Traditional employment dynamics have given way to new realities that many people, particularly white-collar workers and those who have been in the workforce longer, are unequipped to deal with.

Characteristic of the stories that were included in this article are the stories of the following employees:

> Leslie Goldberg, 45, of Los Angeles, considered herself lucky to find a new job in her field, employee training and human resources, after a year of looking—but she had to swallow a $10,000 pay cut. Shirley Martin, 52, of Maryville, Tennessee, had been working at a Levi Strauss plant for 11 years when her shop shut down. . . . Martin found a job in a smaller sewing factory after about two years, but her pay dropped from $8 an hour to $4.25. She was recently laid off from that job as well. Says Martin: "It seems like you're always starting over—from the bottom."[24]

Late in 2003, as the United States was going through a second jobless recovery, similar to the one that had led to the stories above, an article in the *New York Times* highlighted some of the other changes I have described here:

> Employers are being extremely picky, the few jobs being offered pay less than they once did, and they do not come with the bountiful benefits and sterling opportunities of the 1990s boom, job seekers say.[25]

These stories illustrate how the changing terrain of the working world has made individual employees more vulnerable to unemployment.

These dangers primarily manifest themselves in three ways: increased financial risk; more hours spent working, particularly for middle-class families; and increasing debt. In addition, there is a growing sense of general insecurity which, of course, manifests itself in many ways.

A June, 2003, survey conducted by the Heldrich Center at Rutgers University found that 56 percent of the respondents said they or a family member had been laid off at least once in their lifetime. Furthermore, 44 percent of those with a college degree reported they had been downsized.[26] Most of these people lost their jobs not because of personal performance issues but because of strategic changes or cost-cutting moves on the part of their employers. Peter Cappelli, a noted scholar in this area, wrote in 2001 that restructurings "may well be continuous" because "these competencies [that companies seek in their employees] change with consumer demand and the reactions of competitors (competencies are determined relative to competitors)."[27]

For those who are downsized, the prime objective, of course, is to get another job to replace their lost income. According to Princeton University researcher Henry Farber, who has studied the phenomenon of displaced workers extensively, even those who lose and find a job during good economic times take a financial hit, but if the job loss occurs during a downturn, the results are then quite serious. He estimates that job losers with some college education who were able to get another full-time job within six months lost an average of about 6 percent of their former income in 1997–99 (during good economic times), but lost about 20 percent if this happened in 2001–3 (during the last recession). For those who had 16 or more years of education, the average loss in earnings increased from 4.5 percent in 1995–97 to 21 percent in 2001–4.[28]

Working longer hours is a second manifestation of the increased risk for workers in today's working world. The authors of *The State of Working America* write: "Over the last 30 years, workers in middle-income married-couple families with children have added an average of 20 weeks at work, the equivalent of five months. . . . By 2000, middle-income black families worked the equivalent of twelve full-time weeks more than white families."[29] This additional work has been done primarily by women, who have become more active as earners in their families.[30] There are many reasons for the overall increase in working hours: the need to replace wages lost through displacement, the desire of women to work outside the home, additional job responsibilities as a result of the elimination of positions, or the fear that declining to work overtime may make one a candidate for downsizing. Whatever the reasons, longer workdays certainly produce more stress in most people's lives.

Data reported in *The State of Working America, 2002–03* also illustrates the third indicator of increased risk on the part of middle-earners. This book reports that by 2001, total U. S. household debt exceeded total disposable income by nearly 10 percent, with those households in the middle of the income distribution absorbing the largest increase in debt. Some 14 percent of middle-income households carry debt-service obligations that exceed 40 percent of their income.[31]

Many white-collar and managerial employees were caught by surprise in the downsizings and restructurings of the 1990s. Most thought they were performing well and so they never expected to lose their jobs. For them, it was like what happened to Dorothy in "The Wizard of Oz." They were going about their daily lives, a storm came up, and suddenly they weren't in Kansas anymore. Not only did they have to weather the shock of losing their jobs (i.e., the storm) but getting new jobs was much more difficult for many and took longer than they expected. Often they had to settle for what they could find and work for less as well. They did the best they could in a difficult situation with little preparation or understanding of how the situation had changed.

Those who tried to help people in these situations to respond to the circumstances they found themselves in argued strongly that being flexible and willing to learn was what was needed.[32] That was a good answer then, but it is no longer a satisfactory response now that the ongoing pattern of the changed employment dynamics has become clear. Now employees need to be ready to change employers more often. They need to think about how to be ready to meet other employers' increased expectations about the relevant experiences or knowledge their new hires should have about the challenges these employers are likely to face. Also, simply being flexible and constantly ready to learn does not necessarily lead by itself to a career that individuals can build and shape over the long term in order to seek the kinds of rewards they want as individuals and hedge against the greater risks within today's labor market.

Other Trends Affecting Employees

Other trends in our society are also encouraging people to seek ways to become more proactive with respect to their careers. One of these trends is an increase in our average life span. Since the turn of the century, approximately twenty years have been added to the expected lifetime of men and thirty years to that of women. And now women can expect to draw a paycheck for 30 years in comparison with only 15 years in 1950. This increase in the years spent earning by women makes their participation in the earning world comparable to that of men whose time spent in the labor market has ranged between 30 and 40 years since 1900.[33]

Thirty or forty years is a long time to work in one occupation, and so the simple length of time modern employees spend in the workforce is itself causing a growing number of people to want to redirect their careers in mid-career. This phenomenon was first "discovered" in men in the 1970s, when it was often seen as a part of the "midlife crisis."[34] Today, increasing numbers of women are also arriving at midlife and asking, "What do I want to do for the last half of my career?"[35]

Another trend encouraging people to take more control of their careers is the human potential movement. In the 1950s, Maslow's hierarchy of motivational needs, with self-actualization needs at the top, provided psychologists with a model of, and many others with a validation for, the desire to have personally meaningful work lives. *Do What You Love and the Money Will Follow,* published in 1987, has become a classic in the career literature and embodies in its title the hopes and desires of a large number of people. Many, many similar books about how to find personal fulfillment in work continue to be published.

So people are not just being pushed into taking more responsibility for shaping their careers over the long term, they are also being pulled by the desire for more personal fulfillment in their work. This is a lucky confluence of motivations because developing a proactive response to the changed employment dynamics will take additional time and energy, particularly at first, and individuals tend to be better motivated to change by the desire to gain something positive than by the fear of experiencing something negative. But to change their behavior people not only need to have a positive desire, they need to have a reasonable expectation of getting what they desire if they invest the time and energy.

The Changed Landscape of Career Opportunities

Another trend that makes it feasible for individuals to take more responsibility for their long-term earning careers is the growing variety of work specialties and organizational settings for work within our society. Of course, the impact of new technologies to create new jobs while making others obsolete has been described in the popular media. But there are other changes that are increasing an individual's options for building a career path and having more rewarding work. James Brian Quinn contends that the evolution of our service economy has provided a whole new set of service specialties or "industries," such as direct marketing and inventory control. These second-generation industries or specialties include jobs that are integrated into the traditional industries as well as creating specialized work organizations.[36]

Another well-documented source of new work opportunities is the increasing impact of technology on all facets of the economy. Barley has pointed out that the occupational category for technical and professional positions has had the largest growth since the 1940s.[37] The point of this fact for mid-career individuals is that technologies of all kinds are being integrated with various types of work, providing opportunities for people to specialize and build their careers.

Finally, as our economy has evolved and become more complex, many consulting businesses have appeared in all sectors and a variety of business service firms also add to the options for shaping the type of career an individual can have. A panel of nationally recognized scholars, brought together by the National Research Council to study the changing nature of work, has highlighted the increased variety of types of work within general occupations and contends that there will continue to be more ' variety as technology, market demand, demographics, and employment policies interact with each other.[38]

Let's look briefly at just one example of the career options currently available to individuals in the general work arena of human resources (HR). An individual can become a "generalist" doing a range of HR activities, or he can learn one of a variety of functional subspecialties (e.g., compensation, recruitment, training and development). With such a specialty, he could work within HR in a large firm or join a consulting or business services firm, thereby seeing a wide range of organizations and the challenges they face in relation to that specialty. He could become a solo practitioner/independent consultant which would involve knowledge of a specialty as well as the opportunity to run his own business. He could use his knowledge of HR to develop and sell products (e.g., software, instruments, or kits) that help HR professionals get their work done. He could go into the management of a subspecialty or the whole HR function. Or he could specialize in the HR challenges that are faced by a particular type of business or industry. Or he might work in government to design or monitor regulations governing employment practices, or work for one of the professional organizations that support the profession.

This list just hints at the variety of experiences and knowledge you can develop and the variety of career paths individuals in mid-career can build within a particular work arena. People can build in a variety of ways over time and for example, this individual need not even retain his focus on HR. Over time he could shift into software design, sales, or even general management within one of the industries in which he has worked, using his knowledge of HR to provide value to the employer while he learns about his new work focus.

With some forethought and an understanding of the expanding work options, the choices you make as you change jobs and employers can become a career path. By choosing jobs that build knowledge and experience in chosen areas, you can prepare to meet the current needs of potential employers and make choices that also help you build a career that you will find more intrinsically and extrinsically rewarding. This ability to make choices that will help you enjoy your work and that integrate it better with your larger life is one of the silver linings for individuals in the changed employment dynamics.

Gone are the days when employment options were all about the same, and people selected jobs primarily on the basis of the employer's corporate culture, pay, and benefits. These are still important factors in an individual's job choice, but because most workers are now likely to look for new employment more often, the experience and knowledge you can gain from a particular employment opportunity and how it fits into your long-term career development has become very important to job choice as well. Most people in mid-career do not need to go back to school to get more skills and knowledge in order to compete for jobs even with the criteria for hiring constantly being raised or changed. What they need is new ideas about how to manage their long-term career, see their current knowledge and experience in a new light, and figure out what additional information they need to maintain or increase their worth as employees.

The general trends I have described are fine, but you need to find out what employment options exist given your particular interests and experiences and work preferences. You need to figure out how to test the options so you make wise choices. And you need to have techniques to change your career direction even when employers are seeking experienced new hires. You need information, and you need a way to turn that information into knowledge you can use.

Information is more easily accessible and there is more of it than ever before. In particular, long-term career management requires information about how various kinds of work are changing. It turns out that libraries have become a major source of such information about work—even better than the Web in some ways! The development of databases that bring together literally tens of thousands of professional and industry publications, along with the capacity to search through all of them for particular information, has greatly increased access to information about how work of various kinds is evolving, what the issues are, and which companies and organizations are involved with those issues. In essence, what you find out at the library will set the scene for using the World Wide Web and for networking much more effectively.

So the information is available and there are many more options within the workplace now to allow people to build and shape their careers. The change in employment dynamics has opened the door to the freedom and opportunity to build more rewarding, proactive careers, in addition to bringing new risks into the workforce. What is still missing is a conceptual structure to help people reorganize what they already know and learn what additional information they need in order to move forward and manage their careers more effectively.

To develop a proactive, long-term approach to career management, people need a way to focus their information gathering. They need a category system with which to think about employment possibilities across employers that not only identifies job types but also their potential for career enhancement and their possible lifestyle impacts. They need plans for preparing for their next job search, so that they will be ready for the type of work they want when they seek new employment. Finally, they need an understanding of the various stages and cycles they will go through as they manage their careers.

These are conceptual tools that will be new to most employees. Our increased access to information makes that information useful in ways that we have not been able to imagine before. In the next chapter, I will provide an overview of these conceptual tools for turning information into knowledge that can be used for success in mid-career.

CHAPTER TWO

Four New Strategies for Career Management: The "Employability Plus" Model

One's philosophy is not best expressed in words; it is expressed in the choices one makes. . . . In the long run, we shape our lives and we shape ourselves. The process never ends until we die. And the choices we make are ultimately our responsibility.

—Eleanor Roosevelt[1]

The psychological contract between employers and employees after World War II was that if employees were good corporate citizens, did steady work, and took on the jobs that their employers asked them to do, in return their employers would provide them with job security—that is, in the future they would always have a job with their employer, at equal or higher pay. Chapter 1 tells the story of how the larger economy changed, competition increased, and employers found it harder and harder to keep up their end of the deal. Peter Cappelli writes that in the late 1990s most large companies rewrote their policies to describe the "new deal" they were offering in the changed circumstances, and some of those companies suggested that, instead of job security, they would now offer "employability." That is, these companies considered promising that employees at their companies would obtain the skills needed to be able to secure jobs elsewhere if they were let go.[2]

The exact nature of that promise of employability never was clear, in particular whether it included being able to obtain comparable salaries and benefits. Cappelli, who has long studied corporate human resources practices, questioned the ability of companies to deliver on such a promise.[3] And by 2004 there was at least one published study suggesting that it was not practical from the companies' perspectives to make such assurances.[4] This makes logical sense. Managers have a prime responsibility to do what is best for their organizations. Concern for the futures of those who leave their employ falls somewhat far away from that responsibility.

For most workers, this new deal hasn't been such a good deal. Employability at its minimum simply means that you have qualities that make it likely other organizations will hire you. But this is not all people want: they want assurances that they will be hired at the same or at increased levels of reward. This is what I call "Employability Plus," and it is a laudable and attainable goal for most white-collar workers and professionals in mid-career. But it is something individuals must do for themselves.

Employment dynamics and the earning world have changed so much in recent years that what you need to know to remain highly employable has also changed. You need a new perspective on your career, one that is less dependent on a single employer for definition and direction. That perspective should provide you with a way to learn what you need to know to stay current, to see employment options offering growth or change, and to be constantly developing your knowledge and skills to meet both your and your potential employers' future desires.

This approach to career management demands a broader knowledge than most workers have had about their work in the recent past, but luckily advances in information technology, together with a set of guidelines about what to look for, and focused networking on the part of the individual, can make this accomplishable. And this additional perspective and knowledge will enable more active career management and a greater understanding of career cycles that can be very helpful to the worker in mid-career. These are the primary components of what I call the Employability Plus model for mid-career management and are the focus of this book.

One goal of this chapter is to introduce four strategies for success and show how together they form a holistic, proactive response to the business and employment trends described in chapter 1. A second goal is to highlight how this approach is different from—though not a replacement for—the traditional activities associated with mid-career management. Think of it as an infrastructure to support your use of the more traditional job-search and career-management skills. The activities that make up this infrastructure will need to be managed well so that they fit into your already busy schedule, but this is possible for most. At the end of this chapter I will begin to discuss the time management challenges you may face and how to overcome them. A final goal of the chapter is to describe how I have organized the rest of the book.

Snapshots of Careers in Progress

I will start by describing the approaches that three individuals took to their mid-career management after learning about the Employability Plus model.[5] While these three snapshots will certainly not be a complete description of the four success strategies, you will begin to see how the model works. Next I will explain how the model enables you to respond to the trends identified in chapter 1 and how it differs from the approaches to mid-career management typically used today.

Snapshot #1: Emer

Emer is a software engineer about ten years into his career. He has decided that his long-term career goal is to eventually start a firm to either develop or adapt software to the needs of his home country. He is already a software engineer, but he has decided he needs to know about three additional areas in order to do well as a business owner. He needs to know how to run a start-up firm. He needs to know how companies produce and distribute software. And he needs to know more about the software needs and economic dynamics of his home country. He has decided to focus on the first two areas in the next four or five years.

Emer has obtained a full-time job in a large software company. His goal for this employment is to experience how software products are developed, readied for production, and introduced into the market. He is not necessarily seeking promotion in the positions that he applies for but rather exposure to what he considers the prime functions in bringing software to market. He is also keeping an eye on how the software industry as a whole is changing because he recognizes that he is in an industry that evolves on a worldwide basis. To learn more about running his own business, Emer has enrolled in a part-time MBA program that has a focus on entrepreneurship. Eventually he plans to gather some information about his home country and its software needs. He returns home for vacation annually and he intends to make time for such projects as his move home comes closer.

Emer believes he will have completed his MBA in about four years and will have sampled at least two or three of the major functions that are currently a part of the software introduction process. At that point he has committed to reassess his long-term goal and he believes he will be able to say with more specificity whether he still believes that he will enjoy and be successful in starting a firm in his home country. If he decides against it on the basis of the information he has, he knows that his experience and education will continue to help him get interesting jobs in the software industry. If he decides to continue to pursue his current goal, he will have much more information with which to determine where he needs to focus his learning in the following few years; then he will identify new activities and maybe a new employer to facilitate that process.

Snapshot #2: Sue

Sue is a manufacturing engineer who is aware of the decline in the number and size of manufacturing facilities in the United States. She also has noticed that her interests have changed since she entered the workforce. She has decided to change careers and her long-term goal now is to do marketing for a company that produces medical devices. Like Emer she started a part-time MBA program to get a broad understanding of the function of marketing that she is now interested in. She has networked with people working for medical device companies in her MBA classes in order to learn about those companies and, in particular, about any job opportunities for which she might qualify. Sue is aware that medical device companies are likely to be very different from other types of manufacturing companies in their corporate culture and business concerns, so she also wants to test whether she will enjoy working in that environment. Also, she knows that working in the medical device industry will make it easier to obtain experiences and knowledge that will help her make the career shift to marketing later. After about 18 months into the MBA program, Sue obtained a job in a medical device company as a manufacturing engineer.

Snapshot #3: Joe

Joe made a major career change a few years ago. He'd begun his career as a musician and minister. He did this for a number of years and is still committed to both, but for a number of reasons he decided that this should not be the focus of his earning career. He got a job in a call center and was quickly promoted to manager. Joe really enjoyed this work and decided that the opportunity it gave him to "minister" to the often underappreciated and overstressed employees in call centers was an excellent match with his life values. He also liked that the job ended at the end of his shift and that he had time for his other life interests.

I worked with Joe in the mid 1990s. Downsizing, restructuring, and outsourcing were well under way by then, so it was easy for him to realize that in order to provide himself with increased employability, he needed much more information about call center work than he would be able to get by doing his job at his current employer. Joe looked for articles in the business press about the challenges and issues faced in call center management.

By using the library's resources and doing some networking, he discovered that there were two major challenges to call center management at that time. First, new and improved software was constantly being developed. Knowing what was on the market and what it could do was very important to companies making decisions about when to change software and what software to purchase. Call center managers were often involved in such decisions. Also, Joe realized that the process of actually making the shift to new software was very stressful for the workers; often it decreased productivity, and it was happening with increasing frequency. He concluded that knowledge of and experience with change management was something that could make him particularly attractive to a number of employers.

Armed with this information, Joe decided to make time in his schedule both for learning about new software and for attending workshops and experimenting with various change management techniques and ideas. This would be a challenge because his day was already busy, and these activities would take him away from interacting with his subordinates. He started by identifying activities that were feasible in his schedule, as well as articulating for himself how they would contribute to his learning process.

Joe committed to either attending two workshops or reading two books on change management (or some combination thereof) in the next eight months and making notes about how he might use what he learned as he managed his current group. At the end of the eight months he would assess how this approach to learning was working. To explore his goal of keeping current about software products, he decided to begin by seeing some of the software vendors who regularly contacted him; he would see at least one vendor every two weeks. After four months he would reflect on what and how much he had learned, and who his best information sources were.

Success Strategy #1: Articulating a Personalized Work Focus

The previous three snapshots of individuals managing their careers illustrate the four success strategies of the Employability Plus model. First, each person is well into the process of articulating what I will call a personalized work focus (PWF), that is, a description of the kind of contribution each wants to make to their potential or actual employers' organizations. Joe's and Emer's descriptions of their work are the best articulated at this point, whereas Sue is in a more exploratory mode. Each personalized work focus has an objective dimension, (e.g., software engineering or call center management) which communicates to employers what skills and knowledge the individual could bring to the organization; it also has a subjective dimension (e.g., starting a business or "ministering" to subordinates) that expresses the individual's selfhood and helps them generate energy to learn more about their work.

This description of the personalized work focus is key to the Employability Plus model. Employers own jobs, but individuals own their work. A person's description of their work centers around some theme such as helping businesses meet their software needs or helping people who answer phones in call centers to have a positive experience while accomplishing their jobs. A personalized work focus is something that could be helpful to a number of employers, so it helps individuals to see their mobility. In addition, it is something that is interesting and engaging, motivating the individual to become more useful to multiple employers rather than just focusing on their current employer. Recognizing that their work belongs to them and not their employer provides the launch pad for using the freedoms of the new employment dynamics to build more interesting and fulfilling earning careers.

Of course, people have always been engaged in identifying and preparing for work they think they will find interesting. In most cases, however, this defining process has traditionally taken place before an individual's entry into the full-time workforce. By mid-career workers generally have let their long-term employers shape the nature of their work by means of the transfers and promotions they offer. By making a more conscious effort to articulate the contribution that you want to make to multiple employers, you can take more ownership of your future and prepare for it—whether you want to stay with your current employer like Emer and Joe or to make a change like Sue.

Much has been written, mostly by career counselors and psychologists, about how individuals can "find" or articulate work that interests them or that they can be passionate about. The vast majority of this writing focuses on individuals and their internal processes. Such a focus is very important, but it is only half of what needs to be considered, particularly in mid-career. What the earning world needs and how it categorizes the work to be performed should also be a part of the process. An earning career is an ongoing conversation with the world. My approach will help you to articulate your personal preferences within real-life, earning-world contexts.

Success Strategy #2: Learning about the Near Future of Your Work

A second success strategy proposed by the model and illustrated in these snapshots is how the individual undertakes to learn about the *near future* of their work (i.e., the next three to five years). This process involves gathering information from sources not only within their current place of employment but outside of it as well, then turning that information into knowledge that they can personally use. Sue and Emer are both in degree programs, but I do not think this is a prime learning option for most in mid-career. Experience or more targeted formal learning, such as Joe is pursuing, is probably more effective.

In the post–World War II era of employment there was little need for individuals to gather future-oriented information about their work arenas and about alternative employers. They could rely on the management of their organization to provide the information they needed about their work as well as training when needs changed. Today you are much more likely to change employers mid-career. When that happens, you need to be ready to compete for jobs in other organizations and with a much larger group of fellow job-seekers who are also experienced workers. To be prepared you need a greater knowledge of the challenges faced by your potential employers. With this knowledge you can then shape your experience to show you are able to meet those challenges.

Further, during the past era of more stable employment, even if workers had wanted to find detailed information about their work, their ability to get it was much more limited than it is today. Of course, there were professional associations and informative articles, but finding this information was often a major challenge. Professional associations were expensive and provided limited information about the work itself. Public libraries in that era needed to be able to pay ongoing subscription fees to individual publications in order to gain access to them. Funds for subscriptions being limited, libraries didn't buy many work-specific periodicals.

Today, the world in which public libraries exist has changed dramatically. Not only are there many more sources of quality information, but most libraries today lease access to Web-based databases that contain tens of thousands of business and professional publications rather than subscribe to individual publications. Their subscription budget goes much further now. Also, patrons can search these databases very easily using words and phrases, which is a huge advantage for people looking for information about specific types of work and/or topics. Furthermore, the World Wide Web provides additional resources and networking opportunities for those who have learned how to search it effectively and to assess the quality of the information they find there.

Individuals who want to manage their mid-career so that they will be likely to continue to maintain or achieve increasing rewards, need to develop the skills to use these new information resources and to keep themselves current. I and my colleague Janice Kragness have worked together to provide you with guidelines about how to use these resources to gather the kinds of information you need in order to deploy the Employability Plus model. Armed with this information, you should be

able to work in tandem with your local librarian to develop your knowledge of how your work arena will change in the near future and what the employment options will likely be in your preferred locale.

Success Strategy #3: Acting to Shape Your Career

The third success strategy of the Employability Plus model that you can observe in these snapshots is that each person has designed a set of actions to further develop their career. Sue has taken two major actions toward a work focus in the marketing of medical devices by securing employment at a medical device company and starting an MBA program to learn about marketing. To prepare to open a business of his own, Emer is constructing his own management trainee path by rotating through various departments in his company and exploring the challenges of entrepreneurship in his MBA program. Joe is committed to a series of meetings, workshops, and reading to gain more knowledge about subjects he deems important to maintaining and increasing his worth as a call center manager. While the tasks each person has undertaken certainly benefit their current employer, the individual's motive is his or her long-term career benefit. These are excellent examples of the kinds of more independent, ongoing career development activities that individuals need to add to their working lives.

Until the recent past, career management during employment focused on performing well at your current job, participating in management-sponsored training, and learning to work effectively with your coworkers. Today, because of the increased mobility between organizations occurring throughout an individual's working life, most people need to also be learning and experimenting with how they want their careers to evolve, while they are doing their current jobs. That way they will be ready for the next job search.

The independent, proactive nature of these developmental activities and career "experiments" is new to most people. We have always learned on the job, but in the past that learning was mostly employer-directed and/or casual and opportunistic.[6] This Employability Plus approach encourages individuals to consciously guide their learning by considering the work settings they place themselves in, how they do their jobs, and the extra activities for which they volunteer. This has been called "crafting" your job.[7] By becoming more selective about the work-related learning opportunities you become involved in, you can test your preferences and abilities as well as prepare yourself for future employment options that meet your criteria. This is different from most traditional career advice, which advises simply trying to gain as many different skills and abilities as you can so that you will have a better chance of matching some employer's job description during your next job hunt.

The approach to "planning" used here is also new. The person in each snapshot has a general, longer-term goal and is involved in one or two short-term activities to move toward that goal. I refer to designing these short-term activities as "chunking" the career development process.[8] At the end of a chunk the individual stops and reassesses the process and direction of their efforts. This is in contrast to more conventional "career planning," where the goal is to develop a detailed, multiple-year blueprint and then to follow that blueprint. The pace and complexity of change in our society has made this conventional approach to planning obsolete.[9] A major challenge posed by this new approach is to incorporate it as an ongoing part of our adult lives, like exercising and taking vacations. It is a slower process and the benefits sometimes take longer to recognize. But the overall advantage of doing so is that it allows for a quicker response to changes in the earning world, and thus more personal control over our careers.

By mid-career your work has become a major part of your identity.[10] That fact and the reality that most individuals will need to continue to make money even as they build and change their careers means that a gradual process made up of multiple chunks makes sense. Also, because your earning career is not just about yourself but also about how the earning world responds to our endeavors, these chunks allow us to gather feedback from the larger world each step of the way. This approach to planning is not without structure and systematic thought, but the long-term goals are more general and tentative than in traditional career planning. Furthermore, the regular, short-term milestones encourage you not only to celebrate the chunks completed but also to reconsider your trajectory in light of what you have learned.

Success Strategy #4: Managing Your Career Cycle

As you can see, the Employability Plus model calls for a wider variety of career management activities than traditional mid-career management. Luckily, you don't have to do all of them at the same time. These two facts suggest yet a fourth success strategy: understanding where you are in the career cycle and focusing your career management activities appropriately.

The career cycle is the same as it always was in that it still involves moving from job to job. Furthermore, job performance—the focus of most individuals' career management efforts in the past—is still an important part of career management. Certainly, for a year or 18 months after you get a new job you should be focused on mastering that position and, if you changed organizations, becoming a part of your new organization. Job performance is still one important way that you build your career over the long term. But in today's multiple-employer environment, you also need to add other career management efforts after that initial period. In addition to performing your job responsibilities well, you need to review your personalized work focus, keep current on how your work arena is changing, and begin again to develop new capabilities so that you can maintain your worth as an employee in the larger labor market and achieve your evolving, individualized career goals.

This is very different from the norms established in the post–World War II era, norms that are still part of the assumptions that typically guide our behavior. Those assumptions include the idea that you owe your employer 100 percent of your work time and should think only about your current employer's success when making decisions about your work. This idea worked when your employer was committed to you for the long term, but now you also need to think about yourself.

And you shouldn't assume that your employer is on the cutting edge of your industry—another reason why workers tend to focus on their current jobs instead of actively planning a personal career-management strategy. This assumption is probably based on the idea that we are part of the world's dominant economy and the most technically advanced society. This kind of thinking suggests you don't need to worry about getting any more training or knowledge than your current employer provides. But times have changed. There is much more competition and variety. What you need to know to be successful in one organization may not be what you need to know in others. In addition, these skills and abilities are evolving more quickly. The mobile employee—which includes most of us today—needs to develop their capabilities with multiple employers in mind.

As the world develops, it gets more complex. A thumbnail history of skill development for white-collar mid-career management is outlined in Table 2.1. After World War II, career management for white-collar employees in mid-career focused primarily on job performance, which included the intraorganizational skills of networking and gaining visibility with management.

Starting in the late 1980s, when the downsizing of white-collar workers began to pick up momentum, mid-career management skills were expanded to include job-search skills. Relearning these skills, which career counselors and others understand well, helped people to compete for jobs to replace the ones they had lost. These skills remain important career-management capabilities. But without the "right stuff" in their resumes, many have found it hard to find new positions with intrinsic

Table 2.1
A Brief History of the Evolution of Mid-Career Management Skills for White-Collar Earners

Historical Period	Employment Dynamics of Period	Career Management Skills Needed
1950s– late 1980s	Most mid-career white-collar earners worked long-term for a single employer	Job performance skills, including intra-organizational skills of networking and gaining visibility
late 1980s— 2006	Downsizing begins to include white-collar as well as blue-collar earners. In the mid 1990s the psychological contract between employers and employees is rewritten, making individuals' long-term careers primarily their responsibility	Job performance skills + Job search skills needed when downsized
Post-2006	New era of expanded individual responsibility for long-term career management	Job performance skills + Job search skills + Employability Plus Model's Four Success Strategies

and extrinsic rewards comparable to those they lost. Today, individuals need to pursue more, and different, activities than before to help them improve their success in the job market.

Many academics and others have pointed to the changes in our workplace and called for changes in career-development theory and career-management strategies to meet these changes.[11] The Employability Plus model is an answer to those calls.

Some Words about "Making Time"

As you have read this chapter, you may well have been thinking, "Makes sense, but where am I going to find the time to do all this?" People in mid-career are also in the middle of their lives. Most have families, hobbies, responsibilities, and community involvements; in addition, many are working longer hours than before. So this approach to career management, while it may offer greater potential for success, also presents many with what appears to be a huge time-management challenge.

Clearly, to learn about the various components of the Employability Plus model and to change some of your career-management habits will take additional time and energy. But, once you have made some of these changes, I think you will be surprised at how easily some of these components can be integrated into your daily working life.

For those who have lived with the norm that our employers deserve 100 percent of our earning energy and time, the idea of having a "parallel" career-management track devoted to pursuing the potential of a career within a multiple-employer context seems like heresy. It also feels like an either-or decision: *Either* I am being a good employee for this employer, *or* I am pursuing my own career interests. But, if you are generally happy with the work you are currently doing, this work will be the foundation from which you begin using the Employability Plus model, and what you learn about your work may well be useful, not just for your future, but for improving your job performance in the present as well. Remember that employers face increasing competition and many want more creative answers for their work dilemmas. Your added knowledge about the work can help you to discover such answers. Also, learning more about your work in a multiple-employer context helps you to understand the goals of your current employer better.

When downsizing occurs, those who survive are often asked to do more. These demands can keep them from thinking beyond their current job. While I realize that the time pressure in many jobs has increased, I also think there is an opportunity to manage that time better. The job redesign that should accompany new strategies and new organizational configurations often is not done by management. By understanding what management's critical path is—that is, what management sees as most crucial to the current and long-term success of the organization—I believe most individuals can set priorities and redesign their work schedules themselves, so they can complete the most important tasks in the time available. I will discuss this in more detail later in the book.

Most people in mid-career have learned a good deal about their part of the earning world as well as about their interests. The challenge of the Employability Plus model is to use that knowledge to more proactively direct your career. Often it just involves looking at what you already know in new ways. For example, I worked with one executive who had decided to remain a manager in his industry but wanted to manage in a new setting with different challenges. I was surprised, then, to find he was at a loss to identify his industry's major issues and challenges. As we talked, it became apparent that when he read the industry magazines, as he did regularly, he had "blinders" on. That is, he looked at the articles solely from the perspective of his current management responsibilities. Those blinders made it hard for him to see how the industry was changing generally and what new challenges he might enjoy managing. He needed to take his blinders off to think about his own future career.

The Employability Plus model will help you understand what you need to know to more effectively manage your career, and it will help you change your perspective and find the information you need but don't have. Of course, this will take time and effort, but that effort can be broken down into reasonable chunks so you are not overwhelmed. This approach to mid-career management is something you do in an ongoing fashion; you start slowly and build. This book will make suggestions about reasonable first steps related to each component of the model.

Once you have found a work focus that truly interests you, this will provide natural momentum for the process. Every time you find a source of information or make a new, important contact, you not only achieve a small goal but also feed your true self as well. This naturally builds strength and momentum into the process as it moves forward.

How to Read and Use the Rest of This Book

The next four chapters describe the four success strategies of the Employability Plus model in much more detail. Chapter 3 helps you to shift your perspective from job-centric to work-oriented, so that you can more easily think of your capabilities as assets that you develop and carry with you from employer to employer. I will also stress looking at your work not just in terms of what interests you but also in terms of how employers will see those interests as contributing to their goals. At the end of the chapter, I describe three levels of career-management intensity and focus. At various times in your life you will choose different levels of career development intensity, and this is one way that you manage your career in tandem with the other aspects of your life. Throughout the rest of the book, I will speak to differences that I see among these intensity levels in terms of how individuals will implement the four strategies.

Chapter 4 focuses on learning how your work will be changing in the next three to five years. Taking this larger, multiple-employer perspective on the work helps you to identify what will be important to employers and what new developments are of particular interest to you. Looking forward a few years gives you enough time to develop the skills, knowledge, and experience in relation to these developments to maintain or improve your worth as an employee.

Chapter 5 then describes how you take this general information about your work and localize it in order to determine how it relates to employers in your preferred locale. This chapter also includes ideas about how you can begin to develop a targeted network around your specific work focus and design career-management chunks to increase your capabilities in your chosen areas.

In all three of these chapters, I try to show you how even people with full-time jobs and busy personal lives can accomplish these activities. I describe how to design tasks in chunks and suggest questions to ask and other methods for connecting the chunks. Clearly, this model calls for more independently managed learning than many have engaged in before, but I think the examples and stories I include provide assurance that what is described here is feasible.

I also show how you can use the resources of your library to further your information-gathering, networking, and development efforts. As knowledge workers, we should be able to use our expanded access to information to help us shape our careers. I've also included an Appendix by Janice Kragness that provides a more detailed description of library resources and many more ideas about how to use them to answer mid-career–related questions.

Chapter 6 continues with an overview of the whole mid-career management process. This overview explains how the Employability Plus model affects the more traditional career-management activities of performing well on the current job and refining your job-search skills. This allows you to implement success strategy #4 of knowing where you are in the career cycle and letting that determine how you direct your career management activities.

I suggest that you read all four chapters before diving into the change process. While I have presented the strategies in what I consider a logical sequence, that sequence may not be the best one for you. For example, some people may decide to gather information about a work focus (my second strategy) in order to articulate their personalized work focus (my first strategy). Also, I have tried to be economical and not describe any information-gathering tactic more than once, but that does not mean that you should use a tactic solely for the strategy where it was highlighted in my discussion.

As you read these four chapters, determine how your current knowledge about the earning world fits into what the Employability Plus model requires. Since you are in mid-career, you are likely already to have some of the knowledge and to be taking some of the needed actions. Your second objective as you read is to identify major gaps in your thinking and/or information gathering. At the end of Chapter 6, I will provide some questions that will help you decide how to begin to use the model to your best advantage. Today there is a greater variety of activities needed for successful career management. It is possible that you will want to seek out other sources of aid and support for some of them. I have also included a discussion of these resources and when they would be most helpful in Chapter 6.

This book is focused on explaining the new skills and concepts that I believe mid-career individuals need in order to manage their careers in the twenty-first century. I do not describe the basics of networking, time management, or other well-known topics. Nor do I discuss resume writing or job interviews. There are many good books on these subjects. I do, however, describe how some of these basics need to be updated and redeployed to accomplish the new, more complex tasks that mid-career people need to do today to manage their futures.

The endnotes throughout the chapters are meant to provide you with the sources of specific facts or research so you can read more about them if you want. I have also included a short essay on suggested readings at the end of the book for those who are interested in continuing to read on this subject. Finally, I will be setting up a web site at www.employabilityplus. com for people using the model. It will provide some additional information and a place where you can leave feedback about what works well and what challenges you experience; there will also be a place to volunteer for research studies if you want.

The final chapter of the book looks into the near future and how implementing the success strategies of the Employability Plus model changes the relationship between individuals and potential employers. One of the downsides of the changed employment dynamics has been that employment deals have become too one-sided, favoring the employer. This model helps individuals get the knowledge and capabilities they need to move into stronger negotiating positions when they feel the need for that. It sets them up, then, to negotiate for the rewards they want from their work. Over time, these negotiations should also produce patterns of agreements that will lead to new employment norms which will facilitate the development of independent career management in this new era of employment dynamics.

CHAPTER THREE

Success Strategy #1: Articulating a Personalized Work Focus

Choose a job you love and you will never have to work a day in your life.
—Confucius[1]

Virtually everyone in the earning world has an answer to the question, "What do you do?" Usually, people just state their current position title or briefly summarize their current job and the conversation continues. The Employability Plus model asks you to revise and upgrade that brief description so that it better serves you in the process of managing your career and living your life. I call this upgrade your personalized work focus (PWF). The PWF is meant to be a starting point to help you identify the following:

- the work that you personally find interesting,
- the employers who are likely to have jobs that you would enjoy, and
- the skills, knowledge, and experience you need to maintain or develop so that you can do the work you want to do well.

Notice that this is about the work itself. Work is the activity that brings the employer and employee together. It determines the primary criteria used in hiring and the thresholds that are set for them. That is, with only a few exceptions, candidates who cannot show skills, knowledge, and experience in the work they would be hired to perform, do not make it to the final rounds in job searches. This is particularly true for people in mid-career.

Until the 1980s employees' choices about the work they did were pretty much limited by their long-term employers.[2] Their jobs were configured by their employers to meet each organization's needs and strategies, and the primary way to build a career and income was by moving up within that organization. Employees in that environment had relatively few choices for directing their careers.

As I have noted earlier, greater employee mobility brings not only challenges but also more opportunities for individuals to have more freedom to shape their careers by their choice of jobs. Furthermore, the growing complexity and variety among employers in our economy means that the variety of jobs that are potentially available has greatly expanded.[3] These trends present more opportunity for mid-career white-collar individuals to reenergize their careers around topics that interest them and add to their value to employers.[4] You can enjoy this freedom more fully by using the success strategies of the Employability Plus model. The first step is to identify and articulate a PWF. Then, using the other success strategies, you will further sharpen that focus in terms of what employers need and want, and in terms of your own work style and lifestyle preferences.

This chapter will focus on helping you to articulate at least a starter PWF. Even if you think you know what you want to do, I urge you to read this chapter. The shift from thinking about your job to thinking about your work involves some important changes in perspective that you will need in order to take full advantage of the rest of the book. Then, in the next two chapters, I will help you assess your knowledge about your work, learn how to generate any additional information you need, and turn this knowledge and information into actions that you can take to manage your career.

Your Work Is Not Your Job

Employers own jobs and rent them out to the individuals currently holding the positions. **Your PWF is more than your job; it is what you can or want to contribute to multiple employers.** This definition of your PWF expands on the common understanding of "what you do" in three important ways. First, it is future-oriented. You cannot manage your past career; that is over. You can, however, have a significant impact on your future by thinking ahead.

The second difference is that your PWF is not just about what you can do; it is about what you *want* to do. If those two things are different, you should begin moving toward what you want to do. This part of the PWF concept has seldom been a big part of the decision-making calculus for mid-career individuals. People did what their organizations asked them to do—if not, they usually found that they had made "career-limiting" decisions. The Employability Plus model aims to reintroduce more personal interest and engagement into individuals' careers.

The third difference between the PWF and a job description is that it is not focused as much on the specific tasks you do, but rather on how what you do contributes to the larger enterprise where you are employed or might be employed. So, for instance, "I design Web sites" ideally becomes, "I design Web sites that help users quickly gather information." This kind of thinking helps you see in more detail how your skills, knowledge, and experience could contribute to work organizations. For example, a person with this work focus would want to identify potential employers with Web sites that primarily provide information. Furthermore, you begin to see how your skills and knowledge would need to be augmented in order to contribute more in that specific type of environment. So, continuing with the Web design example, our worker might want to become familiar with new ways of communicating statistical information more effectively or ways in which Web sites can become more interactive allowing visitors to manipulate data in their own ways. These skills would be very different from the skills of those Web designers who were focusing on Web sites that specialize in sales or entertainment.

Notice also that your PWF is not about things other than your work. It is not about having a good supervisor or compatible coworkers or a harmonious organizational culture. These are all things that are certainly important to consider when choosing a job, but you are not thinking about whether to accept a job at this point. You are thinking about a major theme that can tie together a series of jobs in your career.[5] This PWF will also by help you see how to build expertise in work that you find interesting and which multiple employers will find valuable.

Articulating Your PWF

At this early stage in your understanding of the Employability Plus model, my aim is to help you articulate at least a "starter" PWF. Managing your career in today's ever-changing world requires a good deal of information about work opportunities and challenges as well as about your own abilities and preferences. To gather that information or to organize the information you already have, you need a focus. That way you can begin to determine what streams within the torrent of information we all wade through every day might be most useful to you. A starter PWF provides such a focus.

As you gather more information, learn more about the Employability Plus model, reflect further, and respond to changes in the world and in your own preferences, even a PWF that you thought was certain will evolve to some extent. The two threshold criteria for a "starter" PWF are: 1) it ties your work to a specific part of the earning world and 2) it captures enough of your interest that you are willing to independently take the time and energy to gather information about it.

Some people already know what kinds of contributions they want to make. This is great! Here are examples of some good starter PWF descriptions:

- I want to combine my knowledge of technical writing and corporate training to design Web sites.
- I like to drive advanced software engineering efforts.
- I want to augment my public affairs/public relations background with more knowledge of business and move into investor relations.
- I want to become a product manager for a medical device company, where my knowledge of engineering as well as the many functions necessary to bring a new device to market will increase the introduction success rates.
- I want to build a private clinical psychology solo practice.
- I want to move into the nonprofit sector.
- I want to open a franchise.
- I want to work with retirement-aged people to help them get health care services.
- I want to manage the engineering design and production process for medical devices so that more individuals can live healthier, longer lives.
- I believe that computer memory is an important part of the computing process because it determines the size of the problem you can solve. I want to build computer memory devices to increase the capacity and flexibility of personal computers.

As you can see from reading these PWF descriptions, some are much more elaborate than others, but they all begin to describe a specific contribution to the earning world. None of these PWF descriptions says things such as "I want to work with people" or "I want to seek management positions with more responsibility." Such statements, while they may reflect your preferences, are so general that they could describe work in almost an infinite number of positions and organizations. Employers hire people at mid-career incomes to make much more specific contributions, and they assume these candidates already possess such general traits.

Obviously, if you are changing your focus in some significant way, your PWF will be more general at first. For example, "I want to open a franchise" and "I want to move into the nonprofit sector" are very general statements, but they do begin to provide some specific connection to the earning world. These are fine as starter PWF descriptions.

The Personal in Your PWF

The brief examples of PWF descriptions just given do not adequately communicate the source or intensity of the individuals' interest in their work. They concentrate on the contribution the individual wants to make to employers. This is a crucial part of an individual's PWF, but personalization is also important because it provides individuals with their personal connection to the work. It allows them to describe what they enjoy about the work itself and what motivates them to pursue building their skills, knowledge, and experience in certain ways. This personalization can be crucially important for long-term career satisfaction. To illustrate how this personalization can work to reenergize someone's work life, I want to tell Joel's story.

Joel was an engineer who had become a manager in a medical device firm. He had defined his role as a manager in terms of coordinating the projects and completing the paperwork necessary to make his unit run. In his mind, the manager performed the necessary, albeit onerous, bureaucratic work that allowed the real work of the organization to be done. When he began to explore what really interested him about the work he did, however, he discovered that it was the way he and his colleagues improved the lives of patients by designing and manufacturing new devices. He loved finding articles that highlighted devices his unit had produced so he could generate ideas about how to improve them.

As he pondered his role as manager, he realized that he could accommodate his interest without neglecting his coordination work. As a result, Joel began gathering more information about how the innovations his unit developed fared in clinical trials and about other related device innovations. He began sharing that information and using it to shape assignments and motivate the people in his unit. And he made time for this change in his activities and focus by delegating some of the coordination and paperwork to the supervisors who worked for him. They welcomed these new tasks because they were getting more managerial experience.

Joel reported that he felt reenergized and no longer saw his position as a sacrifice for the good of the company. The process also allowed him to articulate his PWF as motivating people to do quality engineering on medical device prototypes, something he found much more compelling than "pushing paper."

Besides the energizing aspect of Joel's experience, please note that his company and supervisor probably never knew the specifics of his change in career focus, even though it made such a difference to Joel. The personal reasons for your work focus, as well as your longer-term career direction, are yours, not your employer's. The employer can no longer make long-term commitments to its employees; that means you need to make a long-term commitment to yourself. Sometimes, as Joel did, you will discover a significant overlap between your own goals and those of your employer. When that is not the case, you owe it to yourself to begin preparing to shift positions and/or employers to move toward work you find more personally rewarding.

The interest and engagement embodied in the "personalized" part of your work focus can take many forms—you may experience it as intellectual interest, a commitment to the importance of the work, enjoyment of the work itself, or a true love of learning about it. The intensity of interest or engagement in their work varies for different people. Earning careers play different roles in different people's lives or at different times in a single person's life. The level of interest or engagement you currently have is likely to be a result of your personal preferences, your past, the role of work in your life generally, and your cultural background.[6]

Interest or engagement may be signaled by your increased animation when talking about that aspect of your job or by the fact that you keep returning to that part of your work. Another indication may be the wealth of knowledge you already possess and the interest you have in learning more. In articulating your PWF, look for projects or challenges or tasks in which you were fully engaged and did things you considered particularly important, interesting, and/or fun. Often you will lose track of the time when you are so engaged.[7] Table 3.1 provides a set of general questions to ask yourself to help you recognize your focus of interest in the working world.

The Five Aspects Exercise to Help You Articulate Your PWF

It is not surprising that many people have difficulty describing a PWF. Early in our careers, most of us know relatively little about the options in the working world or how we will react to the work styles required by the jobs we choose. Some of us get jobs in areas we enjoyed or excelled at in school, but there is no assurance that, just because we were attracted to a subject in school, we will enjoy working at it in the earning world. Furthermore, after completing our formal educations we typically choose jobs from whichever ones are available, often by comparing salaries and benefit packages but taking little else into account.

Furthermore, we realize that the jobs we have in the early years of our careers will change, and the common wisdom has been that choosing a

Table 3.1

General Questions to Facilitate the Articulation of Your Work Focus
With what activity or effort at work do you most identify?
About what aspects of the working world do you feel passionate to learn more?
What activities at your current and past jobs have fired your interest and imagination?
What work do you see yourself performing in the next 3 to 5 years?
What work activities or efforts do you read about even when not required to do so by your employer?
What types of outcomes of your work give you the greatest sense of satisfaction or feeling of accomplishment?
What types of work outcomes do you end up talking about in social situations with coworkers?

Originally published in: Power, Sally J. and Teresa J. Rothausen. "A Work-Oriented Midcareer Development Model, An Extension of Super's Maintenance Stage," *The Counseling Psychologist* 31, no. 2 (March 2003), 178.

"good employer" was more important than a specific job or type of work because employees were likely to stay in those organizations a long time. Once inside an organization, most of us let management shape our careers. This has meant that many of us now in mid-career have not actively sought interest or engagement in our jobs during most of our earning careers.

People who are trying to articulate their career interests or goals often begin with a blank sheet of paper and try to focus only on their personal preferences as they answer the question, "What do I want to do now?" Unfortunately for most, the answer does not spring to mind when they take this approach—probably because they are not used to thinking about their interests and their employment in the same context!

I have devised a different approach, the Five Aspects Exercise, for people trying to articulate their PWF. It helps you begin to define some of the details about your experiences and preferences in order to express a more tangible connection between yourself and the earning world. It also helps you recognize which facets of your various jobs you have found most interesting and/or energizing. Finally, it encourages you to look at the work not in terms of the particular combinations found in any one job, but in terms of larger conceptual themes or "aspects" that connect the jobs to one another. Each aspect can become a focus of your expertise and a theme for building your career.

The five aspects of work are 1) industry/sector, 2) function, 3) product/service, 4) customer/client, and 5) contribution. The vast majority of jobs have all five aspects. They occur in particular industries, involve particular organizational functions (e.g., marketing or engineering), often are tied to particular products/services, serve particular groups of customers, and make contributions to the organizations and/or to society.

These aspects are general categories. Don't worry about what makes up "the" list of industries or what precisely a sector is. Table 3.2 provides some examples of each aspect in commonly identified sectors of the economy so you can get a better idea of the category system. Most employees in mid-career have a general idea of the major components of each of these categories in the areas in which they have worked, and the information gathering that is part of the next success strategy will help you focus on exactly what terminology is used to describe your interests. The aim at this point is to discover your interests.

After you have done some thinking about your experiences, it often really helps to talk it over with someone, who can see your interest and engagement much more easily than you can. I discovered the importance of this step in the process when I first started using this exercise in my evening MBA classes with working adults.

From the very first, the working adults had trouble shifting from thinking about jobs to examining their interests in various aspects of their work. To see if I could show them how to identify their interests, I decided to try talking to one of them, while the rest of the class listened. When I started talking to a student who worked in marketing at a big packaged-foods company, she said she was in marketing, and then corrected herself to specify that she was really in direct marketing (direct marketing is described by the Direct Marketing Association as businesses who "advertise their products/services directly to consumers by mail, telephone, magazines, Internet, radio and television"[8]). She went on to describe the customers and the products on which she was focused, but she kept returning to the ins and outs of direct marketing and describing the "cool" quantitative analysis she could do on the job. In a

Table 3.2
**Examples of Work Focus Descriptors for Each Aspect of Work in Various
Sectors of the Earning World**

Remember, these are just examples *of descriptors people might use to describe different aspects
of their work if it was in one of these sectors.*

Aspect	Education	Business	Government	Non-Profit
Industry	K–12, Higher education, Private, Liberal arts, Research universities	Packaged goods, Telecommu-nications, Software Design	Federal, State, City, Military	Foundations, Health care, Public service, Social action
Function	Teaching, Administration, Librarians, Counselors	Direct marketing, Compensation (part of human resources), Logistics/ Inventory, Research and Development	Finance, Regulation, Investigation, Administrative Services	Development (raising money), Administration, Service providers
Product/ Service	Textbooks, Specialized educational software, videos/DVDs, Specific programs (e.g. drug programs)	Hard drives, Leadership training, Hotels, Cereal, Hair care products, Health insurance	Specialized software (e.g., novusgov.com) or equipment, Web design and computer security	Affordable housing, Environmental conservation, Employment opportunities of the disabled
Clients/ Customers	11–14 year-olds, Girls, Immigrants, Science teachers	Senior citizens, Other businesses, Military, Retail consumers	Special disadvantaged populations, Criminals, The public	Particular disadvantaged populations, Those with particular issue concerns
Contribu-tions	Helping children see the wonder in nature and the power of science to understand it	Providing people with security against catastrophic loss (property insurance person)	Serving the public by writing fair regulations that are true to the intent of the legislation	Helping those in need of financial assistance to find the sources for that help

few minutes it became obvious to everyone in the class, as well as to the student, that her work focus revolved around the analysis that provided information to better manage direct marketing efforts. Of course, she still had to know about the products she was marketing and the industry in which she was working, but she was most interested in analyzing data related to direct marketing.

Because this interactive approach is so helpful, talking about one's work to someone else has become a permanent part of the Five Aspects exercise. It also often proves helpful to ask significant people in our lives when they have observed us being highly interested or engaged in our work.

The Five Aspects exercise centers on your past experiences because it is likely that you have been interested and engaged in at least some aspects of your work in the past. After all, while employers usually determine your options, most mid-career workers have been at least generally satisfied with their employment. Furthermore, workers themselves do play a role in the promotions and transfers they are offered, through their performance and/or by actively applying for positions.

Sometimes surprise interests pop out during the Five Aspects exercise which have nothing to do with your past jobs. Perhaps this is because it is the first time in a while that many people have thought seriously about their interests at work. Once, while doing the Five Aspects exercise and talking in front of the class to one person to help him identify his interests, Mike, who was sitting a few seats away, began bouncing up and down in his chair. He was the supervisor of a department of graphic artists and others involved in designing marketing materials and ads for a large electronics retailer—work he had described as "managing creatives." I asked him, "What's happening for you?" and he replied, "Cereal!!"

What he had discovered as he listened to my conversation with the other person and thought about his own interests was that he wanted to describe his PWF in relation to cereal. He had never worked in the food industry before, but, for him, cereal had a mythical level of importance, and, he believed, this was also the case for millions of Americans because of their positive experiences as children eating cereal for breakfast. He immediately began gathering information on the major cereal makers in the United States. Mike enjoyed what he was learning, and planned to move into a company making cereal as quickly as he could.

Generating Options for Your PWF

Some people have trouble articulating their PWF because they haven't thought much about the larger, multiple-employer context of their work. They may know the general area in which they want to work, but they aren't sure about any specifics because they don't know what employment options exist. Some people might seek different rewards from their work, but still want to focus on the same general work content. (Examples of different rewards might include more autonomy in their daily work roles, a new sense of accomplishment, a different interpersonal environment, more money, etc.) Or some people might want to capitalize on their past experience and also begin to move in some very different directions. Also, people with a seemingly limited number of possible employers in their preferred locales might want to try to expand their employment options. I think that this lack of knowledge about career options is understandable, because we have been so job-centric and employer-centric in the last era of employment dynamics. I have two ways of looking at your work that will help you begin to see more of the options open to you.

The first way to generate options to consider for your PWF is to look at the possibility of specializing in some facet of the work you are interested in, or the work you are currently doing. For example, if you are in accounting you might decide to focus on cost accounting or tax accounting. A list of the major specialties within a job function can usually be found on the Web sites of the relevant professional associations, or are often listed in general textbooks on the subject. A related option to consider is becoming a generalist. Most of the time, generalists work in smaller- and medium-sized companies, or are in the entry positions at big companies. These people perform a range of subfunctions often needed by their unit or organization rather than specializing in one subfunction.

Remember that you do not have to focus your PWF on a function to be able to specialize it. You could specialize your work by focusing on two of the five aspects of your work rather than just one—for example, work with computer hardware (a product) might be further specialized by focusing on hardware for personal computers or computer systems for large businesses (adding a particular customer group focus). Or, you could specialize by the size of the companies you work with inside an industry (e.g., small companies in the defense industry). This approach to building your career by specializing is well known and, in fact, the opportunity for employees to sample various specializations is one of the attractions of large organizations. But some people in mid-career hear "specialization" and think it means they would have to commit to significant formal education and time out of the workforce. That is not the case for many specialties that are based on practical knowledge of specific niches within the earning world. These are perfect for mid-career individuals. Some new learning is, of course, needed and I will discuss how to identify what you need to know (Chapter 4) and then how to go about getting much of it (Chapter 5).

The permutations of specialties have grown partially because the variety of employers that are available has grown. Increased employee mobility opens up the possibilities for building specializations by changing employers. Today there are consulting firms or firms that offer contract services for almost every function and industry/sector. These firms are designed to provide specialized services to their customer organizations that range from the routine (e.g., product testing in the information technology industry) to the highly specialized (e.g., consulting on marketing strategy and implementation). For their employees, these firms provide opportunities for specialization in a way that a single, large employer cannot. First, your knowledge of the specialty is enhanced because you are likely to work with a number of client organizations and be exposed to a range of challenges. This builds both flexibility and knowledge in the work. Second, it introduces you to a number of potential employers. Third, the breadth of exposure can help you build your knowledge of trends in a work specialty as well as major challenges in the work that need to be met. And fourth, it can provide a bridge to management of the organization for some people who began their careers in a role seen as a support or staff function in most organizations (e.g., accounting or human resources).

A second major approach to generating PWF options is to look at the "work arena," that is, to look at the larger earning environment in which the work exists and consider the major ways the work is shaped so that it fits into the larger flow of providing products and services to society. The different components of the work arena share much of the same knowledge about the work but use it in different ways. Figure 3.1 is an abstract representation of the work arena that you can use to think through the options for work that are related to your current work focus. You put your current work focus into the burst in the middle of the figure and then ask yourself what types of work and which employers provide the functions in the boxes around the burst. Of course, you will probably not be interested in all the options, and sometimes the number of jobs playing a particular role may be small or not available in your preferred locales. Some of the options generated in this way will require more new learning than others. But by beginning to see how your current or ideal work relates to the various types of work other people do to provide related products and services, you will begin to see more options for where your current knowledge and skills might be useful.

I will use K-12 teaching as a general work focus to show how to use the Work Arena Figure to build a list of work focus options you might consider. I won't use a particular specialty within this general occupa-

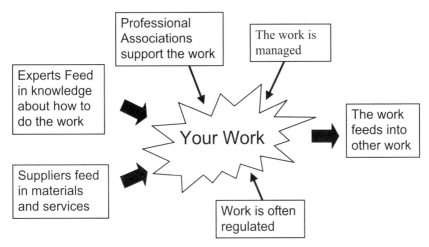

Figure 3.1
The Work Arena

tional focus because that type of example would involve too much description to make it understandable to most individuals. But, if you were an English teacher or a third-grade teacher, you could certainly place that specialty in the burst and specialize the list of options that you generate more than I will here. As you move counterclockwise around the burst, starting in the lower left, here are some of the examples of the types of work related to K-12 teaching that could be placed in the boxes of Figure 3.1:

- Teachers today use lots of different educational software. If you have a growing interest in technology, you might join such a firm to learn the technology while providing your coworkers with valuable insights into what teachers would find particularly useful. Not interested in the technical portion of the software? You also have knowledge and experience that would help you become a good sales representative or marketing person.
- States have departments of education to monitor and manage the educational endeavors in the state. Your knowledge and experience might be valuable in some of those functions.
- In one view of the larger context, your work as an educator helps provide structure and supervision for children of varying age groups. If working with children in a particular age group is still a major interest, you might consider working in another venue with that same age group, such as an after-school program, private tutorial work, or, if you teach high school, becoming a recruiter for a company that hires a lot of high school graduates. Another context in which you can see your

work as an educator is in providing people with information and knowledge in a formal setting. In work organizations, this is often done by "training" personnel, so you might consider working further down the flow of the work by becoming a trainer.

- You could become an educational administrator, running a school or working in the school district office.
- You could work in one of the professional educational associations.
- One prime resource that educators use is textbooks and other curricular guides. You might want to move into providing those kinds of materials using your experience as a teacher to help you shape your products or services.

Of course, writing a textbook or developing and showing that you have the skills and knowledge to join a software firm, a consulting firm, or working successfully as an administrator often means learning and doing new things. This is the new reality of career development: you have more choices about what you do, but you have to manage your own career development to get there.

A potential benefit of using these methods to generate options for your PWF is that these two methods encourage you to build on your current knowledge and past experience. Furthermore, you can choose a new focus not simply to learn more about a different facet of the work, but also to change the nature of the impact of your work on your larger life. For example, someone who has been working as a manager might want to develop a specialty and move out of management because he would like to move away from the long hours and stress involved in most management positions. Or someone who is a specialist in a large organization but wants to increase her income might join a consulting firm.

Another benefit of these option generation techniques is that they can also be used to help you devise a path or "bridge" toward your chosen PWF. This is necessary when your current work is significantly different from your ideal work. In that case, you may need to change jobs a number of times and build your skills and knowledge as you go. I call this process "bridging" because it involves using your current skills and knowledge to help you change work units and/or employers so that you get access to new learning opportunities as your career interests evolve. It also allows you to sample new types of work environments without completely "burning your bridges" in terms of your past work.

Here's how bridging worked over 15–20 years of one person's career. Jennifer began her career as a dental hygienist. After a few years, she tired of that work and began to look for something else. She used her knowledge of dentistry and of the procedures used in a dental office to become an investigator of complaints about dentists made to her state attorney general's office. She enjoyed that work for a number of years before she changed her job (and her employer) and became a researcher for the state dental association. She highlighted her investigative skills as well as her knowledge of the dental community and its practices as a hiring edge to get that job. Eventually, she was promoted to the executive-director position of that association. Each shift she made in her career used some of the knowledge and skills she had developed in her then-current job in order to give her a hiring edge for her next position. And each new position gave her opportunities to learn new capabilities. When she was making these shifts, her career looked unusual because she not only changed employers but also sectors as she moved from a dental office to government to a nonprofit association. But her career was founded on her knowledge of dental health procedures and shaped by the different roles she played within that work arena.

You also could see this idea of bridging being used by Sue, the manufacturing engineer who eventually hoped to become a marketer in a medical device company and who was highlighted in one of the snapshots in Chapter 2. Early in her quest to realize this PWF, she decided to change employers and sought a job as a manufacturing engineer in a medical device company. She sought out a small firm who would be attracted by her years of experience as an engineer and her work in some particular facets of manufacturing engineering. By bridging into the medical device firm as a manufacturing engineer, she increased her ability to learn about the medical device industry on the job without sacrificing her current expertise. If she finds that the medical device industry and/or marketing is not to her liking, she still has her expanding experience in manufacturing engineering to help her get jobs.

This set of options for specifying your PWF should help you see more possibilities to change or build your work in a multiple-employer environment. People have asked me, "Isn't there a good chance that I will make myself too specialized if I pursue a more specific PWF?" Yes, that could happen if you constantly choose to specialize without considering what employers are likely to need. But employers today want successful mid-career job candidates to have directly relevant work experience for the jobs they are being hired to do. Specialization and a knowledge of the likely needs of employers in your preferred locale are both necessary in order to successfully develop your career.

Learning about what employers are likely to value in their new hires requires gathering new kinds of information about the earning world. I will discuss this in Chapters 4 and 5. For right now, however, you should be thinking about articulating your interests in the earning world. This is a first step in focusing your information gathering. As you gather more information you can refine or even redefine your PWF based on what you learn.

Some Words for Aspiring Business Owners

The 2004 Merrill Lynch Retirement Survey reported that 13 percent of baby boomers say that their ideal work in retirement would be to open their own businesses.[9] The AARP Working in Retirement Study in 2003 reported that 16 percent of pre-retirees who intended to work in retirement want to work for themselves or start their own business.[10] With these statistics in mind, I'm going to include sections in this and the next three chapters that address how my approach to career management might be used by those aspiring to own their own businesses.

This book has been written using the language "employers" and "employees," which you may assume implies that the employers are organizations. But if you think about it, business owners need to be "hired" by their customers to do the work that they do, just as employees seek to be hired by employers to do the organization's work. Furthermore, heightened competition is a serious factor, both for people seeking jobs and businesses seeking customers. So the career challenges for business owners and non–business owners in terms of relating to the external environment are very similar. Thus, the four success strategies for the Employability Plus model of mid-career management—articulating a PWF, learning about that work focus and how it is likely to change in the near future, taking action to shape your career, and managing the career cycle—should apply to managing both types of career development.

Those considering changing their careers to become business owners, however, face some unique challenges that arguably make their situation more demanding than that faced by others. The root of this added challenge is the range of skills and knowledge such individuals need to have.

I have argued that most people, while they must know something about all five aspects of their jobs, can build a career by focusing on building their knowledge and skills around one or two aspects of their work. This works for those seeking employment from organizations where they will be one of many workers and where their responsibility for the organization's success is limited. But aspiring business owners really need to have a good deal of knowledge and skills related to all aspects of their work, because they will be taking responsibility for their entire enterprise. In essence, aspiring business owners need to focus on all five aspects of the work. For example, they need to pick a business that has the product/service focus (knowledge of product/service) that customers want (knowledge of the customer group), and that is different enough from other organizations' offerings in the industry to attract enough customers to sustain the business (industry knowledge and one form of contribution). In addition, owners often find themselves doing all or most of the organization's functions at various points, ranging from management to selling and from operations to financial analysis (knowledge of functions).

While the potential range of duties may be daunting, there are factors that make it feasible to manage. The most important of these is that business owners often run small operations, and that makes it easier to cover all the bases. Also, it may be possible to cut down the size of the responsibilities by affiliating with a franchise, getting a partner, or hiring some specialized help.

If you are serious about becoming a business owner in the next few years but have not thought much about your business, other than that you want one, I suggest that you begin now to articulate in your PWF the general focus you want for your business. Is it a product or service that you are interested in providing? What industry are you interested in? What types of customers do you want to serve?

You do not need to specify the exact product/service focus of your business if it will be some time before you actually make the shift to business ownership. But by specifying the general type of business you can begin to gather, through your career management efforts now, the information and experience needed to understand the dynamics of that business environment. Of course, this becomes even more important if you are thinking of opening a business with a focus different from that of most of your earning career. These efforts can help you both to pick a more specific business focus when it is time and to manage your business more successfully in the start-up phase when resources are often most stretched.

Just as with other PWFs, to identify a general business focus, you begin with the aspects of the work you find most interesting. You will find that many functional specialties can be converted into small businesses that serve other businesses. Products/services are constantly being improved by new organizations. Or you can study an industry in which you are interested, looking for the gaps in services or products that exist, or focusing on the type of customer you would like to serve and thinking about their needs. Then, as you learn about that aspect, you can branch into the other aspects.

For People Still Having Trouble Articulating Their Work Focus

If you are still having trouble articulating a starter PWF, you may want to consult a career counselor. Helping individuals to discover their interests in the earning world has long been a primary task of career counselors. But before you take that step, I have other ideas that might help you deal with the challenge on your own, or that at least may help you to articulate the nature of your challenge more clearly when you do contact a helping professional.

My preferred first option asks you to assess your reaction to a greater variety of work. You can begin that process by quickly scanning some periodicals focused on various parts of the earning world. Table 3.3 is a list of some of them, with brief descriptions of their focus. Your first task as you read through the list in Table 3.3 is to be sensitive to your interest. What periodical names cause you to think about situations you find personally important or interesting in some way? Check off the names of those periodicals and find out which libraries in your area have paper copies of them. Then plan a trip to briefly scan the last year or two of those periodicals. If the library only has the periodical available in an electronic database rather than as "hard copy", never fear—a librarian can usually show you how to access the periodical by issue, or the publication may have a Web site that you can explore. If your interest is in some area not mentioned in Table 3.3, talk to your local reference librarian about professional or industry publications related to that area that you could look through.

When you get to the library, your task is to scan the periodicals you have selected and make notes on the subjects of the articles that you find interesting (I suggest you actually write down a list). Then, read a few paragraphs of the article and see if you are still interested. Again, briefly note what you read and your reaction to it. Continue this process of scanning and making notes for no more than three or four hours. At the end

Table 3.3

A Listing of Examples of Major Periodicals Focusing on Different Sectors, Types of Businesses, Functions, or Industries

Type of Focus	Periodical Name
Management of non-profits	Nonprofit Times
Nonprofit fundraising and management	Chronicle of Philanthropy
Small Business	Entrepreneur, Venture, Inc.
K-12	Education Week
Higher Education	Chronicle of Higher Education
Finance	CFO
Information Technology	ComputerWorld
Health Care Management	Healthcare Executive

Table developed by Janice Kragness.

of that time, reread your notes and see if any ideas or patterns are apparent. If you have not gotten some ideas and if you have not been able to better articulate your interests by then, move on to another approach for identifying your interests in the earning world.

As you scan the magazines, consider your larger life interests—the issues that concern you, the services and products that are important to you, and the people with whom you interact, who you perceive as interesting and involved in their work. Could you be interested in doing work that is related to one of these?

I worked with one woman who really agonized over her PWF until she began thinking about what had been truly important in her personal life. A number of family members had had serious bouts with cancer. She had come to really appreciate the treatment she and others in her family had received. Once she had focused on helping others deal with the challenges of living with cancer, a number of work options opened up for her PWF.

Another possible explanation for difficulty in identifying an interest in the earning world is that you may be caught up in the desire to find your one true calling. This desire can range from wanting to go through this kind of process only once and to get it right, to believing that God or fate has a plan for you and your task is to discover it. Here again, I think that a career counselor or spiritual director can be helpful. If you want to work independently, it may be helpful to read and reflect on *What Should I Do with My Life?* by Po Bronson, which was a *New York Times* bestseller in 2002.[11] Bronson tells the stories of people seeking their one true path and of the lives they lived during and after that search. The book offers no solutions, but it may help you to better articulate your issue and see how to move forward.

Poet David Whyte, the author of *Crossing the Unchartered Sea,* a book about the emotional challenges of pursuing a career that is anchored in your personal uniqueness, argues that to live out your unique personhood in the world requires a "conversation" or interaction with the world.[12] As a way of starting that conversation, I suggest you articulate a tentative or starter PWF and then gather knowledge about that focus (the subject of chapter 4). See how you feel about it and observe the response you receive from the larger world to your endeavor as you pursue it. Use that information to help you better articulate your interests and what you want to contribute. Keeping notes and looking for patterns can be useful. Career management is a journey with ups and downs and side trips; unless you start the journey, you will get nowhere.

People often hope that they can go to a career counselor or other helping professional who can administer a "test" and tell them what career they should pursue. While career assessment tools exist, they have fairly general category systems and so do not usually lead to specific career options, particularly for people in mid-career. These instruments may be a way of seeing your interests in a different light, as well as a good discussion starter with your career counselor, but in my experience, few people in mid-career view them as particularly helpful.

Yet another possible explanation for having trouble articulating your work focus is that you are burnt out. If you have been working very long hours or have been under a lot of stress, you may be reading this book because you know you want a way out. Recognizing that you want out is good, but I'm not sure that this is the book for you at this time. I believe that if this is your situation, you first need to create some space and regain your energy. Create a break for yourself. Take a vacation or go on a retreat, even if it is only for 24 hours or a weekend. During that time, make some commitments and identify some concrete strategies to limit your working hours and more effectively manage your stress.

Also, I advise setting a time frame—perhaps three to six months—to assess your progress in managing your time and gaining some perspective. Put that date on your calendar. Breaking old habits is one of the hardest things adults do, so it will take time and energy, and will probably require repeated efforts with different tactics. Making space to focus on new activities is part of the challenge of personal change. If the goal is worth it, why not spend the time? Many books have been written that discuss how to make personal changes, and you may wish to consult these books in your quest for personal change. You may also want to seek a personal coach or counselor for support and ideas while you work through this challenge. At the end of the process, you can return to this book and have the energy as well as the motivation to do what is suggested here.

Finally, I have found that a number of business executives have difficulty moving to a more independent stance. They have spent their whole lives as team players, and they have trouble not relying on their employer's support structures. Also, many executives are used to having others come to them with ideas and opportunities. The approach to career management discussed in this book asks you to turn the tables and develop your own ideas.

There are many creative solutions to the challenges facing those who wish to manage their own careers more independently. One executive I worked with who had been downsized found that he was very uncomfortable without an "organizational home base." His answer was to create his own one-man organization with a Web site and an organizational name to put on his business cards.

Creative solutions notwithstanding, this model may not be for everyone. Certainly, some individuals will continue to have long, productive careers in a more traditional long-term relationship with one employer.

A recent small but longitudinal study of MBAs indicated that after ten years about one-third of the group still had these types of careers.[13] And some people will find jobs with comparable or better compensation in days or weeks after being downsized. Finally, this model—while it makes sense logically and appears to be feasible for individuals to implement— is not intended to be "the answer" for everyone. At this point, the Employability Plus model is for pioneers—individuals willing to step out and do some new things in order to increase their odds of personal and career success.

Chronicling Your Journey

At this point in the chapter I hope you have at least a "starter" work focus description. I urge you to set up a notebook, or an electronic equivalent, and dedicate it to your independent career management. Your first entry can be your starter PWF or a description of your challenge in articulating it and what questions or ideas you have about it. Writing something down often allows you to examine your thoughts in a different way and furthers your thinking. Also, it makes what you are thinking more concrete.

We are all busy, and adding one more thing to our to-do lists is hard. Seeing your career journal on a table you pass every day or next to your bed can act as a reminder that you should be thinking periodically about your career. If you use electronic media, try to design an electronic equivalent to that reminder (perhaps an icon on your electronic calen- dar). A journal also helps you recognize that career management is a journey; it is not a one-time acquisition.

You do not need to write in your journal every day or even every week, but you should try to make notes (with dates) about such things as your major thoughts and decisions about your work and career, ques- tions you need answered, goals you set, and ideas you have for building your skills and knowledge. This will help you remember your good ideas, connect them to actions that will implement them, and check to see if your implementation is a success. I also suggest taking an hour or two every few months to review your notes and your progress toward achieving your goals.

We all know there are many challenges to living up to our New Year's resolutions. Independent career management has a lot in common with those annual goals: both are about the future, both are usually private, and both need a support system of action options, specified goals, and what I call "review and recommitment breaks," times when you take stock of where you have been, what new challenges you are facing in terms of achieving your goals, and what you can do differently to meet them. Supportive friends and family are helpful too! You are trying to do something that is not the norm in mid-career, so you should expect the process of making this a regular activity to be challenging, at least until you develop some momentum and have experienced some of the rewards of this type of career management.

Moving Forward

Once you have a PWF (or a starter PWF that you want to investigate), the next step is to assess your knowledge about how that work is likely to change in the next three to five years and to establish or reaffirm your information-gathering techniques so that your knowledge is always current. Then it's time to turn that knowledge into concrete actions that you can take in order to better manage your career. These are the subjects of Chapters 4 and 5.

While what you need to know about your work focus will certainly be unique to you, PWF descriptions can be divided into three general categories based on the magnitude of change between your PWF description and what you are currently doing in your job and career. Or, put another way, these three categories indicate the intensity of career management you are embarking on to reach your goal.

I call people in the first category of career management intensity "Maintainers." Maintainers are building and changing, but the level of their career management is less intense than it is for others. This is because they generally want to continue doing what they are doing now. Their main career management goal, then, is to build their skills and knowledge in line with how their work is changing. They also want to keep an eye out for changes in the work that might significantly reduce the number of jobs available (e.g., automation or moving the work off-shore). Finally, they may want to consider ways to gain more flexibility in terms of their work by working with a variety of customer types, technologies, or products to increase employment options.

Joel, the engineering manager in a medical device company whose PWF story you read about in the section on personalizing your work focus, is a good example of a Maintainer. He did not need to change his job or his work focus to build toward his interests. What he needed was to integrate his interests more into his current job. In his future career management, he can build his capabilities and highlight how his interests help him to motivate others and build better device prototypes.

The people in second category of career intensity I call "Builders." The crucial feature of these individuals is that their PWFs build to a large extent on the skills and knowledge they have already developed in the earning world, but the nature of the work that they want in the future includes significant changes. Thus, they have a medium level of career management intensity.

Table 3.4
Levels of Career Management Intensity

Comparison of your PWF to your current job/career	Shortcut term	Level of career management intensity
Your PWF description is very different from what you have done in the working world	Changer	Highest Intensity
Your PWF description builds on the skills, knowledge, and experience you have been using in your employment but takes it in a somewhat different direction than before	Builder	High Intensity
Your PWF description is very similar to what you are currently employed to do	Maintainer	Low Intensity

Today, building does not always mean moving up in the organizational hierarchy or ladder. The opportunities to build in all kinds of directions have increased substantially with the growing complexity of our economy and the increased freedom of individuals to move among organizations. For example, technical and professional positions have increased more than any other category of occupations since the 1950s.[14] And these positions often pay very well. This can open the door for careers that are more flexible and personally interesting.

Amy is one example of a Builder. By the age of 34, she had a good career in marketing. She had recently married, and she and her husband were committed to starting a family after a few years, yet she also wanted to have an active career. With that in mind, she decided to build on her current knowledge and network in marketing, but shift her PWF to becoming a marketing researcher. Because that type of work involves so much individualized work and is usually done to support longer-term marketing decisions, she saw a high possibility for flexible hours and perhaps telecommuting. She also could become a solo practitioner selling her research services to organizations who needed them. This seemed like an excellent fit for her coming family responsibilities. Furthermore, she believed that her increased skills, knowledge, and experience would make her more valuable not only to companies with market research units but also to marketing research firms. She saw the potential for many career development options in the future, as her family became more self-sufficient.

The third and most intensive career development category is that of a "Changer." Nancy's story is a good example of this third category. She had been a very successful corporate attorney, but grew weary of what she perceived as the very confrontational and cutthroat work environment of the law. After a long period of experimentation, reflection, and information gathering, she decided that her PWF was to become the executive director of a nonprofit agency. This would be a big change, as she would leave behind the practice of law to become a manager in a very different part of the earning world. Many individuals, particularly after spending 25–35 years in one work arena, long to make a major change in their earning life. This type of shift calls for the most intensive amount of career management, because of the scope of new things that Changers will need to learn.

None of these three categories of career management intensity can be said to be better than any of the others. The category in which you fall is a result of your current personal preferences and your unique situation. But the questions you will want to answer via your information gathering will vary somewhat given your category, and so I will use these terms—Maintainer, Builder, and Changer—as a useful shorthand as we move on to the other components of the Employability Plus model. A summary of these categories is provided in Table 3.4.

CHAPTER FOUR

Success Strategy #2: Learning about the Near Future of Your Work in the Multiple-Employer Environment

Today knowledge and skills now stand alone as the only source of comparative advantage.

—Lester C. Thurow[1]

The PWF you have articulated is mostly a result of your personal preferences and experiences. To turn it into a viable, longer-term career-management tool, you need to understand how the work you are interested in is changing and whether there will be a demand for it in the near future. This will allow you to shape your skills and abilities in ways that are attractive to potential employers as well as of interest to you.

The information gathering described in this chapter is not focused on jobs or on specific employers, as in traditional career development. The need for that kind of information comes later in the Employability Plus model, when you are closer to switching jobs (see Chapter 5). At this point, you want to get a sense of the larger, multiple-employer picture of the work. Specific jobs and employers will come and go, but the work is much more likely to persist and evolve. This is another reason why a focus on your work (versus on a job or an employer) is a better foundation for individual career management.

For individuals in mid-career, it is particularly important to project how the work is likely to change in the near future (i.e., the next three to five years). This is something experienced workers are usually more able to do than entry-level workers or outside observers because of their experience (although career changers would perhaps be an exception to this statement). In addition, such predictions give you time and direction for developing the skills, knowledge, and experience that will make you particularly valuable to your employer or give you a "hiring edge" with other employers. By "hiring edge" I mean a particular combination of skills, knowledge, and experience that is at least somewhat unique and will make you particularly attractive to certain employers.

I will use the phrase "skills, knowledge, and experience" repeatedly in the next two chapters because it describes the primary assets that you bring to a new employer. These capabilities are what you want to manage and develop throughout your career. As the quotation that opens this chapter highlights, this is your source of competitive advantage. I have included "experience" along with "knowledge and skills" in my phrasing because people in mid-career often get much of their knowledge and skills through experience. Experience was once simply having worked in a particular industry, but in today's more competitive job market is likely to include specific situations in which you have worked—for example, you may have had experience managing projects on a tight budget, or successfully marketing a product within multiple, diverse cultures. Experience today is no longer roughly equivalent to seniority or years on the job, which is how it was defined by many in the past; it now means gaining experience and knowledge about the problems that are and will be important to employers.

To illustrate how this works, I want to tell you Jane's story. She was a young accountant whose employer had adopted accounting software in the early 1990s. She was very involved in her company's adoption process and found that, for her next two jobs, her hiring edge turned out to be her experiences with that process. In Jane's case, it was a happy accident that she got such experience, but had she been able then to read about what was new in her work as easily as people can now, she could have actively sought those experiences in order to create that hiring edge. This chapter is designed to give you the abilities and sensitivities to help you identify such skills and knowledge—that is, the hiring edge that will be most advantageous to your career. Then Chapter 5 will discuss how you develop them.

You have been gathering information about the working world for years. But what you need to do now is review and revise your information-gathering techniques so that they are more future-oriented, work-focused, and have a multiple-employer perspective. This chapter will help you do that by describing the types of information you need in order to manage your career in the twenty-first century, as well as providing an overview of and some creative ideas for ways to get that information.

Why This Task Is Possible

Most people roll their eyes when I suggest that they should be gathering information about the near future of their work in a multiple-employer environment. Even though they can see the logic for career development, their gut tells them it is an insurmountable task. This is understandable because in the past you couldn't easily get a broad view of how work was changing and so, until recently, it was an almost impossible project. Moreover, many note that it has always been chancy to try to predict the future! Let's explore both of these concerns.

Predicting the future has always been seen as a difficult undertaking because predictions so often are wrong.[2] But I am not suggesting that you really "predict" the future. Rather, I'm encouraging you to extrapolate what is likely to happen in the next few years from what you are able to learn about the present. Peter Drucker, the business guru who has often been touted as a gifted seer of the future, had a similar approach. He said that he did not "predict" the future; what he did was "look out and see what is visible but not yet seen."[3] You can use information about what is happening now in your work to "see" what skills, knowledge, and experience are going to be needed to implement the changes currently underway. Also note that this attempt to see a few years into the future is focused specifically on your chosen work, something that you have a good deal of knowledge about, not the earning world in general or any specific organization. This ability to "see" the near future is something that experienced workers are more likely to have than people new to the workforce or those not involved with the work. It is an edge that can come with experience, but it needs to be cultivated.

You have the time to develop this hiring edge because the adoption of changes by multiple employers is usually a relatively slow process.[4] "How can that be," you ask, "with so many, including this author, pointing out that the pace of change has accelerated?" The appearance of rapid change is more about the increased number of innovations being introduced and the increased competitive pressure to change. The process for any one change to be implemented still involves organizations and individuals first finding out about an innovation and becoming convinced that it will, in fact, improve their performance. Then the change must be considered important enough to command the resources necessary to make it, when compared with all the other changes that might be implemented in that organization. Finally, in most cases the change must be completed while the units involved continue to perform their normal duties. You can imagine the time involved for one organization to adopt a change. Now imagine it for all the organizations that might benefit from an innovation. The understandable slowness of the adoption process across a number of organizations gives you the time to learn the skills and knowledge that will be needed to perform the work in the new environment when it arrives. And if you learn the skills and knowledge early, as Jane did in the case of accounting software, you can use those abilities to help organizations make the change.

If your first response to my call for learning about the near future of your work was that information about what is happening to your work in other organizations is not readily available, you would have been right until about ten years ago! Revolutionary change has been occurring at your local library! With the help of Web-based technologies, large numbers of professional and industry publications have now become much more available via electronic databases. Ten or more years ago, libraries seldom had the funds to subscribe individually to enough of these kinds of periodicals to provide a broad overview, so very few subscribed to any. These professional publications still cost money to publish (and there are fewer advertisers, so subscribers have to pay more). But today, databases that include such periodicals are often leased to libraries for a cost based on the number of actual users, thus making their cost relatively reasonable.

Individuals interested in particular types of work or special topics can now search thousands of periodicals for articles in a matter of minutes. The database then provides you details about the publication of the article, a summary of the article, or often the article itself—all just a click away.

Most libraries today subscribe to a number of these databases in different fields (e.g., education, psychology, business), so individuals can relatively easily take advantage of this information explosion. These publications are generally not available for free on the Internet unless you have paid to join the group that publishes them, so the library is definitely the most cost-effective way to gain access. These databases, along with the other high-quality, wide-ranging resources that libraries habitually provide, go a long way toward providing the kind of information that individuals need to learn about their work in today's global, multiple-employer world. Furthermore, what your library doesn't actually have on-site, they can often get, at very modest costs, through interlibrary loans or sharing agreements. Also, many libraries have built their Web sites so that users can get access to at least some of their databases on-line once the user has registered for these services (usually this requires going into the library and having your library card scanned).

So, gathering this kind of information is possible. Now let's see how to make it feasible. Having a focus and knowing what kind of information you want to gather pares the task down considerably. Your PWF describes your current interests, and in this chapter you are essentially getting ready for your conversation with the larger earning environment by asking what employers are interested in.

It also helps to reframe the task and not approach it like you are doing a college research paper. (I'm assuming that was probably the last time you used the library to gather information!) Your job in writing a research paper was to get all the information you could in order to arrive at formal conclusions and present those conclusions as a finished product. The purpose of this information gathering is to develop ideas to explore and test in real conversations with others in the earning world. Your library and Web-based information gathering is designed to sensitize you to what others are thinking and doing so that you can ask good questions, have more enlightening conversations, and build your knowledge more quickly.

Finally, to make this information gathering possible for people with full-time jobs and busy lives, I believe it needs to be divided into manageable "chunks." I will use questions to help you understand exactly what kinds of information you are seeking. At the end of a chunk, you will have a natural opportunity to reflect upon and redirect your information gathering.

Where to Begin

I have said that the more predictable parts of the near future can best be discovered by looking at the concerns of people involved with the work now. Specifically, begin with this question: "What are the current changes, challenges, and controversies connected to my work?" *Changes* are solutions to past challenges or controversies, while today's *challenges* or *controversies* are usually described in that way precisely because they do not yet have clear solutions. The exact definitions of these words are not as important as how they focus your attention on what those managing, monitoring, and doing the work see as the most important current topics within the work. People who are willing to learn about these topics and to experiment to develop methods to address them are likely to be seen by employers as the most valuable workers in the years to come.

You can "discover" what is likely to happen in the near future of your work in a number of ways. Often your particular situation or preferences will determine which information source you start with. For example, let's suppose Linda is a nurse who wants to know if, when she retires to the Southwest in a few years, she can become a drug rehabilitation counselor specializing in how spirituality can aid that process. She knows nothing about whether such a specialty exists within drug counseling, what extra training she might need, or if such jobs might be available in the Southwest. Networking where she is living now is not likely to help her very much. Web searching would be hard, because she doesn't have good search terms yet. But in an hour at the library working with a reference librarian, she could find out that there indeed is such a specialty, as well as obtain some names of people and programs, from which to begin finding specific answers to her questions, both about the training needed for this specialty and about her interest in working in the Southwest.[5]

The library is not always the answer. When Lilly went to the library to discover local job possibilities for working in the importing/exporting of oriental foods and drinks in her new city, she found no information about her locale. She turned to networking and began with the owners of the local oriental restaurants that she liked. From there she began to talk to the oriental food distributors about how they saw the import/export business developing in the next few years.

If there are no special circumstances leading you toward one information source rather than another, it's better to choose your source based on how efficiently and effectively it can provide the information. I believe that reading periodicals is by far the best way to begin to gather information on the changes, challenges, and controversies in your work. Here's why:

1. Your current work-related network is likely to be too limited for this task. You want to get a good overview of what is happening in your work *worldwide*, because knowledge of the newest techniques and approaches is how you identify high-quality hiring edges. In the past, what was happening elsewhere in the world did not matter much to our daily work activities, but, with increased communication and competition, those days are over. Yes, you will likely be limited to publications in English, but periodicals focused on particular types of work are likely to monitor the important changes in the work worldwide.

2. Professional associations can be good sources of information about some topics, but are likely to view them from their own professional bias, which is often related to the standards and practices of the profession. You, on the other hand, are interested in the changes that are important to employers.

3. The managers at your employer—a major source for such information in the past—are often less concerned about the future, even the near future, than they were in the time of more stable employment. Their focus today is on performance in the present!

4. Periodicals employ writers whose job it is to look for changes, challenges, and controversies related to the work and to report on them (these topics are dramatic and make "good stories"). Thus, you can greatly increase your informational reach by using their "leg work."

Why use the library when the Web is so readily available? There are two main reasons. First, libraries are in the business of providing high-quality information. What I mean by "high quality" is that the facts and figures have been checked for accuracy and the opinions edited for their reasoning and thoughtfulness. On the Web, there is very little quality control, so you have to carefully assess the source and nature of each piece of information.

The second reason to use a library is that librarians are there to help you find the answers to your questions. Today, there are many different types of resources—both print and electronic—and part of the librarian's job is to know where different types of information reside and how to use the resources. They can greatly speed your ability to get answers. Even Craig Silverstein, Google's director of technology, recognizes the value of libraries versus Internet searches, saying, "My guess is about 300 years until computers are as good as, say, your *local* research library in doing search"[6] (Italics added for emphasis). Developing a relationship with a librarian who can help you to find the information you want quickly can save you lots of time and frustration! Rather than focusing on where to find the information, why not focus on deciding what questions you want to ask? The questions are the key to building your knowledge about how your interests play out in the earning world.

While the Web is limited in some ways, it is particularly good for gathering some types of information. For example, it can be used to locate current details and resources, such as names and addresses, or speech texts. It is also very good for finding very recent information. Once you have the specific terms referring to some new technology or concept, you can often find great information on the Web, and not have so many hits from the search engine that you could never get through them all. Job search Web sites can be good places to look at postings to see what kinds of hiring criteria or tasks are highlighted for certain types of positions, or what kinds of employers hire people who do the work you are interested in. And while there are many people who put highly biased information on the Web, there are also a lot of people who are experts and provide wonderful information for free via their Web sites.

Because many are unaware of how to use library databases and of some of the details about how to move back and forth between the library and the Web most effectively, this book contains an appendix by business reference librarian Janice Kragness. We have worked hard not only to provide you with the basic library information to increase your comfort about your first visit to the library's reference section to gather information about the near future of your work, but also to integrate tips about using the library with the concepts of the Employability Plus model and the questions highlighted throughout this book.

This chapter, the next one, and the appendix will focus on helping you articulate the appropriate questions as you gather your information. Having good questions is one of the keys to working well with librarians in putting the Employability Plus model to use. This model's approach is different from what is usually found in basic career sourcebooks. White-collar workers in mid-career often need more detailed information than most traditional career resources provide. If you just ask most librarians for career information about a subject, they are likely to send you to those traditional resources. So, by asking specific questions about the work and its challenges or how to find certain types of employers, you signal the librarian that you are looking for more sophisticated information.

Identifying Changes, Challenges, and Controversies in Your Work

Your first task is to get an overview of how your work is changing among multiple employers. Look for the changes, challenges, and controversies currently under discussion in conjunction with your work and make a list of them. I will call the items on your list your work's "hot topics."

Those with a wide personal network that includes those managing the work may well already have a list of hot topics in their heads, or could quickly generate one by networking. That's great, and maybe such individuals don't need to take this trip to the library, but I advocate trying this library-focused approach to information gathering at least at first, because of its broader reach. It is a good check of your network's usefulness in predicting how the work is changing. If the information from your personal network turns out to be comparable to the results of your research, you can rely on it in the future.

Begin making a list of the hot topics in your work by searching the database most appropriate to your work using key words that identify your work (e.g., "direct marketing" or "training") along with other general key words such as "challenges" or "trends." Also, begin by limiting your reading to the last two to four years. (The appendix provides details about how to use databases, along with specific strategies for getting information.) The database will provide you with a list of articles, summaries of them, and often the entire article. If your search comes up empty, talk to a librarian! Articles are probably there, but the key words you use might need to be different. Different databases often use different key words and determining the appropriate words to use for a search is one of the things that reference librarians specialize in.

Electronically generated article lists are seldom perfectly focused for an individual's purposes, but you can scan through them, looking at the titles and "marking" those you think hold most promise (another common feature provided by electronic databases allows you to "mark" arti-cles you are particularly interested in and generate a list just of those articles). Next, quickly read the most promising articles. Regardless of how the topics are presented, try to identify the growth points for your work and/or potential opportunities to add value for employers while doing the work. As you read, briefly list the challenges, changes, or con-troversies in relation to your work, and any special terminology con-nected with them. You will know that you have done enough searching when your database mostly turns up articles on hot topics that you already have on your list.

The next question to guide your thinking about these hot topics is to ask yourself which of them are likely to have direct and widespread impact on large numbers of people doing your work. These are hot top-ics that you will want to learn more about and develop strategies to deal with, regardless of your personal interest in them, because they are likely to affect your value as an employee.

For example, John was working in an administrative unit of an insur-ance company in 2000 and found himself on the Group Administrative System (GAS) committee. He was casually reading a local newspaper and came across an article on a change that would affect his work in a major way. The article was about e-signatures and announced that a law was taking effect that made e-signatures as binding as actual, pen-on-paper signatures.[7] Suddenly, the committee service, which he had seen as simply one more thing to do, began to make sense to him in a whole new way.

Approximately 60 percent of John's work entailed putting informa-tion from a number of different forms into one form and then getting the appropriate signatures on that form. The GAS committee was charged with consolidating the four or five different software programs that pro-duced the different forms he consolidated, and now he could see where management was going with that task. Once the forms were consolidated into one software package and the e-signature software was added, the company would be able to eliminate many of the tasks he did in his job. Clearly, his administrative unit was on its way toward a major downsiz-ing. He quickly began planning to move on!

As with Jane's story in the beginning of the chapter, John's insight that his employer was getting ready to consolidate the administrative work in his unit was the result of a series of accidents. But if you have information about such changes in advance and are thinking about them as employ-ers would think about them, you are much more likely to recognize such moves and have the time to appropriately adjust your career trajectory.

There are usually options to revising your work focus when something like that happens, if you have time to think and prepare. Let's look at how people might adjust to such a situation from the perspective of each of the career management intensity levels. For example, someone working in John's unit who is a Maintainer might consider what cases would still need special handling even with the more automated system (e.g., those involving funds over a certain dollar amount or those where important information is missing) and become an expert in those kinds of cases. Someone who is a Builder might consider moving to an information systems focus by using his knowledge of insurance processes as a bridge into helping design the specific application of this software package to consolidate the forms. Or, if someone wanted to move toward management (i.e., someone who is a Changer), that person might get deeply involved in the transition process to build a specialized knowledge of managing such transitions.

For the five or six hot topics of most interest to you, next ask yourself, "What employers will find this topic particularly important?" The answers I am looking for here involve specific concerns or needs of the organization's management—not the actual names of employers. To begin to develop this kind of information, you need to think about exactly what the change does for the larger organization and describe what kind of employers would find that change particularly valuable. Those early-adopter employers will be willing to pay a premium for knowledgeable employees. Then, as more and more organizations adopt the change, the premium for those capabilities will gradually decrease and the capabilities will increasingly become "expected."

An Illustration of a Library Visit

To illustrate the points I have been making about the practicality of this type of activity, I want to describe how a round of such information gathering might unfold. Because this round might be somewhat truncated for Maintainers and Builders who know a good deal about their work, I have decided to describe the first round of information gathering for the more complicated situation of a Changer.

Let's suppose for this illustration that I am a midlevel manager in business who is interested in changing my career focus to the nonprofit sector. I am tired of my current work and what I am increasingly seeing as a meaningless "rat race" in business. In the next phase of my career, I would like to make my work count for something I feel is important. I have been thinking about the nonprofit sector. Although I have volunteered in a number of organizations, I am uncertain exactly how my skills, knowledge, and experience might translate into a job in this sector. Also, I don't have many contacts with people actually employed by nonprofits, and I don't know exactly what I'm really interested in yet. So, I have decided to do some library-focused information gathering to get started.

Here's a description of what one library visit might look like written from the perspective of the person doing the search so that you can see the thought process that guides the actions:

I started with the question: What kinds of changes, challenges, and controversies are "hot" in the nonprofit world and which of them interest me? In discussion with the local reference librarian, we decided to start by gathering articles just over the last five years from one publication, The Chronicle of Philanthropy (its prime audience is the nonprofit sector), and some general key words. The librarian showed me the database that included that publication and helped me set up the search. Specifying that journal plus the key word "competition" (I know, awfully "business" oriented, but I just wanted to try it!) brought up 14 articles since 2000 (see Figure 4.1). And, when I specified the journal and the key word "trends," I got 27 articles (see Figure 4.2).

I read through just the titles of the articles online and marked three from the group of 14 and seven from the group of 27 (see Figures 4.1 and 4.2) for further reading. So far, the database search had taken about 30 minutes. What I wrote down in my journal notes at this point in the process was the following:

- *Searched C of Phil. since 2000 using "competition" and "trends" as key words*
- *Comparing the article titles that I chose to look at further with those I didn't: I am pretty uninterested in the development side of nonprofits, at least for now. That's good, because there is certainly a lot to learn about that, if these searches are any indication! But it's bad because in order to run a nonprofit (if I decide to aspire to that), I would certainly need to know about fundraising!*
- *I think I see a trend in wanting to become more "like business"—at least to adopt the good things. My skills could be useful there.*
- *Hiring good people seems to be a hot topic and something where my management experience might help. There do not seem to be clear answers—I will read those articles carefully.*
- *Not much here about how the nonprofit world tends to be divided up into subgroups—I'd like to look at that to add detail to my focus. This may be a question for the librarian next time.*

Then I read the 17 articles I had selected and made short notes on the information I found useful, using the article title to show where I got it. The articles were short, so it took about one hour.

- *"Human Resources From Scratch": Need for this service—seems not to be a full-time job for most organizations and to be paired with the administrative manager—that's a job that might be a good fit for my current skills, knowledge, and experience.*

Figure 4.1
List of Articles Resulting from a Search of *The Chronicle of Philanthropy* between
January 2000 and June 2005–Key Word Used Was "competition"

1. <u>Business-Plan competition Draws 460 Applications, Awards 4 Top
Prizes</u>. By: Wallace, Nichole. *Chronicle of Philanthropy*, 6/23/2005, Vol. 17 Issue
18, p41, 1 p, 1 chart   **HTML Full Text**

2. <u>Human Resources From Scratch.</u> By: Klineman, Jeffrey. *Chronicle of
Philanthropy*, 11/25/2004, Vol. 17 Issue 4, p25, 2p, 1c   **HTML Full Text**

3. <u>10 Charities Win Awards for Marketing and Fund Raising.</u> By: Prest, M.
J.; Preston, Caroline. *Chronicle of Philanthropy*, 11/11/2004, Vol. 17 Issue 3, p34,
2p, 3c, 1bw   **HTML Full Text**

4. <u>United Way Drives Dropped 3.2% in Most Recent Campaign Season.</u>
By: Wolverton, Brad. *Chronicle of Philanthropy*, 10/14/2004, Vol. 17 Issue 1, p19,
1/2p   **HTML Full Text**

5. <u>Better Press Skills Could Help Relief Groups.</u> By: Greene, Stephen G.
Chronicle of Philanthropy, 3/18/2004, Vol. 16 Issue 11, p51, 1/4p   **HTML Full
Text**

6. <u>Appeals With Appeal.</u> By: Marchetti, Domenica. *Chronicle of Philanthropy*,
10/16/2003, Vol. 16 Issue 1, p27, 3p, 4c   **HTML Full Text**

7. <u>Charities Venture Into Business.</u> By: Wallace, Nicole. *Chronicle of
Philanthropy*, 5/15/2003, Vol. 15 Issue 15, p29, 4p,3c   **HTML Full Text**

8. <u>Charities and Foundations Must Confront Shrinking Labor Pool,
Research Says.</u> By: Joslyn. Heather. *Chronicle of Philanthropy*, 10/17/2002, Vol. 15
Issue 1, p22, 3/4p   **HTML Full Text**

9. <u>Community Foundations Facing Crossroads.</u> By: Carson Emmett D.
Chronicle of Philanthropy, 5/16/2002, Vol. 14 Issue 15, p39, 2p   **HTML Full Text**

10. <u>77 Foundations Win Honors in Competition for Communications
Efforts.</u> *Chronicle of Philanthropy*, 5/2/2002, Vol. 14 Issue 14, p27, 3p, 6c   **HTML
Full Text**

11. <u>14 Charity Solicitiations Win Honors.</u> By: Hruby, Laura. *Chronicle of
Philanthropy*, 11/01/2001, Vol 14 Issue 2, p65, 4p, 6c   **HTML Full Text**

12. <u>Tech Mogul Mulling Which University Will Receive $150-Million
Donation.</u> By Sommerfeld, Meg. *Chronicle of Philanthropy*, 6/28/2001, Vol. 13
Issue 18, p16, 1/5p   **HTML Full Text**

13. <u>TAX WATCH.</u> By: Schwinn, Elizabeth. *Chronicle of Philanthropy*, 5/31/2001,
Vol. 13 Issue 16, p40, 1/2p   **HTML Full Text**

Figure 4.1
(*Continued*)

14. Direct-Marketing Awards Honor Fund-Raising Creativity, Success.
Chronicle of Philanthropy, 10/19/2000, Vol. 13 Issue 1, p29, 3p   **HTML Full Text**

Source: Academic Search Premier, an EBSCO Host Research Database.

Figure 4.2
List of Articles Resulting from a Search of *The Chronicle of Philanthropy* between
January 2000 and June 2005–Key Word Used Was "trends"

1. Donations to Churches on the Rise. By: Jensen, Brennen. *Chronicle of
Philanthropy*, 4/28/2005, Vol. 17 Issue 14, p14, 1p, 1 chart   **HTML Full Text**

2. A Misleading View of Employment Trends. By: Salamon, Lester M.,
Chronicle of Philanthropy, 9/16/2004, Vol. 16 Issue 23, p39, 2p   **HTML Full Text**

3. Hiring Stalls at Nonprofit Groups, Study Finds. By: Jensen, Brennen;
Wolverton, Brad. *Chronicle of Philanthropy*, 9/2/2004, Vol. 16 Issue 22, P23, 3/4p,
1 graph   **HTML Full Text**

4. Big Business Doing More for Charity. By: Wilhelm, Ian; Kerkman, Leah;
Krauze, Stanley W.; Moore, Cassie J.; Schwinn, Elizabeth. *Chronicle of
Philanthropy*, 8/5/2004, Vol. 16 Issue 20, p7, 5p, 1 chart, 4c   **HTML Full Text**

**5. Foundation Funding for the Humanities: An Overview of Current and
Historical Trends (Book).** By: Kronstadt, Jessica. *Chronicle of Philanthropy*, 8/5/
2004, Vol. 16 Issue 20, p44, 1/9p   **HTML Full Text**

**6. State Officials Are Trying to Hinder Fund Raising by Advocacy
Charities.** By: Cohen, Rick. *Chronicle of Philanthropy*, 6/24/2004, Vol. 16 Issue 18,
p47, 3/4p   **HTML Full Text**

7. Foundation Giving Trends, 2002. *Chronicle of Philanthropy*, 4/15/2004, Vol.
16 Issue 13, p10, 1p, 6 charts   **HTML Full Text**

8. Many Charities Report Success in Coping With Fiscal Challenges. By:
Greene, Stephen G.. *Chronicle of Philanthropy*, 1/22/2004, Vol. 16 Issue 7, p32,
2/3p   **HTML Full Text**

9. Giving and Investing by Financial Institutions Examined. By: Anft,
Michael. *Chronicle of Philanthropy*, 1/8/2004, Vol. 16 Issue 6, p25, 1/4p   **HTML
Full Text**

10. Nonprofit CEO's See Salaries Rise. By: Schwinn, Elizabeth; Wilhelm, Ian;
Larose, Marni D.; Krauze, Stanley W.; Murray, Matt. *Chronicle of Philanthropy*,
10/2/2003, Vol. 15 Issue 24, p27, 4p, 1c   **HTML Full Text**

Figure 4.2
(*Continued*)

11. **Foundation Giving in 2003 Likely to Drop, Report Says.** By: Kerkman, Leah. *Chronicle of Philanthropy,* 8/21/2003, Vol. 15 Issue 21, p10, 1p   **HTML Full Text**

12. **Britain's Largest Charities Face Slowdown in Private Donations.** By: Greene, Stephen G. *Chronicle of Philanthropy,* 8/17/2003, Vol. 15 Issue 20, p11, 1/4p   **HTML Full Text**

13. **A Look at Investments, Borrowing Trends, and Charity Views on Finances.** By: Anft, Michael; Wallace, Nicole; Wolverton, Brad. *Chronicle of Philanthropy,* 7/24/2003, Vol. 15 Issue 19, p42, 2/3p   **HTML Full Text**

14. **Nonprofit Popularity Contests.** By: Berkshire, Jennifer C.. *Chronicle of Philanthropy,* 3/6/2003, Vol. 15 Issue 10, p8, 11p, 1c   **HTML Full Text**

15. **Survey Identifies Troubling Trends for Nonprofit Organizations.** By: Lipman, Harvy. *Chronicle of Philanthropy,* 11/14/2002, Vol. 15 Issue 3, p13, 1/4p **HTML Full Text**

16. **Seeking a Smooth Reentry.** By: Anft, Michael. *Chronicle of Philanthropy,* 6/27/2002, Vol. 14 Issue 18, p7, 2p, 1c   **HTML Full Text**

17. **Charitable Giving Slides.** By: Lewis, Nicole; Lipman, Harry. *Chronicle of Philanthropy,* 6/27/2002, Vol. 14 Issue 18, p27, 2p, 1 graph, 3c   **HTML Full Text**

18. **Social-Service and International Groups Were Winners in 2001, Report Says.** By: Lewis, Nicole. *Chronicle of Philanthropy,* 6/27/2002, Vol. 14 Issue 18, p28, 2p   **HTML Full Text**

19. **Head of Humanics Group Wants to Spread 'Best Kept Secret'.** By: Greene, Stephen G. *Chronicle of Philanthropy,* 6/27/2002, Vol. 14 Issue 18, p44, 1p **HTML Full Text**

20. **Forging Links Online.** By: Wallace, Nicole; Larose, Marni D.; Voetz, Martha. *Chronicle of Philanthropy,* 6/13/2002, Vol. 14 Issue 17, p23, 5p, 2c **HTML Full Text**

21. **Press Clippings.** By: Lewis, Nicole; Williams, Grant. *Chronicle of Philanthropy,* 6/13/2002, Vol.14 Issue 17, p40, 3/4p   **HTML Full Text**

22. **The Nonprofit World: Financial and Employment Trends.** *Chronicle of Philanthropy,* 3/21/2002, Vol. 14 Issue 11, p32, 2p   **HTML Full Text**

23. **Education Is Top Cause for Grants.** By: Hruby, Laura. *Chronicle of Philanthropy,* 3/7/2002, Vol. 14 Issue 10, p17, 1/4p   **HTML Full Text**

Figure 4.2
(*Continued*)

---

24. Trends in Planned Giving Highlighted in 2 Studies. By: Blum, Debra E. *Chronicle of Philanthropy,* 10/18/2001. Vol. 14 Issue 1, p22, 1/3p   **HTML Full Text**

25. On Their Word: Authors' Tips for Raising Money in the 21st Century. By: Lewis, Nicole. *Chronicle of Philanthropy,* 03/22/2001, Vol. 13 Issue 11, p21, 1p **HTML Full Text**

26. Church Giving by Protestants: Report Cites 30-Year Trends. By: Blum, Debra E. *Chronicle of Philanthropy,* 01/11/2001, Vol. 13 Issue 6, p23, 1/4p   **HTML Full Text**

27. American's Social Ties: Trends Affecting Nonprofit Organizations. *Chronicle of Philanthropy,* 10/5/2000, Vol. 12 Issue 24, p38, 2p, 1 graph   **HTML Full Text**

Source: Academic Search Premier, an EBSCO Host Research Database.

- *"Charities Venture into Business": Reports on a competition for business plans in the nonprofit sector. Sponsored by Yale (need to look at their Web site and see if they have other interesting stuff). A very interesting idea!*
- *"Charities and Foundations Must Confront Shrinking Labor Pool, Researcher Says": Study from Brookings Institute by Paul Light—I'll have to see whether it is available on the Web for free.*
- *"A Misleading View of Employment Trends": letter to the editor mentioned another study ("Nonprofit Employment Data Project") that is supposed to be better—I can go to the Web and see if it is available.*
- *"Hiring Stall at Nonprofit Groups, Study Finds": This is the article that the letter responds to.*
- *"Nonprofit CEOs See Salaries Rise": These people don't seem to be hurting for salaries—$200,000+! I bet it is only the very big organizations.*
- *"Survey Identifies Troubling Trends for Nonprofit Organizations": Just focused on development.*
- *"The Nonprofit World: Financial and Employment Trends": Great article about "The New Nonprofit Almanac and Desk Reference"—table lists subgroups within the nonprofit world—library have it?—also summaries of findings at www.urban.org and www.independentsector.org, both sponsors— Printed article.*
- *"American's Social Ties: Trends Affecting Nonprofit Organizations": good historical overview—seems to be based on "Bowling Alone," a recent book. Lists some of the old nonprofits—again, something I should spend some time with. Printed article.*

So, after an hour spent reading, I have printed two articles to read, have Web sites to explore, and one report I want to try to find on the Web. I have identified two hot topics. Hiring employees is hot topic #1. Employers who would be most interested in such a skill would probably be those who hire a lot of people—so, the larger nonprofits. Hot topic #2 is developing a business venture. Employers who would be most interested in that would be nonprofits in need of money (most of them!) who produce products/services or have an expertise that other organizations might want (a much smaller subgroup). So, when I start networking with nonprofits, I will have some ideas about how to find employers who might be interested in either topic, if one of these hot topics becomes the focus of my interest going forward.

After such a round of information gathering and note-taking, I suggest that you wait a few days and schedule some thought time to review your notes and identify the next questions you want to pursue (perhaps over a cup of coffee at a favorite coffee shop?). This would probably take about one-half hour, and I suggest you build it around the three headings listed below. Here's how this person's notes might look:

- *Personal Conclusions:*
  I'm still interested in both hot topics and in working in nonprofits generally. Before I go too much further, I need to do a broader search for hot topics—this search was in only one publication!
  I realized that I will not want to work for just any organization, and I do need to think about what part of the nonprofit world I want to focus on.
- *Prime resources:*
  John's Hopkins University site looks good—particularly "Listening Post Project"
  I want to read those two articles I printed again and look at the summaries of the report on trends on www.urban.org and www.independentsector.org—that last site may be good generally.
- *Best next steps:*
  I want to find out more about the local employment options within the nonprofit world and see their range. My question for the librarian: "What nonprofit organizations are in this region?" Then I will make a list of what I am drawn to. I really need to do another round focused on what changes, challenges, and controversies exist in the nonprofit sector—key words might be "nonprofit" and "management" or "trends" or "operations", pulling articles from throughout the database over the last three years. Questions for the librarian: Which database is the best for articles on the nonprofit sector? What database has the Nonprofit Times? (listed in Table 3.3)

The library visit took about two or two-and-one-half hours (without counting commuting time or reading this book!). The next round looks to be about a two-hour commitment with maybe an hour on the Web, and reading at home to finish off the first information-gathering session. Of course, Changers may need to go for a number of rounds at the library to get a feel for their new work focus. But, for Builders or Maintainers, I would imagine two library sessions (approximately four to six hours) would provide enough information about hot topics to move on to the next success strategy.

Notice how using questions to frame the information gathering helps to divide it into more practical chunks and gives the process a sense of progress. It keeps you moving forward and encourages you to assess what you have learned and make midcourse corrections. The questions you ask of the information are crucial to your ability to use it to manage your career. Throughout the rest of the book, the general questions I highlight will help you see the steps and logic of the Employability Plus model. Later in this chapter, in Table 4.2, I have listed all the major questions I have focused on in this chapter.

Finally, notice how I carefully made notes about the terms and limits I used on various database searches and on what the interesting articles said. This is important for a number of reasons. Writing down your conclusions as you go through the process will help your thinking to crystallize. Also, because you are doing this information gathering in small chunks and it is an ongoing process, you may not remember the details of your past efforts without having notes. And, finally, as you learn more and begin to make decisions, you may well want to return to some articles to find the names of various organizations or experts. These notes will make that more easily possible.

Selecting Your Career Development Focus

Now that you have a list of hot topics that are likely to be important to your work in the near future, you will have a good sense of the current concerns and interests in your work focus. If you are interested and excited about at least some of these, it is a sign that your PWF was well chosen and can be a firm foundation for your career management. If you were not very interested in them, then you probably need to reconsider your PWF (see Chapter 3).

For those ready to move forward, the next step is to select one hot topic from the list as a beginning focus for networking and career development activities. I suggest only one topic at a time. This is a list of cutting-edge topics precisely because most workers don't have the skills, knowledge, and experience to deal with them effectively. By focusing your developmental efforts, you are more likely to develop them more quickly than most others and thus use them to maintain your value as an employee or to build a hiring edge to get positions that are of more interest to you.

Occasionally, your hot topic will be decided for you because you have discovered a topic that has significant potential for widespread and direct impact on great numbers of those doing the work. I have already discussed this possibility. More often, you will need to make a choice. This can be difficult when your knowledge of the larger environment and of the topic itself is relatively limited. To make this choice more comfortable, consider it an experiment for a given period of time—say, six months or a year. If the topic does not seem to provide a viable hiring edge or if you lose interest in it, then you can move on to another hot topic.

Still, you want to make as wise a choice as you can about the topic you select. Interest is very important, but there are three additional questions that can help you pare the list down to a single topic.

Question #1: How far along is each hot topic in its development?

The ideas you are reading about are in various stages of development. It is important not to focus on a topic that will take a good deal of time to develop into a recognized solution if you are concerned about the possibility of imminent job loss or are seeking a change in the near future. It's hard to develop a set of skills, knowledge, and experience if the solutions are still being developed!

Development time should also be a concern if you have thought of a hot topic but have been unable to find it in the databases. If you have such a topic, get a librarian to help you look for articles about it (the key words you are using may be inaccurate). If you still find no relevant articles, then this is a great opportunity to do some networking. You may have identified something of value that most people have not yet recognized. This is how innovations are born! But also be aware that in order to build a career around it, you will need to develop the topic and "sell" the solution to various employers. This is a longer process than simply developing the skills, knowledge, and experience regarding a topic for which the solution has been pretty well worked out.

Question #2: Which topics are best connected to the goals of your PWF?

In addition to that "raw" indication of interest, it may well be useful to look at these topics in terms of how they can help you achieve your long-term career goals. I will illustrate what I mean using the career intensity levels as the basis for a general description—that is, Maintainer, Builder, and Changer.

Maintainers want to continue doing the work they are currently doing. But to do that in today's earning world, Maintainers can develop their abilities in three different ways: by keeping current with new developments in their work, by showing excellence in the performance of their work, and by building the flexibility to do their work in various settings. So, as Maintainers look at the topics they have listed, they might want to consider which of these three ways of developing their abilities is most important to them at that moment in time.

Joe, the call center manager whom you read about in Chapter 2, was a Maintainer who was focusing his career development primarily on managing change well. When I was working with him in the mid 1990s, he wanted to show excellent performance as a foundation for staying in that work. Today, with organizations increasingly outsourcing call centers, his methods for maintaining his value would probably be different. Perhaps he would be focusing on developing his flexibility to manage different types of call centers. To build a hiring edge so that he would continue to be attractive to other employers, he might need to focus on hot topics that relate to the different types of call centers (e.g., call centers dealing mostly with complaints, call centers dealing with very complicated information, etc).

Builders are individuals who want to build on their current experiences and move toward new work situations or new roles. Some of the topics on their list may be more or less attractive to them, depending on the nature of their goals. For example, in the next chapter you will read about Natalie, who was an accounting manager but wanted to move out of management and into more of a specialist role in accounting. When she reviewed the hot topics in accounting on her list, forensic accounting drew her attention particularly because she believes there will be many jobs for individual contributors in that area in the near future.

Changers want to look at the topics in their new field of interest that can help them "bridge" into their new work. That imaginary midlevel manager interested in the nonprofit sector, for example, has already identified two possibilities for bridging—working in administration, particularly finding and selecting job candidates, and starting a business venture related to a nonprofit. Whether that manager wants to do that kind of work long-term or not, it could serve now as a bridge into the nonprofit sector, so that the manager could learn about it in order to more easily prepare for something else he or she may be more interested in.

Reviewing the list of hot topics in which you are interested while keeping your longer-term career goals in mind should help you identify two or three topics that might be useful in helping you achieve your long-term career goals. Move those topics to the top of your short list and move forward to consider more carefully how many potential employers in your preferred locale are likely to require the capabilities that you are thinking of developing.

Question #3: Are there at least two or three likely employers in my preferred locale?

Some people do not need to spend very much time on this question. If you live in a large metropolitan area and are interested in topics with broad applicability within a number of industries or types of organizations, it is likely that there are at least three or four local employers who will be interested in your capabilities. Or if you are extremely interested in some topic and are willing to move, you won't need to think much about likely employers in your region.

However, many people in midlife and beyond have strong preferences about where they live. These preferences often are stronger than the attraction of most career opportunities. If you are one of these people, it may make sense for you to consider the likelihood of employment opportunities in your preferred locale before getting too far into developing capabilities related to the topics at the top of your interest list. You will gather much more information about potential employers as you proceed with your career development activities. But, for now, you just want to roughly estimate how many employers in your preferred locale are likely to value potential employees with the capabilities related to the topics that you are considering developing in the near future.

How much time you need to spend on this factor can be determined, in a rough way, by considering the number of employers in your preferred locale and how narrowly focused your topic is. The number of employers has an obvious impact on your employment possibilities. If you are in a rural area with relatively few employers, you need to spend more time considering whether developing an expertise related to a specific topic will enhance your employability in that locale.

The other factor to consider is how narrowly focused your topic is. That is, is the topic likely to be applicable only to a relatively few employers? The topic of how to write and/or modify Web security software, for instance, is narrowly focused with relatively few potential employers nationwide. On the other hand, the marketing of products to older adults is a broader topic, applicable to a large number of employers.

If you have a narrowly focused topic, you will probably want to identify at least two or three employers who are likely to be interested in your services, even if you are in a metropolitan area. If your preferred locale is primarily rural, your employment options could be limited, regardless of the breadth of your topic, and you should spend some time assessing

Table 4.1
Rough Assessment of Time Needed to Identify Local Employment
Possibilities Related to a Hot Topic

Variety and Number of Employers in Your Locale	Applicability among Employers:	
	Broad	**Narrow**
High	**Little time needed**	**Spend some time** identifying the most likely employers
Low	**Spend some time** identifying the most likely employers	**Spend time *carefully* identifying 2 or 3 high-potential employers**

the number of potential matches between your topics of interest and the employers in your region.

Your goal at this point is simply to see if you can identify at least two or three employers in your preferred locale who are likely to want employees with capabilities related to your preferred topics. Divide the topics at the top of your list (i.e., those topics you are interested in, and which fit your career goals) into two categories: those "broadly" applicable to many employers and those "narrowly" applicable. Consider your preferred locale—is it a large, metropolitan area with lots of employers or an area with a limited number of employers?—and use Table 4.1 to help you determine how much time and effort to spend searching for likely employers at this stage.

To learn more about employers in your region, use library resources and the notes you made when you were articulating your PWF about the characteristics of employers who will be most concerned with this topic (see the appendix and Chapter 3). Because information on employers is used both by the government and in business-to-business marketing, there is often a good deal of data about even small employers. Also, remember that in a small community you are likely to be able to network informally with people working as employees or managers at employers in your area, and you can ask them how important they believe your hot topic is likely to be to their organizations.

The general question you want to share with the reference librarian to begin this search might be something like this: "I'm interested in local companies that are likely to _____ (state the characterization you have developed from your reading here—perhaps it is an organization that produces a particular product/service, or an organization that is similar to a nonlocal company identified in your reading, or an organization which is involved in some specific process, or one which is trying to achieve some specific goal) Can you help me find employers who might fit that description?"

If you have trouble dividing the topics into the narrow or broad applicability groups, you may need to go back to the library and find more articles on those topics in order to get a better feel for what types of employers would find them important. It will probably take about 45 minutes to an hour per topic to find the articles at the library, read them, and make notes. Remember, you will not need to do that for every topic on your list—only those you are most interested in pursuing now and can't categorize as either narrowly or broadly applicable.

You should not need to spend more than a couple of hours in the library looking for potential employers, even if you live in a rural area. The prime purpose of the process is just to make sure you choose a topic which is likely to make you more employable in your preferred locale. If you are unable to find a topic that will advance your longer-term career goals and is likely to be attractive to at least two or three employers in your preferred locale, then you should begin networking within your local earning environment to identify the hot topics in your work for local employers. Once you understand your local employers' needs, you can determine which of their needs best coincide with your interests and meet your other preferences for employment. Even though it may seem to make sense to focus solely on employers' needs rather than your own interests when your options are limited, remember that if you are not pursuing a type of work you are interested in, you are not preparing well for the future. Not concentrating on your own interests works against you in two major ways. First, you will be getting knowledge and experience that will qualify you for work opportunities that you will not particularly enjoy. And second, you will generally find it harder to continue to maintain and develop your worth as an employee because you will not be very interested in the work that you do.

In a rural area, you may need to think "outside the box" to identify employers who need the work done that you want to do. For instance, I worked with Sam, who was a manager at a regional hospital in a small town and wanted to stay there. He loved the small-town life and had become very active in civic affairs when he moved there some 15 years earlier. His career progression had been blocked at his current employer and he was looking for other opportunities so he could stay energized by his work.

When Sam talked about his earning career, he described his work as helping people come together to make decisions and work well as a team. These were very generic statements that could apply in many different work environments and, as such, do not usually make a good PWF. In conversation, however, it appeared that he was really interested primarily in Organization Development (OD). It seemed that only one or two employers in town had such specialized positions in their organizations, and those positions were occupied by people who intended to stay in them. As we talked, I also found that one of the things he enjoyed about his community was the opportunity to get involved in a range of civic activities. I suggested that he gather some information, mostly through networking, to discover what kinds of general management positions might be available in local government. Because he was already in a general management position and taking the OD approach to his work in that job, he could consider moving into a management position in local government to follow his interest and build experience in OD.

And, of course, at times—even thinking creatively—you will not be able to come up with a good answer that meets all of your criteria. If that should happen, you should probably seek help refocusing your PWF. With a greater knowledge of your local earning environment, this may not be as hard as it appears.

Remember to allow your interests to play a major role in your decision. Don't simply pick some type of work that local employers are likely to value but in which you have little interest, or rely on the assumption that you will be able to get jobs in your preferred locale because you are already there. Whatever your work focus is or becomes, you will need to continuously and independently build your knowledge and capabilities in that work to maintain your worth as an employee. Interest in what you are learning and/or in how it might be used is a strong motivator for doing this more sophisticated type of career management.

Once You Have Selected Your Hot Topic

Once you have a hot topic, a final mental task will help you prepare for the activities to be described in Chapter 5. This task is making some notes in your career journal about the new skills, knowledge, and experience you think you will need in order to develop a hiring edge in relation to your topic.

To identify the skills, knowledge, and experience you need, review the articles on your chosen hot topic and look not only for direct statements about needed abilities, but also for stories that may have illustrated various points in the articles. You might also imagine yourself working in the situations about which you are reading and think about what you would need to know and what you would be comfortable doing. Make a list of the various skills, knowledge, and experience you would need and then review it asking yourself what level of expertise you have in relation to each.

For example, if you were an accountant reading articles about the need for reforms in accounting practices after the scandals in the early 2000s, you likely read about the challenges that auditors face when they have to tell paying customers that they can't use certain accounting techniques because they don't conform to the Generally Accepted Accounting Practices. Many observers suggested that it was fear of their customers' reactions that caused some auditors to acquiesce to questionable practices. Translated into career management terms, these reports highlighted a "new" skill needed by auditors: the ability to have difficult conversations with customers.

Another example might be the articles in and around 2005 relating to the management challenges of hospitals. One of the topics raised was the need to upgrade standard procedures to decrease the possibility of infections and other complications. These stories, when translated into career management terms, highlight the need for people working in patient care to gather information about the growing body of knowledge on the causes of these complications and to learn how to improve standard procedures in hospitals.

A human resources person whose hot topic is outsourcing work for employers offers a third example. Simply by putting himself in the situation, he could recognize that, in order to perform well in relation to the new specialty, he would need to know more about negotiating contracts (new skill), the implications for organizational managers who would be using contract employees (new knowledge), and who the prime contractors are, the nature of how they work, and their reputations (new groups to know about and understand).

Take a few minutes now to list in your career journal the skills and knowledge that your current understanding of your hot topic suggests would be needed by people engaged in that work. Then, put a check next to the new skills and knowledge that you believe you will need to develop. If you have trouble making the list, you might consider another visit to the library to read a few more articles about the topic.

Some Words for Aspiring Business Owners

One goal of this chapter has been to identify a hot topic that will help individuals to maintain their worth as employees or to develop a hiring edge for the jobs they want in the future. Aspiring business owners need to be involved in a similar process to identify the competitive edge for their business. This competitive edge may be a new product/service, or

Table 4.2

Questions to Help You Turn Your List of Hot Topics into a Career Management Focus
What are the major "hot topics" (i.e., changes, challenges, and controversies) in my work?
Of these hot topics, which will have widespread and direct impact on those who do this work?
Of the rest of the hot topics, which do I, personally, find most interesting?
How far along is each hot topic's development? Identification of a problem? Identification of possible answers? Implementation of an answer?
Which topics are best connected to my longer-term goals?
What types of organizations are likely to want to make this change first? (List characteristics, not company names)
Can I identify at least two or three types of employers who are likely to want employees with capabilities related to this topic in the near future? (See Table 4.1)
What new skills, knowledge, and experience am I likely to need to perform well in relation to my chosen hot topic?

it may be based on location, a particular set of customers, or the way customers are generated or maintained.

For businesses that are based on an innovative product/service, reading articles in the library about the business focus and identifying changes, challenges, and controversies can be very helpful in generating ideas for new products/services. For other types of businesses, such as professional practices that are *not* based on a relatively unique knowledge base (e.g., a solo practice doing general psychology or counseling, as opposed to a practice focused on providing talk therapy to individuals who suffer from Multiple Personality Disorder or schizophrenia) or small businesses that do not offer a unique product/service (e.g., a dry cleaning store), your competitive edge may be more dependent on the number of competitors in the area or the systems you institute for finding or maintaining clients/customers.

At this point in the process, you need to learn enough about the type of business you plan to start in order to make an educated guess about what your competitive edge might be. You will be able to use the library to read about your competitive edge in some cases. For example, if you decide that your business would be best operated on the Internet, you can read articles about how to attract customers there. The library might help you identify professional associations or industry groups where you might find potential clients or professionals who might refer clients to you. Or the library might help you identify geographical regions where the types of people who would be customers for your business are most likely to reside.

But the best way to identify competitive edges that are used in many common small businesses is to visit a number of similar businesses and study their differences. Occasionally, you may also find an owner willing to share his view of the business and what makes it successful. Another place to look for such people might be at meetings of the local Chamber of Commerce or Rotary Club.

In addition to thinking through their likely competitive edge, aspiring business owners also need to think about their capabilities in relation to the business. This is comparable to the final task for individuals described in this chapter, of identifying the skills, knowledge, and experience they are likely to need in relation to their hot topics. I argued in Chapter 3 that starting a small business is more demanding because of the range of skills and knowledge needed. Essentially, there are three main types of capabilities needed by aspiring business owners.

One area of capability is in general management—that is, the ability to keep all the business operations in mind and make decisions that keep the business running smoothly. The facets of a small business are many, including managing cash flow, profit levels, customer/client flow, advertising, and supply levels, in addition to supervising any other employees. A second area of knowledge involves the product/service you are providing. This, of course, is in many respects the basis of your business. Keeping quality consistent is important in all businesses, and if your business is based on an innovative product/service, constant improvement is probably a major focus. The third area of knowledge is about your customer base and how you can maintain and/or increase the numbers of clients/customers.

In different types of businesses these three areas of capability will have different levels of importance. For example, if you are opening a retail store, general management will be a larger part of the picture than if you are opening a sole-practitioner professional practice. Likewise, product consistency may be fairly easy to maintain in some businesses whereas the focus on customer retention or generation may be key to ongoing success.

If your business is part of a franchise, some of the management systems, quality control, or marketing may be done by the franchise (the types and amount of support vary among franchises). Or if you have a partner, that individual may take responsibility for some capabilities while you focus on others. But regardless of how you plan to divide up the work, you could find yourself responsible for the whole enterprise. Assessing your abilities in these three areas as well as your business's likely needs will help you to direct your career development activities, which is the focus of Chapter 5.

Moving Forward

Learning about the near future of your work in a multiple-employer environment provides you with a broader view of what is occurring in your work than you can get at any one employer. You need this information to make high-quality decisions about how to shape and direct your career in today's new employment environment, where you can expect to change employers more often.

One of the benefits of the changed employment dynamics is the new-found freedom individuals can exercise to build their careers the way they want to. But to exercise that freedom wisely, they need to know how to direct their career management activities. Understanding what employers and others involved with their specific work see as current hot topics is a great way to begin to see what employers are likely to value in the future.

In this chapter I have led you through a process of turning that basic knowledge of hot topics into career management knowledge that you can use to provide yourself with direction initially. The series of questions that I have used are summarized in Table 4.2 for easy reference. Occasionally, you will identify a hot topic that is broadly applicable to your work in a wide range of contexts. When you find such a hot topic, you need to manage your career in a way that allows you to adjust to the likely changes, regardless of your particular level of interest in that topic. The story about John realizing the probable impact of electronic signatures on his current job highlighted some of the major options available for such adjustments.

If there are no broadly applicable hot topics on your list, you can let your interests begin to guide your choice of a hot topic around which you can focus your career development efforts. But your personal interest in a topic should be balanced with a consideration of three important factors. First, you want to pick a hot topic where the capabilities you need to develop to perform well around the topic will be fairly clear. Second, you want to evaluate the hot topic in terms of any specific career desires you have, such as more autonomy in your work, or a possible managerial role, to make sure it fits with those desires. And third, you want to consider the types of employers likely to employ people with these capabilities and see whether they exist in your preferred locale. You are probably attracted to at least two or three of these hot topics. Considering these other factors allows you to narrow your choice to just one.

The final question you should ask yourself should focus on what new skills, knowledge, and experience you believe you will need in order to perform well in terms of this topic. Of course, your answers to all these questions will be tentative. Your information gathering and learning activities have just begun. But your answers, fuzzy and tentative as they may be, will help to give you some direction for your ongoing interactions with others and will assist you to ask good questions and pay attention to things that you might well have ignored before.

If your preferred locale appears to offer you few job opportunities in relation to the hot topics that interest you, your actions will be somewhat different at the beginning of the next, more localized, phase of information gathering. Your focus will be on gathering more information about the hot topics for local employers. Your reading about hot topics in your work will generally help you carry on conversations with people working for those employers and learn about their organizational concerns more quickly. You will then be able to select a hot topic where your interests and the concerns of at least one or two employers in your area converge, and then move into career development activities.

Something else I hope I have accomplished in the chapter is introducing you to the abundance of information about the earning world now available in most libraries. This information source is useful not just for discovering hot topics, although it is ideally suited for that. It is also useful for gathering better information about your work, about potential employers, and about people you might network with throughout your career. Using the library for one's own career management seems to be one of the hardest things for people to actually do when they begin using the Employability Plus model. Because of this, it can give the people who do use it a significant edge in managing their careers.

I have focused, for the most part, on what is available in electronic databases. But there are many other resources available as well. Further, in the appendix, Janice has provided a guide for gathering information about your work focus using not only databases, but also the aspects of work that I introduced in Chapter 3, in the Five Aspects exercise for articulating your PWF. This approach to gathering information can help anyone who wants to know more about their work. It is particularly useful to Changers who need to learn more about their new work focus.

Do not let your new information-gathering skills get rusty! Identifying new hot topics is an exercise you should do at least once every two years. Furthermore, these skills can be very useful in supplementing the networking and learning activities that will be described in the next chapter. Ideally, you will want to highlight the people, associations, Web sites, and library resources that you have found to be particularly helpful in gathering information about your work, so that you can easily consult them over and over. I do this by having a personal Web site for my key sources and contacts, but there are many other ways as well.

The final thing that this chapter has done is introducing you to the idea of chunking your career management activities into small, attainable tasks. It's great to say that people should learn about the near future of their work—most cannot argue against the usefulness of such knowledge—but where they have problems is figuring out how to do it and how to make time to do it. This chapter has provided some concrete tools for getting the information and also illustrated how to chunk your efforts by describing in detail the first library visit of a general manager who may be thinking about moving into the nonprofit sector. Chunking will be used even more in the next chapter, so I will go into more detail about the specifics of the chunking process there.

The first step towards learning about the near future of your work is to make an entry in your calendar both for a coffee break to design your first "chunk" and for a few hours on a Saturday or Sunday afternoon to actually do it. Committing to at least one cup of coffee and one afternoon a month for thinking about and gathering information for your career-management efforts should become part of your routine. Your tasks and the goals of those tasks will change, as you will see in the next chapters, but managing your earning career deserves systematic attention considering the greater amount of change, challenge, and opportunity in today's working world. Just like exercising, vacationing, and resting, independent career management should be a regular part of your schedule.

Now you are ready to move forward toward the activities of actually developing your skills, knowledge, and experience to realize your PWF. While information gathering via the library is an important part of the process enabling you to direct your activities well, it is important to move toward taking action as quickly as you can. Do not get caught up in analysis paralysis! You cannot get all the pertinent information because the world is constantly changing. Furthermore, you are living out your life and career in a small pocket of that world, which is unique in some ways. You need to learn about your work generally and locally, and you get that local, more detailed information primarily by taking action. Those actions will then provide you with more information and more opportunities to learn and to shape your career.

CHAPTER FIVE

Success Strategy #3: Taking Action to Shape Your Career

The future will not just happen if you wish hard enough. It requires decision—now. It imposes risk—now. It requires action—now. It demands allocation of resources, and above all, of human resources—now. It requires work now.

—Peter Drucker[1]

Whether you are a Maintainer, a Builder, or a Changer, you hope to remain employed in jobs you find interesting and rewarding even in the face of increased interorganizational mobility and competition in the job market. This is harder than it used to be. You need to be a good employee for your current employer as a foundation for your career. But in addition, you need to be actively preparing for your longer-term career in a constantly changing, multiple-employer environment.

Just as methods for corporate planning and product development have changed in recent years to respond more effectively to the increased pace of change and complexity in the work environment, your career-management strategy needs to change as well. Companies today set a direction, quickly develop a *rough* plan or product proto-type, and then move to testing it in the larger environment, rather than spending a lot of time internally working out the fine details. In that way, they move more quickly to a "conversation" with their customers and/or competitors. They spend their money and resources modifying their plan/product in response to what they learn in the real environ-ment, rather than trying to predict all the details and to make all the decisions before they move into the market.

This is what needs to happen with the management of your longer-term career as well. You already have a personalized work focus (PWF) and you have identified an interest in a hot topic. You have some ideas about the new skills and knowledge that you will need to do this work, and you have identified what kinds of employers would be most interested in employees with these abilities. This is your prototype. Now you need to engage with the larger environment to test your ideas and expectations as well as to get the new skills and knowledge you will need. You are off on an adventure. There will be surprises.

The Employability Plus model relies on three primary activities for engaging the environment. One is targeted networking. A second activity is skill and knowledge development. Some of this learning and development may involve seminars or for-credit course work, but the vast majority of your development in mid-career comes from experience.[2] Furthermore, gaining experience allows you to show potential employers your abilities and interests as well as to check your interests and expectations about the work. The third activity is personal management. The need for self-management has grown inside work organizations in the last ten years as they have gotten flatter, and it is growing in terms of independent career management as well.

After highlighting the questions you should be trying to answer in this phase of the Employability Plus model, I will describe targeted networking. This refines the traditional approaches to networking in ways that give you more work-related information faster. Next I will provide an overview of how to design learning opportunities and experiences to show your potential to prospective employers. If you are a Builder or a Changer, this also allows you to experiment with how it might feel to do the work you aspire to do. As I describe these tactics, I will also elaborate on the kinds of information you will be seeking in this phase of the Employability Plus model.

Next, I will describe some personal management tactics that can help you work on developing your career in ways that interest you, while working full-time and without seriously affecting your larger life. Researchers have found that most people have greater latitude in how they get their jobs done than many have thought. Furthermore, many employees make idiosyncratic deals with their employers. These mechanisms can allow individuals to customize their jobs to meet their responsibilities while also moving their knowledge and skills forward in ways they choose. I will also describe a technique to manage your time on the job more effectively and discuss the need for you to be prepared to invest in yourself.

This phase of career development is challenging. As the chapter's opening quotation from Peter Drucker suggests, the future involves not only action but also ongoing decisions and risk. In the final sections of this chapter, I will explore the major risks involved in these activities. Also, I want to illustrate how the process gains momentum, and can boost your development with unexpected opportunities.

The Questions Guiding This Phase of Career Management

Table 5.1 lists the primary questions that should guide your thinking and activities in this phase of the Employability Plus model. The first two questions remind you that the few afternoons you have spent in the library so far cannot make you an expert in a work specialty, nor are they likely to provide all the information you need. You will need to expand your knowledge about the employers in your preferred locale. Assuming that your preferred locale is where you are living now, "targeted networking" is likely to be your best bet for gathering this information. (See the appendix for some information about how to get information if your preferred locale is not where you are living.)

The third question in Table 5.1 is about your expectations of the work. While Maintainers and many Builders have a good idea about the day-to-day realities of the work they want to do, Changers are less likely to understand the new situation their PWF might put them in. For instance, Dick was an engineer who enjoyed the science, but came to really dislike the interpersonal politics he saw as necessary to advance in his career. He decided to change his career by becoming a middle-school science

Table 5.1

Five Questions to Guide Your Career Development Activities
1. What work capabilities will employers in my preferred locale value?
2. What are the most crucial new skills and knowledge that I will need to develop?
3. How do my expectations about the work seem to align with reality?
4. How can I get the skills and knowledge that I need?
5. How can I show employers my interest in and potential to do this work?

teacher. This would allow him to build on his knowledge and enjoyment of science, but put him in an entirely new work situation, where he would be interacting with young people, something he enjoyed very much.

After a year of schooling to get his license, he was very disappointed in his first year of teaching because he found that, once again, interpersonal politics in his new environment greatly affected both teacher assignments and curriculum decisions. He decided to leave teaching and become an independent contractor, specializing in building design and renovation. Dick might have saved himself that year's work and expense—and focused earlier on seeking work that would allow him more autonomy—if he had spent some days visiting schools (perhaps to give guest lectures) and talking to working teachers about the pros and cons of their daily work. Every job has drawbacks. You want to recognize what those drawbacks are likely to be from your own perspective and test whether you still want to make the change.

The types of new skills and knowledge that mid-career, white-collar employees are likely to be seeking—the subject of the next question in Table 5.1—are usually quite different from those in the general definition of work-related skills and knowledge.[3] They are usually fairly sophisticated and embedded in the work, particularly for Maintainers and Builders, because they rely on a foundational knowledge of the work itself. What this means is that mid-career development needs to be more individualized and practically focused. Although some for-credit courses or professional seminars may be helpful, often the necessary new knowledge is more experience-oriented.

The final question in Table 5.1 speaks to how you will let potential employers know of your activities and learning. If the knowledge and skills are more sophisticated and the way you get them more self-designed and activity-based, then you often will not be able to communicate them adequately by simply listing your jobs. You will need to think about how you can gain experiences that highlight your newly developing skills and knowledge and ways you can describe them in a resume.

Getting Started

The snapshots that follow provide a view of individuals entering this phase of the Employability Plus model. They will highlight how each individual's situation determines what questions they should start with as they begin the process.

Snapshot #1

Ann was an executive well into her career. A division manager in a large media company, she enjoyed managing the creative process among people. She found her ability to lead creative efforts was being increasingly limited by her managers. Because she didn't want to relocate, and more attractive local openings in her current work focus were limited, she began to consider opening her own business.

She spent a number of months considering a market niche for her future business before she read a newspaper article about a new venture that was designed to help others in her age group make transitions. Armed with some terminology and an idea, she spent four hours gathering information in the library. There she discovered what appeared to be enough activity around her interest to indicate that the service she envisioned might be a viable business, and she found two "golden" articles that were very helpful in developing her ideas and basic knowledge about the service.

Her early conception of the business would ideally have the human resources departments of large companies as its primary customers. Her second possible set of customers were individual executives. The questions she felt she needed to answer before she went any further were whether these potential customers felt a need for the service that she envisioned and what specific services they felt were most important (question #1 in Table 5.1).

Snapshot #2

Natalie had been an accountant before becoming a manager of various accounting departments at a big company. She was growing tired of her managerial responsibilities and beginning to resent the long hours and constant stress of the job. She decided that becoming a content expert in something related to accounting might reduce the impact of her job on her lifestyle (i.e., give her more control over her hours and reduce her stress). Reviewing changes in the accounting industry, she found she was drawn by the challenge of identifying potential fraud (generally known as forensic accounting). Natalie was thinking she could build her abilities as a forensic accountant and perhaps move into an interesting new role as an individual contributor.

When she had looked into the near future of this specialty, Natalie felt she was reasonably sure that employers would want people with this specialty. What she needed next was a better understanding of the analytical methods and more information about whether she would enjoy moving back into an individual contributor role. She discovered a beginning seminar sponsored by the Association of Certified Fraud Examiners and decided to take the course. It would provide a preview of the work of a forensic accountant, allow her to meet others exploring the career, and teach her what skills and knowledge she needed to enter the field.

This would provide her with a clearer idea of what the work entailed (a partial answer to question #3) and give her a better understanding of what she would need to do to enter the specialty (a partial answer to question #4). It would also allow her to connect with people both in the field (instructors) and with those seriously considering it (other seminar participants).

Snapshot #3

George worked for a Fortune 100 company and specialized in maintaining very sophisticated heating and cooling systems. He had a long career in building maintenance and really enjoyed this work. Some years ago, he had realized that downsizings were becoming more regular and decided to go back to school to earn a college degree in management and marketing. Just as he finished his degree he was downsized. His next position was writing exams for people getting their certifications as heating and cooling specialists.

George decided that his best opportunity to recoup some of the salary he had lost when he was downsized would be to get into building management. He assumed his knowledge of heating and cooling systems would give him an advantage when applying for some management positions.

George decided that he probably needed to focus on two areas at the same time: gaining some experience to show that he could apply what he learned about management in the classroom to the "real world" (question #5 in Table 5.1) and discovering whether his knowledge of heating and cooling maintenance would help him get particular building management jobs. To begin to show his management abilities, George decided to become more actively involved in his church's governing committees. To test his assumption that his sophisticated knowledge of heating and cooling systems would be a hiring edge for building management positions, he would need to attend local professional meetings and trade shows to see which employers would value his specialty (questions #1 and #2 in Table 5.1).

Can you see the rough logic in the questions? You can't get exact answers to many of these questions and, even if you could, those answers would change as the work, the employers, and the larger environment changed. You want to reach a threshold of assurance that you're likely to be employed with the same or greater rewards for your work, that you can identify the most crucial skills and knowledge that you will need, and that your expectations about the work are realistic.

As you begin gathering the needed skills, knowledge, and experience, keep your eyes, ears, and mind open. This is the time when you are involved in modifying your prototype career aspirations so that they better fit with the immediate environment and with your interests and preferences. Just as most product introductions now involve more modifications during the roll-out period, you can expect to make modifications at this stage as well.

Now let's look at the three primary activities of this phase of your career management: targeted networking, learning through experience, and personal management. Because people are well aware of the basics of these activities by the time they reach mid-career, I will not be describing the basics. Rather, the next sections will further refine these activities to better meet the needs of the Employability Plus model.

Targeted Networking

Up to this point in the Employability Plus Model, I have strongly emphasized library resources. This, of course, was deliberate. I think it is important that people have a good sense of the bigger picture of how their work is changing. Our work is increasingly affected by global innovations and conditions; our organizations are aware of that bigger picture, and we need to be as well. But in order to manage your career realistically, you also need to know more detail about how your work is evolving locally—that is, in the locale where you want to be employed. This is the career-management manifestation of the phrase first developed in the environmental movement—think globally; act locally.

For most people in mid-career, the area where they want to work is their current locale. A book that puts the findings of the 2000 census into its historical context reports that two-thirds of Americans still live in the state where they were born, although their residences appear to change often within that area.[4] With that in mind, I will focus here on gathering this information in your current locale. If you are interested in pursuing your work in other locales, the appendix will provide you with some ideas.

"Networking" has acquired a bad reputation with many. People often think of it as a group of strangers standing around together trying to strike up social conversations, or as a type of "meat market" where people try to show everyone else how much they know or who they know so that they will be offered jobs. These kinds of perceptions are based on the belief that networking is simply a means of getting to know people so that, if and when you need a job, you can call on them to see if they might know of any openings. Such beliefs about networking make it particularly hard for people who do not enjoy socializing with strangers to initiate and sustain a networking effort.

The kind of networking I advocate here is much more targeted. It has specific goals related to learning about your work rather than to simply expanding your rolodex. It targets particular types of people with whom you want to interact. And it is an important component of your career development—not just to generate job leads but to increase your work-related knowledge.

This different view of networking is highlighted in the research done by Robert E. Kelley and his associates and described in *How to Be a Star at Work*.[5] Their larger research goal was to identify what makes someone a "star performer" inside an organization. They define a star performer as someone in the top 20 percent of performers in an organization, as selected both by coworkers and managers. They found that stars could not be distinguished by traditional characteristics such as IQ, parents' status, connections, or what college they attended.

As they studied the stars more closely, the researchers observed that these high performers had a different understanding than other employees about a number of factors. Those differences in beliefs and the actions they led to were connected directly to their "star" status. Networking was one of these factors. In essence, most people defined networking as making sure you are in the loop on the office grapevine, but stars defined networking as developing a knowledge of who knows what with respect to important organizational tasks.[6] What you are aiming to develop over the long term, assuming your interest in the work and/or hot topic continues, is something similar to Kelley's stars' definition of a network—not built around a single organization but rather built around a particular type of work and a set of hot topics.

The primary way to target your networking is to find groups of people who are likely to be interested in your work and in the hot topics that interest you. Of course, seeking out appropriate professional associations is a good first step, although there are other possibilities as well, such as attending related seminars and classes, trade shows, and conferences. Once you have found a local group or event where people interested in your topic are likely to congregate, you can further target your networking by bringing your specific interest into conversations and seeing who responds.

Your library and Web work can provide you the material you need to raise your topic in conversation. For example, you could say, "I was reading an article about X: It seemed like a good idea for companies trying to do Y. What do you think?" You could continue with, "Do you know any organizations that are trying to achieve Y?" which could help you identify other organizations that might be interested in your hot topic. If someone responds with interest, continue the conversation to find out why they are interested and what information they may have.

Exchange contact information so you can stay in touch. If no one responds, move on graciously and bring up the topic with others later.

A primary goal of your networking efforts is to get a better understanding of the current status of the hot topics among employers in your preferred locale. Table 5.2 is a list of questions that can give you an idea of the kinds of information you should be seeking. A second major goal is to identify people who share some of your interests. With this group you can form an informal learning group and work together to build your knowledge and skills about the topic. As your network grows and matures, you will find that various people are particularly knowledgeable or skilled in particular aspects of the work. You are essentially

Table 5.2

General Informational Questions about Your Hot Topic

How many local organizations seem interested in my hot topic and what characteristics related to it do they have in common?

If my hot topic involves a change to current work processes, where do most local organizations appear to be in that change process? Just considering it? Committed and planning to implement the change? Midway through the implementation? Dealing with challenges after the implementation?

What seem to be the major issues or positions in relation to the controversy or challenge I am interested in?

What are the questions related to my hot topic that local employers are seeking information about? Particular skills? Particular groups or facets of the work environment that are important to the change? How to access particular resources? Exposure to the experiences of other organizations that have implemented the change?

Who are the experts about the topic in my locale and elsewhere? What facets of the topic is each specializing in?

What are the major skills, knowledge, and experience that are or will be most in demand by employers who are involved in implementing this change or dealing with the controversy or challenge?

---

identifying a set of mentors, and you will become a mentor to them by contributing your own growing knowledge and skills in particular facets of the work.

Because these hot topics are relatively new and probably not well integrated into many organizations, there should be a number of issues to discuss and a number of people who are interested in them. Your goal is first to find those people and then to move forward with them to articulate the problems and challenges and to discover answers. While you are developing those solutions, you become more knowledgeable about the topic as well as develop a reputation as a committed and knowledgeable individual. Then, as employers begin to look for employees with this knowledge and skills, you become a prime candidate.

If you do not find people who are interested in your topic, there are two possible explanations. First, your analysis of the importance of the topic to organizations might be faulty. To test that possibility, try to specify why you believed it would be important and exactly what types of organizations you thought would be most interested in it. Also articulate your assumptions about the goals of the work in these organizations. If you are still convinced it should be important, begin targeting people from the organizations you think should be interested and not only ask them about the topic but have them check out your thinking about why it should be of interest in their organizations.

A second explanation may be that you simply have not run into the right people. If you think that may be the case, you should try another professional group or some other venue. Perhaps the topic is simply not of interest to people in your first group or the people you've met are not really that interested in their work or its future. Or perhaps the topic is too new to be well known yet. If that's the case, you may need to consider using a more advanced networking tactic as a way of jump-starting your networking.

Such an "advanced" networking tactic would be proposing a program or writing a newsletter article for your professional association on the topic. Most of the time, such offers are welcomed by those in charge. It will give you a great "professional" reason to call association members/leaders in the organizations you have targeted and ask who might have information on your topic. The people you find will have solid information about their organizations, and if you do not find anyone concerned with the topic, you will have information important to your career decision making.

Kelley says this type of work-oriented networking is most often based on the reciprocal exchange of information and ideas that will improve performance. People in these kinds of networks are busy and focused on performance. So, in addition to adhering to the common norms of networking etiquette (which many books describe), you will want to think about how you can contribute to the network to maintain your membership in the network and develop your credibility as a worker. Table 5.3 provides some ideas for work-oriented targeted networking, both for the early stages as well as for nurturing your network after it has formed.

As your network develops and you increasingly develop tentative answers to the questions outlined in Table 5.2, you will be able to see which of the options listed in Table 5.3 might be helpful in furthering everyone's knowledge of the topic. This information then will lead to new questions and new contacts as your network grows.

Some may be concerned that this kind of networking across employers will lead to the exchange of confidential, proprietary information. Remember that you are not talking about organizations so much as about changes, controversies, and challenges with respect to some common type of work, such as marketing research or psychiatric nursing. Also, by focusing on hot topics, you are talking more about understanding and implementation than about organizational outcomes. Finally, if your work is so close to your employer's critical path that it is confidential and proprietary, your place in that organization is probably secure and the organization itself provides you with resources to learn more about that work. You probably don't need to be involved much in this type of networking at this point in your career, unless you want to change careers and thus need to network about another type of work.

Learning through Experience

Getting appropriate and high-quality experience is a major component of managing your career during mid-career. The first role that experience or "near experience" plays, particularly for Changers and for some Builders, is to provide a realistic preview of the work they believe they want to do. Joan was in her mid-thirties and a successful midlevel manager in the insurance industry when she began to seriously consider changing careers to become a medical doctor. As part of the process of considering this change, Joan not only followed a number of MDs around for the day, talking to them about the pros and cons of their work, but she also volunteered at an emergency room and later worked there. In addition, she took a science course early in her deliberations to see how she would respond to the educational challenges.

Every experience helped Joan see that this was something she truly wanted to do. However, sometimes such experience can show people that the work is not right for them. Dick, the engineer who thought he wanted to be a middle-school science teacher, could have benefited from

Table 5.3

Targeted Networking Ideas—For Early Networking and Nurturing Your Network

Early Networking Ideas:

1. Use the information that you have developed from your library information gathering to identify people for your network.
2. Prepare a range of questions about how the topic is developing: Are the expected outcomes occurring? What unexpected challenges have occurred? Who is heading up the effort in a given organization?
3. Take the time to become involved in projects that will teach you more about the hot topic and introduce you to people who are involved with it.

Ideas for Nurturing Your Network:

1. Provide added information and knowledge.

   a. If a question comes up in a conversation with someone in your network and neither of you has the answer, take some time to look for an answer. Here again, your ability to use the library and the Web to find out what others know can be a great help.
   b. If you find a good article on the topic, share it.
   c. If you come up with an idea about the work, set up a meeting or describe it in an email and ask for feedback from others in your network.

2. Facilitate everyone else's learning.

   a. Help on others' related projects. It is also a great way to meet others who are interested in your topic.
   b. Set up a more formal network—if the topic is just beginning to attract attention in your locale, perhaps starting an interest group or putting together a team to work on a program for your professional association on the topic will allow folks who are interested in the topic to meet one another.
   c. Design or help to design programs for your professional associations that explore various issues related to your topic.

3. Add your network's resources to those of others—be willing to help or to suggest other people who could probably help with specific problems encountered by others.

4. Build your knowledge in some aspect of the topic/work so that you will have knowledge, skills, and experience in this facet of the work that others may draw upon. Write memos to the network or newsletter articles for your professional association about subjects related to your topic

talking with other teachers about their work experiences. That perhaps would have saved him two years of effort.

When Changers move to very different sectors of the earning world, they often must learn about new cultural norms in that sector or area of business, and also work to counteract negative stereotypes related to their past employment. Getting experience in the new sector can help you deal with both of these challenges. As an example, I will describe common difficulties businesspeople face when trying to move from the for-profit sector into the nonprofit world. Businesspeople often want to have what they see as a more meaningful impact on society and think that they consider their more refined skills and knowledge about how to get things done will be welcomed by those in the nonprofit world. They are sometimes surprised to find that many nonprofit employers don't value those skills and often question whether the values that guide the corporate world can be successful in nonprofit organizations.

Businesspeople who want to change careers and enter the nonprofit world often have to "prove" their abilities to work in that environment. That can mean getting some experience and becoming known among managers of nonprofits as an individual rather than as a stereotype. Becoming a corporate representative to United Way or to another group of charities is one way to get to know nonprofit managers. Or you can volunteer to do an assessment, at cost, of some aspect of a nonprofit's operations about which you have some expertise. Simply volunteering to help in the programs of the nonprofit does not give you access to the daily earning culture of the organization. Volunteers are treated as a separate group in most nonprofits, because their free labor is so important to the work of the organizations.

Learning new skills and knowledge is a major part of the Employability Plus model for everyone—for Changers, for Builders, and for Maintainers. Experience is the preferred learning mode, because the skills and knowledge you are seeking are likely to be more sophisticated and embedded in the work, and hot topics are often new and not well covered in more formal educational settings. Furthermore, individuals can often design experiences to provide just the knowledge and skills they need to move toward where they want to go in their careers.

People who want or need to change jobs usually don't need to get experience in all of the skills and knowledge they will need to get a new job. But they do need enough experience to provide them with a hiring edge and to give themselves the assurance that they can do the job. Also, experience is more convincing to a prospective employer than desire or education.

The snapshots in the beginning of this chapter examined people who were just beginning this phase of the model. Now I want to use the stories of people well into their career development to illustrate how you get pertinent experience and can often use it to show potential employers your interests and capabilities. I will return to the stories I told in Chapter 2 when I was describing how the Employability Plus model would look.

Joe was the call center manager who in the 1990s was a Maintainer. To build his skills and knowledge, and maintain his worth as a call center manager, he decided to focus on managing change and exploring the differences between call center software systems. He started an independent reading project on change management and began making time in his schedule to consult with software vendors about software variations.

Emer was the software engineer planning to open a software business in his home country after learning about the major facets of the business in the United States. He would be considered a Builder, and he had begun learning by changing jobs within his company and starting an MBA program to learn about entrepreneurship.

Sue was the manufacturing engineer in a traditional industrial company who wanted to go into marketing in a medical device company (a Changer). She had taken her first steps by changing jobs and becoming a manufacturing engineer in a medical device company; she had also entered an MBA program to begin learning about marketing.

What I want to do next is imagine how their learning activities may develop and how they might be used not just to learn but also to show potential employers the capacities they are building. For example, the next step for Joe might be to begin to apply what he has read about change to the management of his call center group. Some of this he may be able to do without management support. But he may also find himself writing memos to suggest strategies and plans for larger-scale changes as well. Over time, his experiences should provide him with some positive outcomes that he can then highlight on his resume to demonstrate to potential employers his specialty in change management. He could also volunteer to write a review of software options the next time his call center considers buying new software. Highlighting that report in his resume or in a job interview would show his expertise in this area.

As Emer's knowledge of the business and of entrepreneurship grows, he is going to want to begin seriously studying the business situation in his home country so he can design a good business plan. Since he goes to his home country for a month each year, he could design a research project to learn about customers currently using software in his country and their needs. He might gain access to these organizations by promising to write a report that he would share with participants. Such a report could be highlighted on the resume he provides to the bank when he needs a loan to start his business. Such a project would provide him with important information with which to design his business and build his reputation among a group of potential customers as a knowledgeable, committed software person.

Sue's challenge is to make the next step into marketing from her current position in engineering at the medical device company. As she begins to take marketing courses in her MBA program, she could focus her class projects on her current employer, allowing her to network with people in marketing and to begin to get a better feel for real-world marketing challenges. She can share her reports with her network in the marketing department at her company as well as use them for class assignments. To the extent that her reports have a positive impact, she has something that can become a bullet point on her resume.

Resumes or recommendations are the first contact potential employers have with candidates. Experience can provide you with people who know of your interests and performance as well as bullets for your resume. Today, many resumes focus on accomplishments, described in a way that communicates not only what you did but also that you understand how that work contributed to the enterprise and showing the depth of your understanding of the challenges you faced to complete the task. For example, here are some sample descriptions that might have been generated by Joe, Emer, and Sue:

- Designed a change strategy for migrating 100 workers to XX call software that exceeded past efficiency levels in three months
- Conducted a marketing study to assess customer software needs of 20 major customers in country XX in 2006
- Analyzed the success potential of the marketing strategy for a product manufactured by XX company and predicted customer sales within 5 percent

Table 5.4 is a set of ideas about activities often used by people in mid-career to get new skills, knowledge, and experience along with examples of possible bullets for your resume to show employers what you know and have done.

Personal Management Tactics

For most people, working more independently to develop their capabilities while also performing well in a current full-time job is a new challenge. It is not only a new challenge but also a major one for white-collar workers in the United States, whose hours spent on the job have increased significantly since the 1970s.[7] A number of reasons have been cited for this increase, including growing perceptions of job insecurity, the triumph of consumerism in the culture, the 24-hour economy that improved communications and global business has encouraged, the

Table 5.4
Ideas for Gaining and Showing Work Related Experience

Idea	Comments	Sample Resume Bullets
Courses and/or seminars	The variety of these available has greatly increased (see the appendix for ideas for finding them).	• Completed course on X with a grade of A • Completed Y seminar
Proposing programs	The program may be for your employer or your local professional group and offers you a reason to seek resources on a given topic. You don't have to be a part of the program, you can just design it. It also allows you to assess the interest of others and perhaps find those who have expertise and/or interest in your topic.	• Designed and developed (or worked with others to design and develop) a program for AB professional association • Presented informational or training program for XX units in ZZ organization on the subject of YY
Writing newsletter or Web site articles	This also provides you with an opportunity to call people in search of information and insight into your topic, although the opportunities for assessing the interest in your topic are generally fewer.	• Wrote article(s) on Y and its impact on organizations for the AB professional association newsletter • Conducted survey of VPs of Marketing asking about the importance of C and wrote a report that was circulated to them and appeared on the DD association Web site
Volunteer experience	Volunteering is generally the easiest and least risky way to get experience and particularly helps to build some specialized interactive skills and comfort in using them. Many volunteer experiences can provide exposure to different types of situations. Seek out feedback about your performance to get the most from the experience.	• Volunteered with BB organization for 18 months to build my skills in YY

Table 5.4
Ideas for Gaining and Showing Work Related Experience

Part-time work or special projects for your employer	Doing small projects that involve you in the work that you are interested in doing can help you learn about that work and demonstrate both your interest and your abilities to others.	• Completed a special project on X to aid organization Y with Z decision or with implementing process P • Worked part-time for nine months at a DD organization to learn EE

crisis culture in many organizations, and work processes.[8] Overwork turns into stress, which complicates everything individuals are trying to achieve on the job and in their larger lives. A 2004 survey by ComPsych Corporation, the largest provider of employee assistance programs in the United States, reported that 67 percent of the 1,000 people they polled reported that they "have high levels of stress, with extreme fatigue/feeling out of control."[9]

When we had the luxury of expecting long-term employment at one employer, we focused all our attention on that one employer. We could also trust our employers to provide us with the skills and knowledge we would need in the future. Today, this is a short-sighted tactic, and career development is not something that can be easily done between jobs. Careers need nurturing to be successful, and that takes time. What individuals need now are personal management strategies that can help them work at both their jobs and at independent career development simultaneously.

If you are in a unit and/or organization whose goals are well aligned with your own career development needs, a lot of your developmental activities can often be done in conjunction with your employment. This is one reason that "bridging" (first discussed in chapter 3) is such a useful concept for mid-career management. If you bridge to a new employer more aligned with your development goals early in your efforts, you will likely gain more access to win-win developmental opportunities for both you and your employer.

If your development needs are taking you in a different direction from your current employer, you will probably need to spend more of your non-earning time doing the career development that will help you get there. In either case, you will need to spend some of your own time thinking about your career. How much time will depend on the extent to which your career development goals can be cultivated at your current workplace. I estimate that most people will need to spend an average of about two to four hours a month outside of normal working hours developing themselves for their longer-term career options.

Although this is not a book primarily about time management, I have three tactics to help you reduce your job-related stress and make it more feasible for you to find four hours a month to focus on independent career management. One of the tactics has to do with managing your career-development activities. The second focuses on making your work time more efficient for your employer. And the third highlights ways to capitalize on win-win opportunities at your current employer, where the activities will further your employer's interests as well as your own.

The Importance of Designing and Managing Chunks for Your Career Development

The major things you need to attend to during the four hours you set aside monthly to work on your career development include the following:

- networking with others, and then finding activities to help you maintain your targeted network
- deciding what skills and knowledge you need to acquire or to show through experience
- occasionally gathering more information at the library
- designing possible chunks of activity that will aid in your career development

All of these activities can be translated into "chunks," that is, sub-units of the overall set of activities you need to do in order to accomplish your goals. This is a concept I introduced in Chapter 2 and illustrated with the example of the first library visit of the general manager who was thinking about moving into the nonprofit world in Chapter 4. I have described the components of a well-formed chunk in Table 5.5. For most white-collar employees, the concept of chunking is not new, although the name may be. Some don't bother with chunking because it seems so commonsensical. But chunking helps you focus your thinking on what you need to do now to achieve your goals. Prioritize your chunks and only work on one or, at most, two at a time. By thinking through what needs to happen, noting these activities on your calendar, and setting deadlines, you give these activities more importance in your daily life. This may provide the extra attention needed to get them done, particularly early in the process.

Perhaps most importantly, chunking sets up natural reflection points where you can review your progress every three or four months. If you

Table 5.5
Components of a Developmental Chunk

Component	Comments
1. What specific question are you trying to answer?	For example, don't just go to "network"–go to network about a specific hot topic or to learn about what employers are interested in about a given hot topic, etc.
2. What activity are you expecting to focus on to gather information or learn about your question?	Try to specify exactly what you will do and when. Examples: commit to go to three professional meetings over the next three months, to go to the library one Saturday afternoon and read on another, or to call four people to try to find out if any units at your current employer are also interested in your hot topic. Put these activities on your work calendar or your to-do list.
3. By what date do you intend to complete what you have planned?	This should be a specific date, and you should set aside time on your calendar for the following weekend to take a walk or have a cup of coffee by yourself and review what you have accomplished and consider next steps. If you can't complete a chunk in three months, identify a time after two months to review your progress.

Remember to keep notes on your chunks and what you learn, so that you can keep track of where you are in your learning process and recall what resources and activities you have found most useful.

have made progress, you can see it, congratulate yourself, and move on to a new chunk. And if you have not completed the chunk, that time provides you with a definite point at which to reassess and decide what tactics you might pursue to help you move forward more successfully. Table 5.6 identifies five possible factors that might have affected your ability to accomplish the activities in your chunk. It is designed to help you diagnose what might be happening and to consider options for resolving the problem.

Of course, it is also possible that expected and important events at work or at home have interfered with your best intentions. In our busy lives this is bound to happen. If that is the case, don't beat yourself up but use the reflection point to recommit and start afresh. Also, be prepared for your daily life to present you with unexpected opportunities for achieving your career-development goals. If these opportunities are better than what you had planned and/or allow you to help your employer while helping yourself, take advantage of them! The work you have done designing your chunks has helped you to see the potential in these unexpected opportunities, so it has served its purpose.

It is a well-established fact that different people learn in different ways. It is also well known that people need different types of support and motivation to maintain their involvement in the routine activities for maintaining healthy lives-activities such as exercising, dieting, and managing finances. Ongoing career management should be one of these routine adult activities. Think about the support that has worked for you in these other areas—from establishing a routine to setting specific goals; to having a support group, celebrations, or rewards to record your progress in some tangible way. Whatever works for you should be integrated into how you design your career-development chunks.

The snapshots have illustrated how you can decide where to begin. Builders and Maintainers are likely to begin with targeted networking but will move quickly to enhance their knowledge and extend their network. Changers probably will want to get as close to experiencing the work as they can and become involved in some learning initiatives before concentrating on networking.

Managing Your Time on the Job

Managing yourself better is also a skill that some scholars see as increasingly important in this more complex and fast-paced world of flatter organizations.[10] Just as I am proposing that you be more proactive in your career development, I want to also suggest that you be more proactive in managing your job responsibilities. This proactive work should focus both on managing how you target your job-performance efforts and on capitalizing on win-win activities that help your employer and further your desired career development.

Many books have been written on time management, and I am not going to restate what has been written elsewhere. What I want to do here is to describe how you can use your understanding of the critical path of your current employer to set priorities in your work. That way you know that the time you spend on your job will have the greatest impact possible on your organization and on your reputation as a good employee. Also, you are less likely to get caught up in doing relatively unimportant tasks.

Establishing the critical path of your unit and/or organization can sometimes be challenging because your managers don't always explain the critical path and how your job relates to it. The critical path is what managers believe needs to be done now and in the future for the organization to be a success. The activities and goals of individual units should be prioritized in relation to the entire organization's critical path. If you are unclear about the critical path of your unit, here are a few ideas about how to proceed. Ask your manager these two questions: Who are the

Table 5.6
Managing Your Chunking Process

Management Dimensions	What a Problem Might Look Like	Some Tactical Options
Managing Your Time	You repeatedly cancel your scheduled time to work on your career-management tasks.	• Reprioritize activities and drop the least important • Delay accepting new commitments • Design ways to do routine activities more quickly
Managing Your Energy	You are simply too tired to go to the library on Saturday afternoons.	• Promise yourself a Saturday afternoon of rest or energy-enhancing activity and go to the library on Sunday afternoon • Divide the task up further and spend a shorter amount of time at the library; e.g., print articles and read them later, when you have more energy
Managing Your Motivation	You find yourself thinking, "It all seems like just so much work with very little payback!"	• Find a career buddy, support group, career counselor, or coach to work with you • Select a reward that you will give yourself if you stick to the tasks or finish a task that you find very onerous • Find something that inspires you to do the work (e.g., a role model, a poem) and incorporate it into your career management activities • Reconsider what you are doing and why
Managing Your Means	I have been trying to network around my selected hot topic at a professional group's meetings for more than three months and have had few results.	• find another venue for networking • go to the library and look for people related to the hot topic and email them to ask about other associations or networking ideas • approach the association program chairperson about doing a program on your hot topic

Table 5.6 (*continued*)
Managing Your Chunking Process

Managing Your Process	I have been working to get experience in stressful situations, but every time I start a volunteer project in such a situation, the organization asks me to do something else. This has happened twice after only a few days!	• Perhaps the feedback you are getting here is that you do not do well in such situations. Meet with the people who have asked you to change assignments and talk candidly about their reasons for asking you to move and their assessment of your abilities.

unit's prime internal or external customers? What are the most important outputs of the unit in terms of the organization's functioning?

Try to ask these questions in a casual, private discussion, explaining that you want to know what she thinks so you can improve your performance. (Some managers will assume that you are about to criticize them if you don't expressly state your objective!) I suggest a private conversation to avoid putting your manager on the spot, because she may not have a good answer for you. She may not have thought much about her unit's critical path and see the manager's role as simply coordinating assignments or making sure that all assigned tasks are done equally well. Or, the organization itself may be confused about its critical path.

If your immediate manager's response is not clear, thank her for her insight into the company (assuming she has said something about how things above her are confused and/or changing) and move to plan B: Logically establish what makes sense as a critical path given the information you are able to gather about your unit and organization. Then use that information to set priorities in your job responsibilities.

This process has three main steps: First, seek out information about what your organization's critical path is likely to be. Find out what its public Web site or annual report says is the organization's primary business and what the organization prides itself on providing to customers (high quality, innovation, good price, or some combination of these three[11]). Read what you can about management's strategy for the future. Identify competitive advantages by reading some industry overviews and seeing how the analysts compare competitors and what environmental factors they see as important to success (see the appendix). And, if you can get access to the information, consider what units are contributing the largest profits to the organization.

Once you have obtained some information about the organization as a whole, your second step is to establish how your unit contributes to the critical path. While all units are important to the company, some are direct contributors to the critical path—for example, their work provides the innovation that is the company's key competitive advantage, or they sell or market a current, high-profit-producing product/service. You identify these units by connecting them directly to what the organization says is or will be their prime competitive advantage or to where the organization's highest proportion of profits are being made. These units' goals are usually pretty clear and relate directly to the goals of the organization. Some units, of course, contribute more than others, and the organization generally contributes more of its resources to those units. Managers of units that are not big contributors to the critical path sometimes add unit objectives in attempts to contribute more.

Other units support the work of the units that are direct contributors to the critical path; they are indirect contributors to the critical path. For example, human resources and accounting are indirect contributor units in many companies because they perform functions that help the other units, usually by helping the workers who are on the critical path become more efficient. These support functions can become critical path functions when they are split off into organizations in which they are the primary business, such as headhunting firms or public accounting firms.

Table 5.7 lists three types of units in terms of their relationship to the organization's critical path (i.e., direct contributors with high impact, direct contributors with low impact, and indirect contributors) and describes how the unit objectives generally can be characterized. Once you have figured out your unit's likely objectives, you have a basis on which to determine what is most important among your job responsibilities. This can help you set priorities for your job responsibilities. Then watch for feedback from others in the organization (particularly your manager) and use that feedback to help shape your job priorities going forward.

This process should help you establish job priorities and free up some time and mental space to spend on career development activities. Unfortunately however, it does not always work. There are supervisors who are micromanagers and/or have unrealistic expectations. And there are jobs that are just too demanding. If this describes your situation, you may need to consider seeking an internal transfer or looking for another job so that you can be employed in a unit/organization where managerial expectations are more realistic.

Such a move may mean postponing your long-term career development to get some skills and knowledge that can let you make a lateral move quickly. While this is not an ideal use of your career development

Table 5.7
Likely Priorities of Units Depending on Contribution to Critical Path

	Unit Makes Indirect Contribution	Unit Makes Direct Contribution with Lower Impact on Organization	Unit Makes Direct Contribution with High Impact on Organization
General priorities for the unit's work	Priorities will focus on serving internal customers well and doing so efficiently	Priorities will be partially specified by the organization and partially dependent on manager's goals (e.g., to move up the pecking order by producing more profits or by demonstrating impact more effectively)	Priorities will be specified by the organization goals and what has worked in the past
Relationship to organization's resource allocation	Organizational resources least available and provided on a project-by-project basis	Organizational resources less available and provided on a project-by-project basis	Organizational resources most available
Impacts on employees in unit	Workers are least stressed, worker training and development is least available	Impact on workers depends on the unit manager's goals and success in obtaining resources	Workers are most stressed, most rewarded, and most actively developed by the organization

time, it will be worth the effort to be able to regularly spend some time on your own development and relieve your level of stress as well.

Capitalizing on Win-Win Opportunities in Your Workplace

You will want to identify and, as much as possible, capitalize on opportunities for your personal career development that also help your current employer. This obviously can save you time, as well as contribute to your reputation as a good employee and improve your organization's functioning. Maintainers, of course, are most likely to have a significant overlap between their developmental desires and their current employer's goals. To begin capitalizing on that potential a Maintainer might casually share with his manager his hot topic and how he sees it improving the performance of their unit. Regardless of the manager's response, he will gather important information. If the manager does not agree with his assessment of the idea's importance, he will learn more about the organization's critical path and thus set better priorities for his job responsibilities.

If his manager likes the idea, he can help with implementing the next steps or become more involved in activities already under way. Whatever the tasks involved in pursuing the idea, volunteering to help will allow the Maintainer to learn more about the topic he is interested in. It is also likely to be considered as part of his job, and his manager will see him as someone with initiative.

Builders also have a significant likelihood of discovering some overlap between what they are interested in doing with their careers and their current employer's interests. The possibilities here are many and varied. Sometimes activities related to your long-term interests can also improve your current unit's functioning. For example, Lorie decided that she wanted to build her career in the direction of computer programming. She saw an opportunity to help her marketing unit, which was learning new software, and to begin understanding program design by becoming responsible for answering questions about the software's application. This led to opportunities for her to work with the software vendor to customize the software, which gave her better exposure to the programming process.

It is also possible that the way you want to build your career is really within the purview of another unit in your organization. If so, the traditional informational interview may be a way to introduce yourself to the unit. Learn more detail about what that unit does, check out the overlap with your interests, and look for opportunities where you might work with that unit to accomplish the goals of your current unit or of the larger organization (e.g., committees that you might join, projects in the other unit that your unit might be able to help complete, or information from that unit that could help you do your current job better).

Even if there are not job-related reasons for you to work with them, interacting with employees in the unit can provide useful ideas and information about building your knowledge and skills. Assuming that your interest and development efforts continue, you might be able to combine your knowledge of the organization with the fact that you already work there as a way to transfer into the department.

Changers can sometimes find commonalities between their current employer and the type of work they want to do—although those overlaps are rarely plentiful. To show how this might work, let's return to the story in Chapter 4 about the midlevel manager in business who was in the first stages of information-gathering about work in the nonprofit sector. He had realized that he did not know much about the range of nonprofit organizations in his locale and that he had few contacts with people actually employed in that sector. One way he might begin to remedy that lack of information and also be a good corporate citizen at his current employer might be to volunteer to work in his organization's annual charity drive. In this way he could gather information about the range of nonprofits that are active locally and begin to meet people from some of them.

Developmental activities outside your employer, such as seminars, professional meetings, or academic courses may also be win-win opportunities. Once you have identified what you want to do for your career development, see if you can make the case that some of the information you gather could also be of use to your employer. Specifically, ask yourself these questions as you search for arguments to persuade your current employer to support this activity:

1. How could my sharing some of the information I gather help my current employer remain current or address important issues?
2. How could my involvement in some activity provide an organizational presence among people or organizations with whom my current employer wants to be involved?
3. How could learning this material make me a more valuable employee for my current employer?

George, whom we have already met, and who is currently working for an organization that produces certification tests in a range of construction trades, might argue that his attendance at trade shows could help his current employer by providing a presence to remind people in construction that the certification process exists. Or Natalie, the woman interested in forensic accounting, could suggest to her current employer that if it paid for a particular seminar in forensic accounting, she would in return prepare a report comparing her current employer's practices with what she learns are good preventative measures.

Does this mean that George or Natalie or you need to explain exactly why you, personally, want to do these things? To suggest, for instance, that you are planning to change careers or get a new job? No. When talking with others at work, stick to what it can do for your current employer. Natalie might say that she was just fascinated by the subject and wanted to learn more. George could say that he enjoys interacting with people in the field and was hoping attending a trade show would provide some ideas for questions about technical aspects of the new methods and equipment coming into use. Just as I argued that the personalization of your work focus is not something you need share with your current employer, your long-term career plans may also be kept to yourself. By focusing on what your activities can do for your current employer and not on what they do for you, you are a more responsible employee, and you limit the risk that management will see you as disloyal or preparing to move on.

Finally, remember that you don't always have to make a win-win argument to get some support from your employer for your career development. Some organizations still provide very flexible educational benefits to their employees. Others provide compensatory leave time if people work excessive overtime. And managers often want to reward their employees but are limited in the type and amount of rewards they can provide directly—thus, for example, your request to attend a seminar might be granted as a reward for your performance or initiative.

Furthermore, the way you do your job can be "crafted" to give you new experiences.[12] For example, volunteering to do presentations about your work to your unit or to other units might provide you with needed experience in public speaking, if this is an experience you believe will help you perform more effectively in your future work.

Some of these developmental opportunities will need to be negotiated, others will not. Don't be put off by the need to negotiate a "deal" with your employer when you need permission or resources to do something you believe will make a contribution to the organization. Idiosyncratic deals are much more common for regular employees than most think. Denise Rousseau, a very well-respected scholar in the area of psychological contracts between employers and employees, has just written an entire book focused on these kinds of agreements.[13]

Investing in Yourself

You may not be able to achieve all your career development via the methods already discussed. In particular, if you are a Changer, some of what you will need to do probably has no relation to your current employer. It is also possible that you are currently working for an organization or for a supervisor who is very restrictive about employee activities, including initiatives to improve your unit's functioning.

The answer to these situations is for you to begin investing in yourself and your career development. For many years this was not the norm, since long-term employment usually meant that an employer trained its employees for what they would be asked to do on the job. Furthermore, educational funds were included as part of benefits packages, and that often gave employees the sense that educational funds should come from the employer. Today, the easy accessibility to both of these kinds of opportunities for continuing education are declining for most employees.[14]

The bad news is that you probably should begin saving for these kinds of expenses. But the good news is that you have much more freedom to choose the type of educational experiences you believe will benefit your career desires most (see the appendix).

You may need to invest some time outside work in your efforts as well. You have already been doing that with the afternoons and coffee breaks you have dedicated to thinking about your career. In this phase of the model, you may invest study time if you take a seminar or course for credit. You may spend some of your free time getting involved in volunteer efforts to increase your skills and get experience that you can use to show your capabilities and interest. This may take away from your leisure activities or family life for a while, but just as you have looked for overlaps between your goals and your current job and employer, look for overlaps between your larger life and your career. Manage your time in these endeavors by reassessing their usefulness regularly and designing exit strategies to spend more time with your family when the developmental helpfulness of these activities has declined.

Your earning career represents the major time commitment in your life, and it provides you and your dependents with funds to live. It is a worthy focus of some of your extra time and investment.

The Risks

As the chapter's opening quotation points out, every action is risky. What you want to do is to manage as many of the risks as you can. When you commit to working to develop your career more independently, you in essence are saying to yourself that you are no longer comfortable taking the risk that your employer's decisions will also be good decisions for you over the long term. Given the turbulence in the working world and the desires of many born during and since the baby boom to have different and/or more rewarding work, this choice makes sense for many people. But let's look more specifically at the risks that will need to be managed if you become involved in the Employability Plus model.

The first risk that may come to mind is that coworkers or your managers will interpret your actions or requests as disloyal and/or an announcement that you are looking for another job. This is a significant risk, particularly if you talk openly about your independent developmental efforts. That is why I have advised that you only talk about your career interests when you can connect them directly to your current employers operations, goals, or challenges.

Your thinking and questions about the critical path should be considered smart thinking on the part of a committed employee by most managers. Furthermore, managing your activities so that your performance is more aligned with the goals of the unit and/or organization should lead to higher performance appraisals. Volunteering to become involved in activities that you see as win-win situations for achieving your employer's goals and your own development also should be interpreted as initiative. The fact that these actions will also allow you to save some time and energy to pursue your own career interests after contributing significant efforts to your current employer can be your secret.

The Employability Plus model does not necessarily encourage you to switch employers. If you can stay at your current employer, still pursue work that you find interesting, and increase your future value as an employee, then there is no need to move. Many Maintainers and Builders can do this. Lots of varied options can be found in many organizations because they are constantly growing and changing and involve so many specialized kinds of work. That said, however, it is the possibility of changing employers that makes more independent career development so liberating for individuals, so don't discard that option!

Another risk that you will need to think about is that the premium value of the skills and knowledge you are focused on developing might have passed by the time you develop them. This might happen for a number of reasons. Your part-time development process might take too long. The employers you thought would need your services might change their strategies and not need those capabilities any longer. Or a new innovation in processes or technology might make your new skills and knowledge less valuable. Your ongoing networking and information gathering can help you manage this risk if you remain sensitive to these possibilities. If technology or process innovations happen, do a mid-course correction to integrate them into your developmental activities. If employer needs change, reconsider your current development direction.

If the change is happening more quickly than you had planned, think about accelerating your development efforts. If that does not look viable, consider getting a job with your current level of skills and knowledge at a smaller organization or at another employer that is willing to grow the ability rather than buy it. Even if you miss the period when the skills and knowledge you obtain are valued at a premium by employers in your locale, you have at least maintained your value as an employee in this work.

Another possible risk is that you will miss major, bleeding-edge innovations in your work. The process that has been described in this book guides you to focus on changes in the earning world whose value has already been largely recognized. These innovations might be considered cutting edge, and the possibility that the abilities you develop in order to work with them will be valuable to multiple employers is higher.

If you are someone who relishes being involved in bleeding-edge innovations, I suggest these adjustments to your process. When you read about the near future of your work; focus on challenges and controversies rather than on the changes, and attempt to imagine innovations that would resolve them. You might also scan magazines looking for innovations in various technologies that might be of use in your work.

If you become enthralled by an innovation or hot topic that you are convinced will be valuable to employers but that the industry and professional press have not discovered yet, give it some close analysis. Review your logic, identify your assumptions, and check at the library and/or by networking to make sure those assumptions are valid. You may be onto something. It will probably take longer to develop the topic and networking will be harder, but if your interest is strong it may be worth the effort.

The final risk that I want to point out is that in the midst of a long development process with several midcourse corrections it is possible you may move away from your interests and veer back to a primary focus on pleasing employers. This is a great temptation because of traditional norms and the potential of short-term rewards. To manage this risk, I advise people to periodically take a time-out, review their career journals/notes, and assess the level of their interest in their current focus. While not all your developmental activities are likely to be exhilarating, you should have a firm sense that the work you are doing is preparing you for what you want to do. If you can't say you still see the purpose of the work in terms of your interests and your future career, take time to generate some other work options (see Chapter 3). If you move away from work in which you have an enduring interest, you lose a major motivator for your continued, independent career development.

Some Words for the Aspiring Business Owner

This chapter has been about how individuals refine their career-development plans and build their capacities for the work they want to do. Aspiring business owners need to do these things as well. But before getting involved in career development, it would be prudent for most aspiring business owners to consider getting some "near experience." Business ownership, like many other endeavors, often is very different in reality from what many expect. Ideas for getting "near experience" include following a couple of small business owners around for a day and talking to them about their activities and responsibilities, taking a part-time job in a business like the one you are considering, or working part-time in such a business.

This is also a time when you want to gather more detailed information about how your business's proposed competitive edge would work. You may need to develop a network that is targeted toward helping you to discover an innovation or to develop a reputation that will lead to business referrals. Or you may need to figure out how to join groups of potential customers where you can bring up the subject of your proposed product or type of business and listen to what they say about that product/service. If you do not get a positive response to your proposed competitive edge, this information may give you ideas about other competitive edges to explore.

Another set of activities would revolve around building your skills and knowledge in the three general types of capacities needed by small business owners: general management skills, knowledge of the product/service, and ability to attract and maintain customers/clientele. As you learn more about your likely business and the form it will take (e.g., partnership, franchise, or sole ownership) the high-priority capabilities that you will need to develop should also become clearer. Then you can look for resources that can help you to build these capabilities, whether they are found through your current employer, by getting volunteer experience, or elsewhere.

While you will not need to "prove" your capabilities in a traditional hiring situation, you may need to demonstrate them by writing a well conceived business plan in order to obtain financing. Also, because you will be taking the primary responsibility for the success of the business, you will want to assure yourself that you are ready for the responsibilities that you are taking on.

You will need to manage your time and your independent career development as others do in this phase of the Employability Plus model. Your career development may or may not take more of your "free" time, depending on how aligned your current employment is with what you need to learn about. The decision of when to move forward and actually start your business involves balancing at least three factors: your financial resources,[15] the development of your capabilities, and the timeliness of your competitive edge. Part of your challenge in this phase of your transition to owning your own business will be to assess these three factors and decide when you are ready to "take the plunge." While the temptation might be to focus on developing the information you need to determine the details of your competitive edge, if you are also not ready financially and in terms of your general managerial capabilities, your plunge will be much more risky.

Moving Forward

In moving forward with career development, many have reported that it is easier to see the "chunks" as experiments rather than long-term commitments. In *Working Identity*, Herminia Ibarra writes that progressing slowly and experimenting is an important approach to managing change in midlife and mid-career. Her rationale, after studying a group of individuals who had embarked on major changes in their careers in midlife, is that individuals are not just changing their careers but changing their identities.[16] I would add that they are also trying to find a good fit between their interests and a constantly changing external environment, and that takes time. In addition, most are trying to make the transition while continuing to make money, and this often necessitates a step-by-step approach.

How do you know you are on the right track? There are two major factors to assess during your experiments. One factor is your personal interest and/or engagement in the activities and topics you involve yourself in. Was the hot topic or type of work as interesting as you expected it to be? What was your reaction to the work itself? Did it energize you? The other factor is the "external momentum" that you experience. By that I mean the interest you are able to tap in others, how quickly your targeted network builds, and what kinds of opportunities appear for you to become more involved in whatever is your focus—in other words, the feedback that the larger earning world provides you.

Ginger provides a good illustration of how this might work, as well as a comment on time management. Her job is in information technology, working as a contract worker. She was no longer excited about her work and was thinking seriously about what kind of work she could do in the last years of her earning career. Artistic expression had always been important to her and she was considering both writing and music. She had been a music educator early in her career but then moved into computer programming. Ginger did some "experiments" with her writing and found that, while she was willing to practice her music, she was not willing to practice her writing by revising and editing. She took this as an indication that writing was not a good focus for her earning career and moved on to experiment with music.

Ginger had sung regularly in a church choir and, when the choir director died, she volunteered to step into his position on an interim basis. She was able to find someone who was willing to help her improve her conducting style and give her occasional lessons. This helped her realize that she could figure out what she needed to know and learn it "without having to go to school for five years!" She was asked to continue on as choir director at the church.

She also started a small summer music class for children at the church. While preparing was hard work, she found she really enjoyed it. This gave her the idea that she might go back to teaching music in her community. In her networking she found that individuals seemed to think that there might be a good business for such work, because the schools in her area were cutting back on music education but many parents still wanted it for their children. Her positive reactions to her experiments/

chunks with music education, the positive responses she got from the people she worked with, and the ease of her networking all were indications of external momentum. Her plan now is to continue experimenting with music education and thinking about how to structure such a business.

Ginger was doing all this while still working full time. In fact, her job assignment as a contract worker changed, and she had both a new organization and different type of programming work to master. When she started doing the independent career development (writing, directing the choir, and teaching), she was concerned about the loss of her personal time. But almost a year into her experiment, she reported that "music is feeding me better than relaxing!" Furthermore, she was learning to draw a line and say to herself "enough is enough," thus providing herself some downtime.

Ginger's story is very positive, with everything working perfectly. Of course, that is not always the case. Jim is a librarian who has worked for almost twenty years at a college. During that time the school has grown and Jim's career has progressed as well, and he is now part of the top management of the library. In the last few years he has become interested in organization development (OD). He has taken a few courses and enjoyed them, and sees it as a logical step building upon his managerial experience as well as upon the training he has provided library patrons. That said, the OD field is very competitive. Jim has been thinking about how he might make the switch. For a long time, he saw no opportunities. He tried networking at the local chapter meetings of a big professional organization but was not very successful. He was beginning to think about moving on and changing his PWF from OD. Then, at a library conference, he saw a program about OD inside libraries. Now, he has begun to network with this group of librarians doing OD and has been learning a great deal.

The career development process is an adventure, and you never know how it might turn out. Life is complex and the earning world is constantly changing. By declaring your interests, testing your abilities, and listening to the response of the larger earning environment, most white-collar workers can build their own career paths. And today the variety among those paths has greatly increased.[17] Does this mean that it will be an easy trip? No. But regardless of the outcomes of your efforts, the journey has more potential of being personally rewarding than before, and the learning you do will help you make better decisions about your future.

The primary way that Builders and Changers will move out of this phase of the Employability Plus model will be to get a new job that takes them towards their independently developed PWF. Your targeted network and growing knowledge of employers in your preferred locale should begin to provide you with job possibilities or at least with knowledge of which employers are likely to need someone with your skills and interests. I will write more in chapter 6 about how the job search changes for people using the Employability Plus approach to mid-career management. But here I will say that I recommend that you apply for jobs that you find interesting as soon as you believe you have the minimal qualifications for the work. There is no better source for information about your readiness and about what is needed than potential employers. Whether you get the job or not, the information you gain is golden.

CHAPTER SIX

Success Strategy #4: Managing Your Career Cycle

To everything there is a season, and a time to every purpose under heaven.
—Ecclesiastes 3:1

Monica has always had a passion for science. She started college thinking she would become a medical doctor, but she later decided that she wanted to teach science. She married when she graduated and began teaching in a high school. When her children were little, she suspended her full-time employment, got a master's degree in physics, and worked on a number of part-time earning projects so she could be at home with her children. When her youngest went to school, she went back to teaching full-time. During the next 12 years, Monica taught in three schools as she worked her way to the school where she wanted to teach.

When Monica's son graduated from high school, she was free to focus on herself and her career. She prepared for and was awarded the National Board Certification as a teacher, the first science teacher in her district to achieve that distinction. Immediately upon getting that award, she and a partner began writing a textbook to share their ideas about how to teach physics. Now, six years after being awarded the National Board Certification, she has a successful textbook, is actively doing the workshops and other events needed to persuade school systems to adopt it, and is at work on another book. Monica believes she is well on her way to a successful career transition that allows her to stay connected to science in her retirement but gives her much more calendar flexibility than teaching ever did!

The New Careers by Arthur, Inkson, and Pringle is a report on the careers of a cross-section of workers in New Zealand in the 1980s and 1990s. They begin the first chapter of their book with a description of Peter's career. He began his career after public school by going into computing. After a number of employers and positions, Peter had risen to be the data processing manager for a travel firm, where he distinguished himself by redeveloping the firm's whole information system. When that project was done, he wanted a new challenge, so he approached the travel firm's software supplier and got a job in that company.

Peter had a fairly long tenure at this company, which provided him experience in a large organization and as a supervisor—both of which he enjoyed. After a few years, he requested a transfer into sales to build his knowledge and test his interest in that part of the business. But he didn't enjoy the pressures of sales, and in a few years he requested another transfer. He went back to the technical and support side of the business. There, he continued to move up and made major contributions to the company using his knowledge of the travel industry and sales.

It looked like Peter would be at that company for most of his career, but that's when the turbulence in the economy caught up with him. The company's multinational parent company ran into financial trouble and began significant downsizing. That downsizing included Peter's company, even though it was profitable. Peter knew he would eventually be downsized as well. Then another manager suggested that Peter and some colleagues become partners in a new company marketing the software they had developed, which the old company would no longer support. Their new company became very successful over the next few years.[1]

These are stories of individuals making successful transitions in today's economy. They are "naturals" in terms of the type of career management needed in today's earning world, or they have been exceedingly lucky. Their stories allow me to make two major points. First, what I am suggesting can be done. If people discover work that they find interesting and engaging, they naturally seek out information about its larger context over time. Knowing how the work is changing and what roles it plays in various organizations and/or for various customers helps them to discover options for maintaining or increasing their value as employees. Depending on the environment (e.g., the stability of Peter's employer) and their personal life choices (e.g., Monica's decision to split her attention between raising her children and her earning career), they can choose the intensity of their career development efforts—that is, whether they want to be a Maintainer, a Builder, or a Changer—at various periods in their lives.

The second point I want to make is that careers are cyclical.[2] If you consider job change—whether within one employer or when moving between employers—as the starting point for a cycle, each of these people has had a series of career cycles. Monica's career *may* have had fewer cycles than Peter's, but both individuals' careers have involved changing jobs often. The outward manifestation of the career cycle (i.e., job change) has not changed, but the changed employment dynamics have increased the frequency of the cycles and made them more pronounced in mid-career because individuals are changing employers more often. Furthermore, the things that need to be done in order to make the career cycle a smooth experience have changed.

Another change in the situation of most people in mid-career, which I have already pointed out, is the greater amount of competition for jobs and compensation. That means individuals need to be more better equipped with the experience that employers are likely to value when they seek new employment. This point is not so apparent in these stories because both Monica and Peter had been so engaged in their work that they were prepared for the changes they made. Monica spent at least three years preparing for the national certification and writing her first book. Peter had spent most of his career preparing to manage a company like the one that was so severely downsized. Both of these people were always doing more than just their current jobs. This kind of preparation certainly makes the cycles easier to navigate.

In the last three chapters, I have focused on a sequential description of what most individuals need to add to their mid-career management activities so that they can move through these cycles more easily, as Monica and Peter did. This approach to writing about the model can be deceptive, however, if readers get the impression that they are gearing up for a one-time transition. A major point of this book is that mid-career individuals in the 21st century need to manage their careers day-in and day-out with the assumption that they will be changing jobs and probably changing employers regularly. Understanding the career cycle, and what is called for in managing it, is the fourth success strategy in the Employability Plus model of mid-career management.

For white-collar workers, the model of the "organizational career" was dominant in the post–World War II era. In that model, individuals were urged to work hard in their current job, and their performance would then be recognized by their managers and they would be promoted.[3] There were some variations to this very simple model, of course. For example, some people found they had to change employers to get the promotions that they wanted, and some people applied for jobs that they wanted in order to build their careers. But, on the whole, the focus of this model was on the individual's current employer and on doing well in one's current position, with job changes usually coming as the natural consequence of their hard work or, occasionally, as the result of a job hunt.

In the first part of this chapter, I will briefly review the major components of the mid-career management cycle that I have ignored thus far. Although generally well studied and understood, the dynamics of these processes have changed somewhat as a result of the new employment dynamics in our economy. Then, I will look at the entire career cycle and the challenges to managing the more varied and demanding set of activities required. I will also include a brief section on other sources of advice and support. Finally, I close the chapter with a set of questions to aid you as you begin to seriously examine where you are in your career cycle and how to begin using the Employability Plus model.

The Rest of the Cycle

The career cycle in mid-career used to be much simpler for most individuals. They had found an employer they were satisfied with by mid-career, and they stayed with that employer for an extended period of time—often until retirement. Inside that employer they had relatively few areas on which they needed to focus in order to develop their career: performing in their current job and becoming savvy about how to contribute to and work with others in their organization. Unless they were particularly ambitious or unhappy, the organization's management took care of their career development needs. It guided their work focus, made the decisions about how their skills and knowledge should evolve, and provided them with the training and development they needed (success strategies 1, 2, and 3). This simpler career cycle is shown in Figure 6.1.

Today, management sees an individual's career development as primarily the employee's responsibility.[4] This adds a major new task to an employee's life, and I have spent most of this book exploring how individuals can take on their own career development and the positive reasons they should welcome those duties. In the next few sections, I want to review how the rest of the career cycle changes now that there is more interorganizational movement in mid-career. I will highlight three major points: that virtually everyone needs to have job-search skills, that the time it takes to find a new position is now generally longer, and that the length of time that you should focus primarily on your current job has been reduced because you will need to restart your career development efforts in order to be prepared for your next career cycle.

Job Search Skills

Job search skills have increased in importance for people in mid-career. Even those not planning to look for a job may need them if they are downsized. Whether you are applying for a job at your current employer or else-

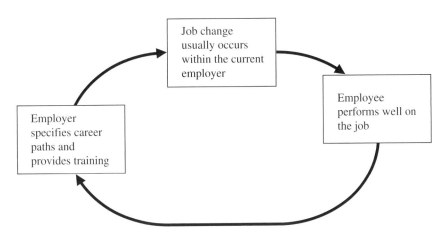

Figure 6.1
Traditional (Post–World War II) Career Cycle

where, you will need a good resume, an understanding of the job-search etiquette in your sector, an excellent network, and good interviewing techniques. Even for jobs inside your current organization, you will probably compete with both internal and external candidates for the position. Simply depending on your internal reputation to sway the person(s) doing the hiring is usually not enough in today's world, where "new blood" often is favored because it connotes different experiences and new ideas.

Job-search skills are fairly well understood because everyone needs them when they enter the work force, and much of career counseling has focused on entry. There are many books explaining these basic skills, many seminars available at colleges and universities and elsewhere, and many career counselors who can provide this information. So if your job-search skills have become rusty, help is relatively easy to find. Here, I want to focus on how the job-search process changes if you are using the success strategies of the Employability Plus model.

When you search for a white-collar job in mid-career, most of the jobs in the want ads are not meant for you; they are meant for entry-level and/or lower-skilled workers. There are, of course, exceptions. For example, many civil service jobs or jobs in higher education must be advertised in the newspaper because the institutions receive federal funds and they are legally required to do so. Also, some industry publications and Web sites include a classifieds section that advertises midlevel and higher-level jobs (e.g., *Wall Street Journal*, Publishers Marketplace). But, for the most part, search firms gather candidates for high-level positions; and word of mouth or personal recommendations alert candidates to the majority of white-collar jobs requiring experience.

Your targeted network can tell you about jobs you would find interesting. Working with the people in your network to learn about a hot topic helps you build a reputation as a good worker who has special knowledge and interests. That can lead to both information about job openings and recommendations. Also, the Employability Plus model suggests that you develop a list of possible employers as you gather information about the near future of your work. These employers should receive more focused attention from you when you are looking for a new job.

People whose capacities are already well developed but who do not have a network in place might conduct a brief survey of potential employers as part of their job-search strategy. Lilly, whom I mentioned briefly in chapter 4, was in that position. She had a master's degree in food science and had run her family's import/export business in Hong Kong but had relocated to the Midwest. Because she had found no import/export businesses in her new city, she thought she would have to change careers and moved into banking. Her particular expertise was oriental foods and liquors, so I suggested as a class assignment that she survey the local Asian restaurants to see how they were supplied as a way to determine whether there might be a market for an import/export business here. She gathered that information, starting by talking to the managers in her favorite restaurants and moving on to the local Asian food distributors. In a few months, she had a job at a large and growing distributor with the potential of opening a small import/export operation within that company.

Another story involves Janet, who was in marketing communications and had been very successful at designing the marketing communications strategy for a product. In fact, she had been so successful that, when her company was acquired by a bigger company, she was asked to help improve the larger company's marketing approach. She worked on that project for two years but came to realize that her new company's organizational culture was not open to the change she was trying to make. Furthermore, she did not like the role of change agent. What she wanted to do was design marketing communications strategies. She began looking for a new employer and was having a really difficult time finding such a specialized job when she came to me.

I suggested that she design a survey that she would be willing to conduct and compile to be shared either as an article for her professional association's newsletter/Web site or as a research report to those who participated in the project. The survey would ask chief marketing officers who in their organizations designed the marketing communications strategies. Janet could prepare a letter or email that explained the importance of the specialty and the difficulty of finding position descriptions that specify it. She could say that she would take no more than 10 minutes of their time to ask three questions about how importantly they viewed this task and where they got this kind of work done. Finally, she could say that the results would be shared with all who participated and reproduced in an article for her professional association newsletter/Web site.

In this way Janet gets good, clear information about the specific problem she is having—finding positions focused on her competency. Also, those who participate in her survey get information about marketing communications strategy and how other companies get that work done. Of course she faces the challenge of finding the names of local people who are in marketing management positions, but the library and a few calls should be able to supply most of them.

She may find that companies are combining the work she wants to do with other positions, or that management does not consider marketing communication strategy important, or that they use consulting firms to do that kind of work. Regardless of the specific outcome, Janet gets good information about how employers view the importance of this particular work and how (or whether) they include the work in other jobs. Janet may even find a potential employer among those she interviews. If not, she still would have data that she could share in a meeting of her professional association to begin building her own targeted network.

I do not suggest this type of intensive networking and knowledge-building activity for many individuals. But if you have well-developed capabilities in a specialized type of work, and your efforts to find employers have been futile, this approach can often help identify the barrier to your job search and assist you in breaking through it. Jobs are constantly being restructured and moved from organizational structure to structure; this provides a way for tracking down what your work is now called in the earning world and who are likely to be potential employers.

The Job Search Period Lengthens

A second change you should prepare for relates to the length of the job hunt. It will probably take longer than you expect. As I have already noted, employers are being more selective. In addition, if you are using the Employability Plus model, you should also be more selective. You now have more specific career interests and goals, and you will want to get a job that is compatible with them. With both sides being more selective, the job search is bound to take longer.

In your job interviews, you will want to obtain information about the potential for experiences that will aid your individual career development. But you will want to get this information indirectly rather than through direct questions such as, "I'm interested in learning about X; will this organization commit to giving me that kind of experience?" Such questions might be taken as a sign that you are more focused on your own career advancement than on the work of the organization. Instead, ask questions about the goals and strategy of the organization in general and your prospective unit in particular. Also, introduce your hot topics into your conversations in an open, questioning way, so that you can assess whether those interviewing you see those topics as useful to their organization.

Get as much information as you can. Later, take time to consider how what you have learned about what you would be doing in the new job is likely to effect your career development. Ask yourself the following questions:

- How would this unit's goals align with the types of knowledge, skills, and experience I want to gain?
- How would doing the work related to this job help me to learn about people, situations, or organizations that are important to my PWF?
- Does the unit and organization I would be joining appear interested in the hot topics in which I am most interested?

As you anticipate a job offer, you will want to assess your value to this particular employer. If you have particular skills that are in high demand by the organization, your value increases. That added value can enable you to negotiate a favorable employment deal, one that might include extra time for personal development, more financial resources for education, or more flexible working hours.[5] This can help you enhance your ability to get the rewards you want from your work as well as increase the time and energy available to you for continued career development.

How Work on the Job Changes

When careers were built mostly within one organization, a worker was doing what was needed for career development by performing the job well and participating in the training provided. Today, the "deal" has changed. Your employer no longer takes primary responsibility for your longer-term career and, in fact, permanent job cuts announced by U.S. companies ran over 100,000 jobs a quarter between the third quarter of 1997 and the fourth quarter of 2002. And ever since the fourth quarter of 2000, the number of cuts has been above 200,000 jobs a quarter.[6] These figures have affected white-collar workers more than ever before, with their rates of job loss rising ever since the early 1990s, except for a brief time in the late 1990s.[7] More than at any time in recent history, people in mid-career need to be ready to go out into the job market repeatedly and compete for new positions against a larger, more experienced candidate pool.

Still, your job performance is also very important to the quality of your career over the longer term. It directly affects your reputation as a worker, as well as your access to developmental opportunities within that organization. In the newly revised and expanded career cycle of the Employability Plus model, you want to focus primarily on your new job—that is, on learning what you need to do to perform well—for a relatively short period of time (12–18 months). After that period, you want to continue to perform well, but to also begin thinking, experimenting, and preparing for what you want to do next.

Learning how to perform well in organizations has received a good deal of attention from business scholars, both because it makes organizations run more smoothly and because it has been seen as the primary method of career progression. With that wealth of information in mind, I'm only going to provide a quick overview of the major areas to consider here.

When entering a new job, you should evaluate four major areas to determine what you need to do to enhance your ability to perform well. In terms of the work that you have been hired to do, assess your knowledge base and experience. If you are a Builder or Changer, you probably have already been developing some of the capabilities that the new position requires, but you also may need to learn on the job. Identify what are likely to be your weakest areas of performance and determine how you might build the knowledge you need or access the experience you need—both in the short term and in the longer term. Your targeted network may well be able to help you with improving your current weaknesses. While you probably cannot be as active with your network in this period as you were before you changed jobs, you should not ignore it. You worked hard to develop these contacts; they represent a knowledge resource about your work and its related hot topics, and you are likely to want to reengage more actively with some of them once you have attained a threshold of job competence in your new position.

A second area to learn about is the organization's critical path and how the unit you have joined contributes to it. I described how you might go about doing this in Chapter 5. Knowing your organization's critical path helps you to set good priorities among your job responsibilities as well as identify activities that could really help your new employer. Taking initiative to help your new employer and perhaps use some particular knowledge or talent that you add to the organization helps identify you quickly as a significant participant in the work of the organization and builds your internal organizational network quickly.

A third area to consider is how well you understand the organizational culture of your new employer. This will be a particular challenge for Changers who have moved into a different sector of the earning world.

Finally, you need to assess whether there are difficult people or groups with whom you need to interact in order to perform effectively. All organizations have difficult people and groups that are not functioning as well as they could. Your task is to identify which people and/or groups could have significant impact on your performance and devise strategies for working effectively with them.

These four components of organizational success, together with some questions to help you identify specific problems and some ideas and resources for meeting your challenges, are outlined in Table 6.1.

After you have worked in your new position for about a year, you should consider how well you have succeeded in building your reputation as a responsible, committed performer who contributes in a significant way to your employer. One way to do that is to review Table 6.1 to determine what tasks, if any, still need attention or require revisiting because of changes within the organization, such as the appointment of a new top manager or supervisor. In addition, ask the five questions listed in Table 6.2. These questions are designed to help you analyze the formal and informal feedback you are receiving about your performance. This allows you to refine your understanding of the kinds of significant contributions you can make in this organization.

Do not get caught in the drive to be the perfect employee! There is always room for improvement, but striving to be perfect in your job will not ensure that you keep it! Aim to focus on that 20 percent of your work that has the greatest impact on the organization and makes you particularly valuable while also completing those tasks that are high priorities, given your understanding of the critical path of your unit and employer. Review your list of potential improvement items and focus only on those that are truly crucial to your overall reputation. If your analysis reveals no crucial weaknesses, *move on to new career-development options!*

Thus far, I have assumed that you have chosen a new job that moves you toward the kind of work that you want to do. Of course, there are other reasons to take a job. People often are forced to take jobs that do not further their career interests if, for example, they are jobless and need the money. If you are in such a job, my advice is to do an assessment similar to that described here, determine what can be done to establish your reputation as a contributor, do it, and then begin looking for another, more favorable position. Even if your managers never seem to recognize your contribution, it's important for you to make your best effort to contribute. This helps you retain your integrity as an employee.

Table 6.1
Checklist of Career Management Tasks upon Assuming a New Job

Task	Action Options
Acquire needed job skills and knowledge	• Find someone in the organization with the skills or knowledge and enlist them to help you learn • Take a seminar or course • Read a book or a number of articles on the topics
Learn the critical paths of the organization and/ or employer	• Read about the organization and its competitors that are relevant to your unit • Have conversations with managers about their plans and what they deem important to the current and future performance of the unit/employer
Learn about the organizational culture, structure, and internal dynamics	• Read what you can about the organization on the internal Web site or in the public library to get ideas to test with others • Ask questions about how important decisions were made by those around you • Listen to conversation to see what captures the attention of coworkers and how they interpret major happenings
Identify any important personal or group challenges you will need to deal with	• Consult with friends and people in your network who might have ideas for resolving the issues • Read up on managing those specific issues or situations (use databases to identify articles and books by topic) • Develop action plans for trying to manage the situation(s) more effectively

Sometimes a new job turns out to be something other than what was promised, or a person or situation at the new job requires coping mechanisms you cannot develop. These kinds of situations are disappointing, and you may need to begin another job search more quickly than you would normally. But job searches are time-consuming, and I would urge you to make a good-faith effort to remedy the situation. Talk to the management and see if the job can be at least partially restructured. Really attempt to develop some approach to working with difficult individuals and think about confronting the problem in a conversation.[8]

Still, the beauty of the earning world today is that changing jobs, even after only a year, is not seen in a particularly unfavorable light as long as quick moves do not become a pattern in your resume. Simply prepare to explain in general, neutral terms why the job was not a fit for you and reenter the job market while your skills, knowledge, and experience for the job you want are still current.

Table 6.2
Assessment of Job Performance and "Good Worker" Reputation

Question	Feedback Focus	Action Items Going Forward
What actions have drawn compliments?	Identifies strengths useful in your new job/setting.	Are there other situations where these behaviors would be seen as useful?
Where have you "dropped the ball" on significant items?	Indicates where your reputation might be damaged.	What can you do to recover the item? What can you do to better manage your time in similar situations?
Can you describe your unit's critical path?	Talk to your immediate supervisor to try to get some clarity.	See Chapter 5 for a discussion of what to do if the critical path remains unclear.
Are there times when your behavior was inconsistent or might have been perceived as inconsistent?	Indicates where your reputation might be damaged.	Talk informally with others to see what their perceptions are and devise action options to remove inconsistencies or the perception of them.
Have you been criticized or received guidance from others about how to handle particular situations?	These appear to be situations of particular concern for supervisors or coworkers and are thus important to your reputation as a good worker.	If you can think of none of these cases, you might consider engaging a few coworkers in a discussion of how they view your performance. This should reveal what they consider important in the work as well as their view of your performance.
Have you made contributions to the success of the unit/organization in addition to your own job responsibilities?	Taking initiative to improve the situation in your unit/organization is important to your reputation. Analyzing what you did also reveals where you may have particular strengths to help your unit/organization.	If you have not made any such contributions, identifying possibilities and working to accomplish them would help establish your reputation as a good coworker. If you have already done this, you have a bullet point to include in the next revision of your resume.

Managing the Expanded Mid-Career Management Cycle

Figure 6.2 is an overview of the expanded mid-career management cycle needed now. In this cycle, individuals take over primary responsibility for directing and developing their careers. After 12 to 18 months in a new job, when they have discovered and developed responses to the unique challenges of their current position, their career-management strategy should become two-pronged: They should continue to be excellent performers who contribute in significant ways to the critical path of their employers, and they should restart their independent career-management activities.

The additional task of independent career development need not take a huge amount of your personal time. So soon after changing jobs, you may still be developing your career potential by learning on the job. In addition, a fair amount of overlap between your interests and those of your employer is likely. That overlap should produce a significant number of mutually favorable opportunities for you and your employer (see the discussion in Chapter 5).

Still, deciding what activities to seek out, designing developmental or information-gathering chunks, and assessing your personal reactions to these activities and to what you have learned about your preferences and abilities will take *some* personal time. In addition, you may want to experiment with new development possibilities outside of your workplace, and you will want to continue to gather information about the near

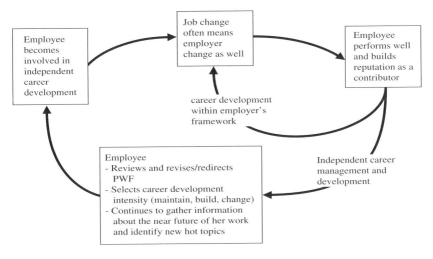

Figure 6.2
The Expanded Career Cycle for the 21st Century

future of your work. But, for the most part, I estimate that the self-management time needed by individuals, once they have been through the start-up phase of the model, will be about an hour a month. In addition, I estimate you should expect to spend one to three hours every month on other career development activities—either in conjunction with your current position and employer or independently—depending on the intensity of your career development (i.e., on whether you are a Maintainer, a Builder, or a Changer).

Think of your self-management time as a long coffee break, taken alone when you can think uninterrupted. Put it in your calendar. Once at the coffee shop, rely on your career journal to help you remember where you are in your cycle and where you need to focus your career-management efforts.

One reason I specify these steps is that actually doing them can be a major challenge. Independent career development goes against norms that have been well established in the earning world since World War II. One of these norms is the assumption that if you just do a good job for your current employer you will be rewarded—or at least not fired. The change in this norm is something that I have already discussed. Of course, people are still fired for substandard performance. But most downsizing today has little relationship to individual job performance; it is instead the result of changing organizational strategies and the drive to lower labor costs.[9]

Another norm that affects individuals' willingness to think independently about their careers while on the job is the belief that what is happening inside your current organization is similar to what is happening elsewhere, so that your on-the-job capabilities will be easily marketable elsewhere at comparable compensation. This belies the growing variety among our workplaces and the increased competition for white-collar mid-career job openings.

Yet another outdated norm is the feeling that it would be disloyal to your current employer not to spend 100 percent of your working time on your current job. Your loyalty to your current employer should revolve around making significant contributions to the organization and keeping proprietary information private. You also need to be loyal to yourself and your family by taking the time to manage your career as well as you can. It is through your own development efforts that you can take more control of your career and direct it toward your preferred work interests and roles. You can't do that when you have not thought about and tested those preferences. Nor can you do it when you are constantly reacting to your current employer's needs or desires.

This is easier said than done, of course—especially given there is usually more work to be done in any job than a single person can do. And while there is disagreement among researchers about whether individuals are actually working longer hours, the perception of overwork is very much a part of white-collar earning life. Still, a long coffee break should not prove too daunting to those who are convinced that they need to manage their careers more effectively.

Much of what needs to be done for ongoing, proactive career management has already been discussed in Chapters 3, 4, and 5. But those chapters were written for people who were being introduced to the Employability Plus model and who were in the start-up phase. The next sections will highlight three additional dynamics you are likely to experience over multiple cycles:

- The importance of punctuating your ongoing career management activities with major periods of reflection and redirection
- The importance of being actively involved in career management even as a Maintainer
- Learning to manage surprises in the external environment

An Opportunity to Reflect and Redirect

The commitment of individuals to more actively manage their career cycles, as called for in the Employability Plus model, helps them to make time to reflect on the changes they have made and to reconsider their career direction. Usually that time would come a few years after a major job change for Builders and Changers, or every three to five years for Maintainers. Of course, a major change in your situation or in the larger environment could also trigger such reconsideration. In Chapter 5, I talked about how corporate planning and product introduction has changed to accommodate the faster pace of change and the growing complexity of the environment. Periodically making time to reflect, refine, and perhaps redirect your PWF is analogous to corporations redesigning major products or strategies after they have been introduced into the market.

Five major factors should be monitored and might trigger a major review of your career:

- Your personal reaction to the work you are now doing
- Instability of your current employer
- A major change among probable employers in your preferred locale
- A major change in the nature of your work
- Life changes you believe may occur for you and your family over the next three to five years

As you approach this assessment, I suggest you do an analysis of the opportunities and threats in relation to each factor.[10] For example, you may have taken a job only to find that important expectations about that work and its impact on you are not materializing. Or, alternatively, you may find that a job that you expected to be a temporary bridge to other work is very compelling.

Make a list of these threats and opportunities and of other ideas about your career development. From this list you should be able to generate at least a couple of options or ideas for your next possible steps. The overarching questions you want to ask are

- What are the threats and opportunities in this larger environment?
- Can I prioritize them by likelihood of occurrence and time needed to fully develop? By what I find most important or fascinating? By the amount of career development time and energy each would require to manage?
- How might my personal strengths and weaknesses help or hinder my response to each of the threats and opportunities?
- Which options make the most sense given my blend of career interests and larger life commitments?

Identify any questions about which you should gather information in order to be able to choose the best available alternative, and explore ways you can experiment with options for your next cycle.

Now, while you still enjoy your current work, is the time to consider your next moves, because you have time to make a relatively calm decision and to prepare for the transition. Sometimes the larger environment will determine your next cycle. For example, concern about a likely downsizing might suggest that you focus on maintaining your current work focus and begin a job search immediately, even if you were hoping to build your career further. At other times, your personal interests or preferences can be your prime considerations.

A major reorientation of your earning career can take multiple years. When *New York Times* columnist William Safire left his job as a political commentator at the beginning of a new U.S. presidency in January 2005, he wrote about his decision never to retire, despite the fact that he was of an age when that might have been his goal. Then he described how he had become involved in an organization to which he had been introduced by a friend nearly a dozen years earlier. He explained how his interest in and commitment to the purpose of the organization had grown until his involvement in the program was running constantly "in the background of my on-screen life." He also reported that he had carefully planned his transition and had informed his editor two years in advance of his departure.[11]

Although most reflect-and-redirect transitions do not take ten years to ripen or involve an advance warning for the employer of two years, this story is a good example of how such a change can evolve.

Maintenance Does Not Mean Steady-State!

Some people have mid-careers characterized by constant building, other careers are characterized by long periods of maintenance in mid-career. The reasons are many. For example, Monica, the teacher whom I profiled at the beginning of this chapter, maintained her career while she reared her family. Others may choose to maintain, rather than build, their careers because they have other interests outside their earning careers that they want to pursue. Still others may choose maintenance because they love the work they do and don't want to change it.

The point I want to make is that today maintaining a career, for whatever reason, should involve more proactive career development and information gathering than it typically has in the past. The world has become more unstable, as was illustrated by Peter's story. Furthermore, technology, organizations, labor resources, and ways of doing business are constantly changing today. You need to stay current and continue to increase your value as an employee, so that you can adjust as your work and your employers change.

At minimum, this means that you need to stay engaged in information gathering about the near future of your work both globally (via the library and the Web) and locally (via a targeted network). Also, you need to build your knowledge, experience, and skills so that you remain current and flexible and can *show* that on your resume. There are a number of ways to build your capabilities and improve your employability without changing the basic nature of your work. Table 6.3 describes three basic approaches, using as illustrations an individual who wants to maintain a position working as a sales representative and an individual working as a lab technician.

Following any of the approaches in Table 6.3—or a combination of them—means identifying what questions you need answered, determining how best to get that information, and designing chunks so that you can track your progress in developing the needed skills, knowledge, and experience. A time will eventually come, however, when most Maintainers need to consider changing employers. There is usually only so much you will be able to do to show flexibility and a range of skills while working for any one employer. In today's more turbulent environment, it is probably good for your career prospects to move at least every five or ten years, even as a Maintainer. It shows employers that you are willing to make changes. It will also build your network and experience base. Three questions can help you to recognize when moving on is a good idea:

- Have I learned most of what this employer and job can teach me?
- Is the organization for which I work becoming financially unstable?

Table 6.3
Four Approaches to Self-Development for Maintainers

Approach	Example Using Sales as a Focus	Example Using Lab Work as a Focus
Hot topics– cutting edge	Start experimenting with augmenting your sales efforts with email and Web sites	Begin working with or reading about new techniques
Build flexibility in customers or products/ services or both	Build knowledge and experience selling to different types of customers (e.g., retail, wholesale, business-to-business, and international customers)	Learn about how the lab work you do changes depending on specimens or applications
Build skills/ knowledge	Analyze your special sales abilities and preferences (e.g., technical sales, government sales, person-to-person sales, big-ticket sales) and then build experience/ knowledge in that type of sales by seeking knowledge about customers or products/services	Analyze the work you do, identify what you find most interesting, build your skills and knowledge around that work
Identify other preferred employers	Pick at least two employers for whom you would like to work, analyze what selling their products/services requires, and focus on developing knowledge and experience in those areas	Find at least two employers, analyze the lab work done there, and build knowledge and experience useful for that employer

- Has a job appeared that I am truly attracted to because of how it will augment my skills and knowledge?

These questions also work well to help Builders and Changers decide when to change jobs.

Surprises in Your Independent Career Management

I have been describing the management of your career cycle almost as though you were the only one who controlled your career decision making. Not true! In this section, I want to highlight three major types of surprises and the methods for managing them.

Your employer may well offer you an unexpected job opportunity. People at all three levels of career-management intensity—Changers, Builders, and Maintainers—who manage their careers in an Employability Plus style are committed to their work and understand and contribute to their organization's critical paths. This is an employer's dream employee, and often management is looking for such people to move into the critical spots within their organizations. In the past, this was the prime method of movement in mid-career. Today, it is just one of the options.

Assess your employer's offer, compare it to the type of work you want to do (as embodied in your PWF) and, if you are a Builder or a Changer, to the types of experiences you need in order to build your skills and knowledge. If it is a good fit, congratulations! If it is not a good fit, explain why that position is not of immediate interest to you. At the very least, provide a careful, articulate explanation of why this is not the direction in which you want to build your career. It will show your employer that you seriously considered the job. Sometimes such an explanation will enable your current employer to find another job that will be of more interest to you. Employers that genuinely believe that fulfilled and engaged employees contribute more effectively to the enterprise often have active systems that try to support and nurture their employees' personal development. These systems can be very helpful, but do not mistake those support systems for a long-term employment commitment.

Management may want to continue to negotiate with you about you filling the position after you initially decline an offer—perhaps because they feel that the position must be filled immediately with someone competent, and they do not want to take the time to do a search. If that happens, be prepared to think about what might be done to make the job more beneficial to your career goals. Could the organization make more funds available for education or training? Could management commit to exposing you to parts of the business that are more compatible to your long-term career goals? Could you do the work and also meet your career goals if they granted you more flexibility in some way? Also consider how long you are willing to commit to doing this job and negotiate an exit from the position. In the end your decision will need to be based on the deal you are able to negotiate and your assessment of its impact on your career goals.

The second possible surprise I want to highlight is being downsized. You might think that if you are on the critical path of the organization, performing well, and in a stable organization; that you are safe, but that is not always the case. Organizations get bought; they change strategies; they change leaders; and they run into financial challenges. Downsizing remains a much-used managerial tactic, so that even the most careful monitoring may not prevent you from becoming a victim to it. Yes, the same companies who downsize often create more jobs than they have eliminated, but that does not always help individuals who have been downsized. The new jobs often have lower compensation than before,[12] involve different work tasks, and may be created in a different location.

While it is not within the scope of this book to discuss personal finance, everyone should have a financial plan for the event that they are downsized, detailing how they would limit their spending and cover their financial responsibilities until gaining new employment. The percentage of workers with a college education or more who have experienced long-term unemployment (defined as being unemployed for more than six months) increased just under 30% between 2000 and 2003, according to the latest figures available.[13]

The third type of surprise you might experience is the realization that job opportunities are declining substantially in your work and/or preferred locale. There are a variety of possible reasons for this. Employers may relocate, move work offshore, or automate jobs. People who repeatedly pursue increased specialization in their career cycles can reach the limits of what enterprises need. Or technological innovations combined with customer choice patterns can lead to a precipitous decline in some businesses. For example, the cell phone business, as it becomes more reliable and widespread, is having a significant negative impact on the pager industry.[14] Such a trend would probably not be happy news for people who were Maintainers in work primarily related to pagers, because it would suggest that they would need to become Builders or Changers. Nevertheless discovering such a trend when you still have at least a few years to prepare for the coming change can be really helpful.

The decline of a particular type of work does not often happen overnight. There are usually signs that things are changing, and the changes create other needs that can either prolong your involvement in the work while you prepare for a major shift or provide opportunities for building your career in other ways.[15] When equipment or services begin to become obsolete, some workers will still be needed to maintain the equipment or services that remain in use. Technology used in the declining equipment may be used in other equipment or form the foundation of new technologies that these workers could learn in advance, if forewarned of the need for change. Furthermore, people who worked selling the previous equipment or services know customers who will now buy whatever is the replacement product/service. That knowledge of the customers can be a hiring edge for them, enabling them to learn about a new, more robust product/service.

People managing such a "surprise" should begin thinking about the various aspects of their current work using the Five Aspects Exercise in Chapter 3. They need to reflect on which aspect of their job/work is most interesting/engaging for them and brainstorm about how they might bridge to other employers and types of work using their knowledge. Of course, this may also involve some information gathering both at the library and through networking. Depending on the likely timeline of the change, it will be useful to prepare a short-term response if your job becomes an early casualty, as well as a longer-term plan for developing a new career that provides at least adequate intrinsic and extrinsic rewards for you.

Getting Additional Help

This career management cycle, when described on paper, sounds very feasible. In the real lives of many adults it is often not so easily accomplished. Real life is messy and demanding. Henry Mintzberg, a highly respected scholar in management, made (academic) history by pointing out that the challenge of management was not so much in thinking as a manager should think but rather in being able to accomplish the goals of that thinking in the midst of a busy, fragmented world.[16] This is one of the challenges of better personal management of mid-career as well.

To a large extent, the Employability Plus model is a model for self-directed, independent learning. There has been a lot of talk in our society about lifetime learning, but today that concept is often manifested more in the "edutainment" of an occasional seminar or retreat than in the sustained attempt to use information and build on it to achieve personal goals. The Employability Plus model provides the outline of a syllabus for enacting a long-term learning plan for your earning career. From time to time it is understandable that you might need help in seeing the larger picture and refocusing your activities or sustaining your efforts.

The variety of activities called for in this model and the recognition that in today's world mid-career individuals are likely to need them repeatedly also means that you may want to seek out experts who can help you refresh those skills when you need them. I have tried to address most of these challenges in the book, but a book can only go so far. Many people making personal changes while also living their complicated and busy lives would benefit from having additional, more personalized support. Figure 6.3 illustrates the expanded career cycle of the Employability Plus model, highlighting the groups most likely to provide the best support for each phase of the model.

Finally, the model may present you with psychological and/or emotional challenges during the process. Such challenges might include anger at needing to take the time and effort to do these things, fear about making choices more independently, and the desire to always make the right decisions even in the face of larger amounts of uncertainty and a constantly evolving situation. The Employability Plus model is a normative model and, for many, that implies that they will be successful if they just

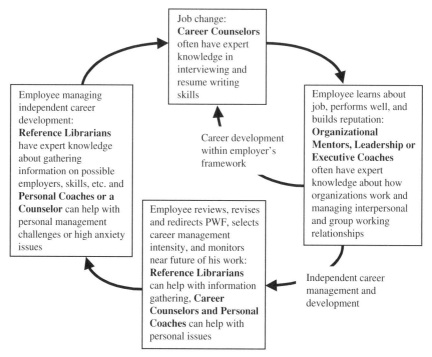

Figure 6.3
Sources of Help for Activities at Various Points in the Career Cycle

follow its guidelines. Unfortunately, that is not always the case because an infinite number of variables affect career success. Unrealized hopes and expectations can lead to serious frustration and disappointment. A high level of anxiety or distress would probably be a sign that emotional and psychological issues need attention. There are many potential sources of help for these issues such as counselors, psychologists, and other trained professionals.

As with all sources of information and aid, the best way to discover the best resources is experimentation. If you do not find one reference librarian particularly helpful, move on to another. Professional groups sometimes list their members by location to facilitate potential clients making contact, but remember that membership in a particular professional group does not assure that an individual will be skilled in the type of support you need or that your personal chemistry with that person will be good. If you know of others who have sought out support, referrals are helpful. Still, to provide yourself with knowledge of their expertise and get a feel for the individual as a person, I suggest that you contact two or three candidates. In that conversation you will want to discuss at least the following topics:

- The specific issue concerning which you are seeking help and/or support
- How the counselor/coach would describe his clients (You may want to directly ask if the counselor/coach is familiar with this book and the Employability Plus model if your challenges are directly related to some of the model's unique characteristics.)
- How the help and support is normally delivered—by phone conversations, one-on-one conversations, or e-mail exchanges
- Cost

Professional associations can also be of help not just in providing networking opportunities but also in providing information. The new challenges of mid-career management should help inform the types of information these organizations provide their memberships. They would be perfect vehicles for finding out the varieties of work roles and employers that their members are involved with as well as keeping track of hot topics in relation to the work and the skills and abilities employers are likely to value most in the next three to five years.

A final source of support is a Web site I have opened to support individuals who are using the Employability Plus model: www.employability plus.com. This site will provide additional information on mid-career management and provide a way for people to ask questions, identify what they are finding most challenging, and share their successful tactics for mid-career management. This book is grounded in scholarly research, but there have been only a few studies about individuals' mid-career development to date. I hope to remedy that lack. The Web site will also allow individuals to volunteer to participate in some of those studies if they wish.

Some Words for Aspiring Business Owners

Because aspiring business owners need capabilities in three major areas (product/service, customers, and management), their career management often extends over multiple cycles of their careers. As I suggested in Chapter 5, the career development tasks can be streamlined somewhat by having a partner or buying a franchise and by looking at the priority needs of the type of business you want to start. But finding a partner or financing and selecting a franchise also take time and energy. And owners still have ultimate responsibility for the entire enterprise.

In this book you have read about two aspiring business owners who exemplify two approaches to career management while pursuing the goal of opening one's own business. Emer, the software engineer first described in Chapter 2, wants to open a software business in his home country in the next ten years or so. He is managing his career now to provide himself with the necessary experience in software engineering. In addition, he is pursuing an MBA focusing on entrepreneurship. So, over the next 10 years, he will get the education and product/service experience he needs, as well as what he hopes will be some valuable management experience. He must also acquire an understanding of customer needs and preferences in his home country as well as of the competition he will face there. He has wisely decided to leave that piece of development until he gets closer to his transition time, so that the information he has when he launches his business is current.

Ann, the media executive you read about in Chapter 5, who is thinking about starting a human resources business, is in a different situation. She has a good grasp of management and customer attraction issues, at least as they are experienced in fairly large companies. She also has substantial financial resources to help her make the change if she decides to proceed. But she needs to find time away from the demands of her current job to explore the new focus of her work (i.e., to gain knowledge about the product/service). Unlike Emer, her current job does not relate to the product/service on which her new business would focus, so she needs to gather the relevant information in a separate venue.

Jeffery's story illustrates a third approach to career management while preparing to open a business. He is an engineer working in a large company and pursuing career development there, but "on the side" he is also developing a small business out of his garage. He had designed a board game during college and is moving toward manufacturing and distributing it. His is essentially a three-pronged career development strategy. He needs to maintain high performance on his current job, prepare himself for his longer-term career in engineering or engineering management, and develop his knowledge and abilities in the area of small-scale manufacturing, marketing, and distribution. Luckily, his wife was interested in helping.

Moving Forward

Now you have read a description of how the Employability Plus model works. You may well have been implementing some of the ideas in this book even before you read about them here. Other ideas—such as targeting your networking or reading about the near future of your work—may have been new to you. Furthermore, as you have seen in this chapter, the Employability Plus model calls for you to focus on different activities when you are in different phases of the career cycle. The goal of this section of the chapter is to help you decide what conceptual tasks are most important for you to address now, as you step fully into using the model.

This book has done two primary things: It has laid out a framework of conceptual tasks needed in mid-career management (i.e., the success strategies and the various questions that need answering) and it has suggested methods for accomplishing those tasks. I have described each method only once, at the point where I think it is the most effective and efficient way to gather information or to build skills and knowledge. When you are using the model as an individual, however, you can use the various methods to achieve multiple conceptual tasks. What this means is that, as you begin to use the Employability Plus model, you will be making decisions both about your conceptual starting point and the methods you will use.

For the vast majority of people, I believe the best place to begin using the Employability Plus model is to articulate your PWF. You need to be interested and engaged in the focus of your work in order to sustain independent career management. Furthermore, since the PWF allows you to limit and focus your information gathering, it is a very important foundation for all your other career-management activities.

The only two exceptions to using this foundational statement as a starting point in the model are: (1) when you have just accepted a new job or (2) if you believe you are in imminent danger of losing your current job. These two situations put you in a different place in the career cycle. A new job suggests that you should focus on learning about your new position and organization so that you can perform well before going forward to articulating or refining your PWF.

If you believe you are about to lose your job, you should focus your career management efforts on staying employed, because unemployment is very punishing for most in this economy. Determine what you need to do to develop a hiring edge in terms of your current job responsibilities, begin a job search, and focus on developing the skills, knowledge, and experience that can improve the attractiveness of your current resume. Once you are secure in your current job or have a new job and have learned enough about it and your new organization to perform well, you will be ready to take up the question of articulating or refining your preferred PWF.

Articulating your PWF for the Employability Plus model requires more than simply describing the work you currently do. So, before moving on to other success strategies, ask yourself these questions:

- Do you believe the PWF you have articulated is something you will want to actively work at for the foreseeable future?
- Will you be willing to spend some of your free time gathering information about it?
- Is it described in such a way that prospective employers would quickly know if your work is part of their organizations? (That is, is it anchored in the earning world and not just a list of the types of interactions you enjoy or of general capabilities that are used in many situations and across industries and functions?)

- Is it a realistic fit with your potential capabilities and the likely job possibilities in your preferred locale?

If your PWF does not meet these criteria, it still needs development. Begin putting the Employability Plus model to use by designing some chunks to rework and refine your PWF.

This is where you want to consider not just the methods highlighted in Chapter 3, but all of the career-management methods highlighted throughout the book. Table 6.4 is an overview of those methods, noting the chapter in which each was highlighted and containing a column that asks you to assess your general comfort with each method. It may make sense for you to use an information-gathering method with which you are already comfortable, particularly as you begin to build your personal momentum with the Employability Plus model. If library research is something you like to do, you could look at the periodicals of the sector that interest you, as was described in Chapter 3. However, if you like to gather information in a hands-on fashion, identify some opportunities to get some experience (volunteering perhaps) or near experience (e.g., following someone around for a day as they do the work you think is interesting). If you enjoy networking, you might ask a variety of people about their work or talk to a series of friends about what work in the earning world they believe would suit you.

Whatever your method and whether you choose to formally "chunk" or not (see Table 5.5 for the conceptual components of a chunk) make some quick notes in your career journal and at least set a future date when you will reflect on your progress in accomplishing what you have set out to do. This date should not extend beyond the next few months. If it is not reasonable to believe you can finish answering the question you have framed in three

Table 6.4
Review of Career-Management Methods

Basic Career-Management Method	Chapter	Rate Your Comfort Level*
Library information gathering	4	
Networking (upgraded to targeted networking in Employability Plus) and gathering information via conversations	5	
Getting experience or near experience	5	
Personal reflection	3 & 5	

*C = comfortable, NW = needs work, ? = don't know

months, set up a reflection time to check your progress at a midpoint. Put a note in your calendar to have a private cup of coffee at a coffee shop or to go on a walk where you can reflect on your progress. During that time, reflect on what you have learned thus far and decide how to make midcourse corrections if needed. Also set aside times or put notes in your personal calendar reminding you to do the necessary activities. Otherwise, the hustle and bustle of your daily life is likely to encourage you to forget your private commitments to your career management, particularly in the beginning.

If you have a well-articulated PWF (i.e., the questions above are all answered), then the next major entry point to using the Employability Plus model is assessing what you need to know about the external environment. The shape of your career over time has been and will continue to be a product of both your initiatives and those of other players in the earning world. For many years most people with white-collar jobs were insulated from that external environment because of their stable employment. Today the situation is strikingly different.

This is another area where your experience in the earning world may be helpful. You probably already have some of the information you need and only have to reanalyze it in light of the new career management concepts in this book. Certainly your knowledge of how the earning world works will help you analyze the information you get. Table 6.5 lists the major questions about the larger environment of the work used in the

Table 6.5
Questions to Determine Focus of Employability Plus Activity Once the PWF Is Articulated

Question	Chapter	Rate Your Level of Knowledge*
What is the near future of my work?	4	
What types of employers will use my work?	4 & 5	
Are there enough of those types of employers in my preferred locale?	4	
What new skills, knowledge, and experience do I need to obtain to develop a hiring edge for the work I want?	5	
How can I go about designing independent career-development "chunks" at my current employer, while also doing my current job?	5	

L = much knowledge, S = some knowledge, and ? = needs more information

Employability Plus model. As in Table 6.4, there is a column that lists the chapter of this book that explores the gathering and thinking through of that information. It also includes a column in which you can note the level of your current knowledge.

To use the Employability Plus model well, you need to have some information about all these questions, but your current knowledge base will vary with your unique set of interests and experiences to date. Use Table 6.5 to help you determine the general question(s) that should be your current priority. Whatever question you choose to focus on, your information gathering should also provide information about the other questions, since these questions are all interrelated. Keep that in mind as you analyze the information you gather. Return to Table 6.4 to choose a method for gathering information about the larger world. Start with a method that you are comfortable with, but use other methods to double check the validity of the information you are getting. For example, while you can certainly begin to identify hot topics through targeted networking if you are comfortable doing that, you really need to check out the list you generate with the databases at the library to assure that you have gotten something approaching a global perspective.

Once you have stepped into the Employability Plus model, you can proceed through the cycle, adjusting your management activities as has already been described. The question that I want to explore next is the following: What will be the overall effect on employment dynamics of large numbers of individuals using the Employability Plus model? There will probably be a number of changes but, in Chapter 7, I will focus on two, hoped-for impacts in particular. First, I will describe why the Employability Plus model relieves our sense of helplessness in the face of the changes in employment dynamics. Second, I will explain how this model encourages support from employers for our independent career management efforts.

CHAPTER SEVEN

Epilogue: Changing the Deal

"No snowflake in an avalanche ever feels responsible."
—from More Unkempt Thoughts, Stanislaw J. Lec[1]

In *The New Deal at Work,* Peter Cappelli describes for employers how employment dynamics have changed in recent years and what new challenges are likely to result from these changes. He also has some points that employees can learn from. First, he highlights the fact that employment is a "deal" between two parties—an employer and an employee. Over the years the norms for the deal (also known as the psychological contract) evolve. *The New Deal at Work* describes how employers unilaterally changed the norms of the "deal" in the 1990s and why. Cappelli also contends that over the last twenty years employers have been the dominant partner in making these employment deals. But Cappelli points out that employees can and should respond to the changed norms during their individual negotiations and writes, "So, for companies, announcing the new deal is only the beginning of a process of arriving at a new employment relationship."[2] It is my contention that, as yet, most employees have not thought through their best response to the current "new deal," and that as a result they are suffering from more feelings of insecurity, finding the shifts they want to make in their careers more difficult, and experiencing more loss than necessary—both in terms of income and other rewards from their earning careers.

In the years immediately after the psychological contract between employers and employees had been changed, employees who were directly affected did not have time to respond proactively. As I have already described, those who were downsized scrambled to do their best to get back into the earning world and maintain their incomes. There have been hardships for many, and the popular press has published many articles about affected individuals—particularly during recessions but also when pension plans revert to governmentally insured funding or traditionally strong industries face new, severe challenges that cause them to restructure. Such economic restructuring promises to continue because of continued globalization and increasing competition. But the scrambling reactions of individuals, while understandable in the early years of the change, now should be replaced by a more proactive response.

To date I have seen two other attitudinal reactions on the part of workers to the new employment environment. One reaction is fairly combative. It rests on the logic that, if the employers' need for long-term loyalty has diminished to the point where they can regularly embrace downsizings, then employees should also cast aside the need for long term affiliation and work as independent agents. I believe this is one reason for the popularity of ideas like those espoused in *The Free Agent Nation*.[3] While being a free agent will work for some,[4] I think many mid-career individuals cannot effectively take on the range of functions needed to be successful solo practitioners—essentially running their own businesses selling their services—nor do they want to do so.

The second reaction, which has been much more frequent among white-collar workers, is denial. Many people think downsizing happens to other people, or they tell themselves that they are skilled and will be able to easily get another job. They are often baffled and somewhat bitter when they apply unsuccessfully for jobs they clearly have the potential to perform. The "hidden" changes in the job market, which include more competition for jobs and more exacting hiring preferences, are things that many are not aware of and thus are unprepared for.

I have an acquaintance who had been a computer programmer in a big insurance agency for about fifteen years. Her job involved working on a software system that was proprietary to her employer. When I first talked to her about her employment almost four years ago, a big downsizing at her company had been announced. She told me that she knew her job would end eventually because the company was going to phase out the unique software she worked with. But she said she wasn't going to worry about it. It was a casual conversation, but I tried to point out that she would certainly need new skills to get a job, and now was the time to begin preparing. I talked to her more recently, and she told me that her employment would end in a few weeks. She would be one of the last to get a "good" severance package from her company and was looking forward to taking most of the summer off. Again I asked what she had decided to do. Her response was that she was done with the corporate life but she didn't know what she would do next. She hadn't really thought about it. I wished her luck, and she is very likely going to need it.

All of these reactions are understandable, but they are not a pragmatic, proactive response to the changed employment dynamics. They do not help mid-career individuals to be more successful in their more frequent employment negotiations and better manage their longer-term careers, for which they now carry prime responsibility. My belief is that individual employees need what Cappelli provided for managers: an analysis of their new situation and some ideas about how to respond to it proactively. That is the purpose of this book and the Employability Plus model.

Negotiating Basics

The basis of any negotiation is simple: Each side has something the other side wants. In employment negotiations, the employers have jobs, income, and learning opportunities and the employees have capabilities to do certain work. But during the era of long-term employment, we got in the habit of taking a less-than-equal position in these negotiations. This was because as entry-level employees we offered employers primarily potential (rather than specific skills, knowledge, and experience) and had little knowledge of the earning world. This meant our employment negotiations were employer-centric focusing on what the employer needed and was willing to give.

The norm of not changing employers further entrenched this employer-centric approach to employment negotiations. Most people do not look for a new employer until they have lost the one that they have. This greatly increases the importance of the reward any potential employer provides—income—and emphasizes the idea that individuals should focus on selling themselves as employees in all instances and simply take their best offer. But now we can expect to negotiate multiple employment deals as experienced workers. We have more specific value to offer the right employers, and we want more than entry-level rewards. Furthermore, because we are likely to have a series of employers throughout our careers, we need to be more selective because we are building our own careers primarily through the work experiences we get. This calls for a rethinking of how we approach employment negotiations.

The Employability Plus model provides the basic knowledge you need to upgrade your negotiating approach. It provides you with a way of articulating a career that you build in tandem with your employers rather than as a result of any one employer's guidance or needs. It helps you recognize your value as an employee and identify employers where your work will be an important contribution. And it helps you see multiple employment options so you have more choices. As a result of this knowledge, you will be able to choose when you should change employment more wisely, usually moving before you lose your job. You will choose your jobs to enhance your earning career as well as because of the rewards and the employer. And you will know when the deal is a good one and when you should make proposals to make it better. In other words, your basic approach to these negotiations will be more as a full partner than as the weaker party.[5]

Obviously, it will take some effort for most individuals to develop the better negotiating base described here, but this book has shown that it is feasible. Furthermore, it is likely that people who choose this course will not only be better negotiators but will also have more personally fulfilling careers and lives. In addition, their work capabilities and interests should also be assets to the organizations in which they work.

Negotiating Strength and Options

Individuals renegotiate their employment deal with each job change. In addition to improving their basic negotiating stance, the Employability Plus model provides employees with a way to strengthen their negotiating position even more, if they choose. This stronger position can pay off not just in salary but in being able to negotiate other rewards as well.

In recent years employers have become increasingly more flexible in the employment deals they negotiate, and the deals are becoming more individualized.[6] One reason for this shift is that employers are now making different deals with many different employee groups—deals with companies who provide workers to do particular jobs on a short-term basis, deals with individual contract workers, deals with highly paid consultants who offer specialized skills, deals with companies that manage offshore workers or with the employees in foreign countries themselves, deals with part-timers, and deals with full-timers. Employers also are being more careful how they spend their labor dollars. They are willing to pay for skills and knowledge that are specialized and important to their goals, but they will pay less for skills and knowledge that are more readily available.

Strength in your negotiating position is certainly helpful for obtaining the rewards you want from your earning career, but remember your employer is not the only source of rewards. For example, Changers often have a weaker bargaining position because they are new to the work arena where they want to be hired. But, for them, the change and its future potential are important rewards in and of themselves. Likewise, Maintainers have made a decision that they are generally satisfied with the level of rewards they have and that they enjoy the work they are currently doing. Because they are not likely to be focused on developing new capabilities, their bargaining position with prospective employers is likely to be somewhat weaker as well. But they are satisfied with the work and their lower career management intensity is likely to give them more time for other activities they find rewarding. And, of course, when individuals believe that the deals they will be able to negotiate will no longer include the rewards they want, or include enough of them, Changers and Maintainers can shift their career management and become Builders.

For white-collar, mid-career employees, the more sophisticated capabilities they develop are seldom "new skills" that they need to go back to school for long periods to get. They grow out of the interaction between employees' general work-oriented skills, recent changes in how the work is done, and the needs of employers. More often than not, they involve complex interactions that involve ambiguity and draw upon an individual's experience and judgment.[7] These new capabilities are ones that experienced workers can identify and develop, if they have an increased awareness and knowledge of the multiple-employer context of the work.

Builders are likely to be in the strongest negotiating positions with employers when pursuing employment deals. They are building directly on their past knowledge and have developed new capabilities around hot topics currently of high value to employers. Occasionally, Maintainers and Changers may also find themselves in strong negotiating positions because of the prospective employer's particular needs or some other environmental factor.

Whenever you are in a strong negotiating position, you owe it to yourself to be ready to negotiate not just for the traditional employment rewards but also for new types of benefits that can help you manage your future independent career development. Hopefully, over time patterns will develop and new norms for the general employment deal between employers and employees will arise that better meet our new need to manage our careers more independently.

What might some these new benefits be?

- Workers might negotiate to have money and time available annually for personal career development that is unrelated to their current job or their employer's goals.
- They might negotiate membership in professional groups or subscriptions to professional literature, which will help them continue to monitor how their work is changing and what is of concern to employers.
- They might negotiate their employers' commitment to allow participation in particular groups or activities within the organization that are not directly related to their current jobs but that they consider important to their longer-term career development.
- Workers might consider negotiating for resources to make more successful transitions to their next positions. For example, employees who will work with technologies or methodologies that are becoming obsolete may want to negotiate a commitment from their employers to provide funds toward retooling their skills and knowledge in the latest work processes.
- Or workers might negotiate the general terms of a severance package to be offered if their new employer's direction or commitment to the task they are being hired to do changes before it is completed. This would give them some assurance that, if the experience that they hope will help them build their skills and knowledge in certain ways does not materialize or continue, they will then have an option to pursue that experience elsewhere if they choose.

There is probably an infinite number of such nontraditional benefits that could be devised; what's best for your situation will depend on how you assess the strength of your bargaining position and what you believe are the major risks in the job you are considering.

Ed has been working as a highly skilled contract worker in computing for a number of years. He has had a long-standing assignment at a large company and has become crucial to their ongoing work in two or three important areas. The company to which he has been assigned now wants to make him an employee. The change in status will lower his current salary, but will also save him money on health care for his family and provide him five weeks of vacation annually. Ed is also negotiating for some other benefits. Here are the kinds of things he is currently discussing with his manager:

- He wants to have access to regular professional development money and time.
- He wants good quality assistance so that his workload is more reasonable. As a contract worker he did all they assigned him, which was a

substantial amount, but as an employee he is interested in being able to limit his overtime.

- And he wants it understood that he intends to continue his relationship with the contractor for whom he has worked in the past. He wants to work with other people that his new employer hires from that contractor to keep his relationships current.

Ed sees this job offer as an opportunity to reap some additional rewards for his current skills and knowledge. But he is also aware that he needs to be thinking about—and preparing for—his next career move. And he understands that it is up to him to negotiate the deal he needs to make that happen.

The earning world is in a period of great turbulence. As the world economy has expanded and our capabilities to move people, materials, and ideas have grown, competition has also increased. We see it among businesses, nonprofit organizations, and in the global labor market. Furthermore, we do not have a societal consensus about the innovations and/or issues on which we should focus our economic efforts in this new era—a consensus comparable to society's focus on growing food in the agricultural age or on the mass manufacturing of products in the industrial age. Such a consensus would help us as a society to set priorities and agree to common structures and norms to support that effort. This lack of consensus has led to a huge variety of endeavors and much experimentation.

Such periods of discontinuity and experimentation can be very exciting but also very unsettling because individuals cannot depend on the old norms and structures to achieve personal success. In such periods, we must clarify and rely on our own personal interests, values, and motivations because they become the basis for our sense of success. Then we must negotiate for what we want.

As individuals each negotiate their own employment deals, patterns of practice will form. Employers will become more sensitive to what their skilled and committed employees desire, and the more progressive among them will begin to institutionalize those opportunities in order to become "employers of choice." As a society, we will slowly rebuild our understanding of how the earning world works and form a consensus about the new norms for the employer-employee relationship.

Let the negotiations begin!

APPENDIX

Career Management Resources

Janice Kragness

You've all encountered the information explosion. Google, Yahoo, AOL, and MSN—these resources make information of all sorts available at your fingertips, literally! While this may sound like a boon for someone who is trying to manage his or her career, the reality is that there is too much information out there. You need assistance, not only to determine *where* you should look, but also *how* to look.

One of the myths of this revolution is that most information on the Web is readily accessible to the everyday user. Current news and information related to leisure activities, hobbies, and health concerns are definitely freely and easily available from reliable sources. Once you are familiar with the subject categories on Yahoo or About.com, you're set. Other information, however, may be part of either the "hidden Web" or the "pay-per-view Web."

A great deal of the information on the World Wide Web is part of the "hidden Web;" librarians are often successful in finding this information by using sources and strategies they have developed over time. In addition, people have gotten used to paying for information on the Internet. You can pay with a credit card for newspaper or magazine articles, images, house plans, mailing lists, etc. Sometimes this makes sense. In most cases, though, it is useful to realize that the same information may be available through a library for no extra charge. The public library is using your tax dollars to pay for these resources so that they'll be available to you!

Purpose of This Appendix

Many adults use libraries regularly to check out books of interest and to get resources for their children; they use the library as a resource to gather information about their earning careers much less often. This appendix has been written to jumpstart your information-gathering efforts regarding your career.

First, I will reintroduce you to the reference librarians and the reference section of libraries and describe the way libraries work together to provide a greater range of resources to potential users. Understanding these library services should help you save time when looking for information. Then, I will suggest some specific resources that you can likely find in a local library and use for the specific tasks described in this book. Armed with this information you should be able to work in tandem with your local librarian to develop your knowledge of how your work is changing and what employment options are likely to be in your preferred locale.

What you will learn about gathering information should provide you with skills and resources well beyond what is listed in this general, starter guide—resources that you can use again and again to improve your knowledge of your work and of the earning world, as well as to gather information about other issues important to your life.

Libraries and Librarians

The Reference Librarian: Your Guide to a Good Start

No matter how helpful and complete you think this guide is, you will want to avail yourself of the services of your local reference librarian. This guide is written with a focus on *types* of useful resources with particular reference to specific, generally available sources. Reference librarians know in detail what information is locally available and—most importantly—how it is related to other kinds of information sources. This knowledge is crucial for making the connection between what you know and what you want to know. Since librarians spend much of their day helping people with research, they also have a grasp of the key words that are used in databases and can often save you time by suggesting different approaches to the databases.

A reference librarian's job is to help you find information and, if possible, assist you in learning how to think about finding information and evaluating information sources. They will find just the right resource to answer your question regardless of whether the resource is in a book, on the Web, or is—in fact—another person. Reference librarians have a master's degree in library science, which I describe as "a master's in finding stuff." While some libraries have changed the title of their reference librarians to Information Consultant, Information Navigator, Cybrarian, or Research Advisor, you can still ask for a reference librarian—the library staff members will know who you're looking for.

The reference librarian generally works in the reference section of the library, which is the starting point for information seeking, since many resources there are designed to *refer* you to other sources. Below I have listed the types of information sources that you'll likely be looking for in the reference section of a library.

- *Library guides* that list resources on particular topics, such as starting a business or learning about an industry
- *Industry surveys* that provide overview, statistical, and trend information as well as comparisons between competitors and referrals to other sources
- *Article databases* that contain references to articles from a wide variety of publications, searchable by key terms
- *Directories* that provide contact information for companies, industries, products, organizations, or people

Choosing a Library

Just because a library is the closest one to your home or office does not mean that it will have the materials you need. Luckily, information about the earning world is likely to be generally available because many people use these resources for a variety of projects.

There are several different types of libraries, each of which provides different resources and types of service. Most libraries are willing to share materials and information with anyone, but the collection and the policies of a particular library have been shaped by the needs of the primary clientele of that library. Librarians know the strengths of various libraries in your area and can find out which library would have the materials you need if they are unavailable in their own collections.

Call the library you would like to use in order to determine if it has the necessary materials. The types of questions you will want to ask in this initial call are the following:

- "I'm interested in gathering some information about the nonprofit sector (or the health care industry, or business, or government/public administration). Is there a particular library you would suggest?"
- "I want to gain access to professional/industry publications through an electronic database. Do you have a database with those kinds of publications? Are there any restrictions on the use of that database?"
- "I am interested in learning more about local employers in the _____ sector. Would you have those resources or would you suggest another library?"

When you find out which library is likely to be best for you, call that library and ask about hours when a reference librarian is on duty so that you have help available when you arrive.

If your local public libraries do not seem to have the types of information you need, try the libraries affiliated with local or regional postsecondary educational institutions. Community colleges and other colleges and universities all have libraries supporting their instructional programs. The library collections will vary with the programs offered at the institution. Academic libraries will have varying hours for reference service and policies concerning the use of their databases by those not affiliated with the institution. Being an alumnus always helps, and at some universities you can pay for a library membership.

Government agencies often contain libraries that collect regulatory, legislative, and statistical information for the region. Such government information is increasingly available through the agencies' Web sites, but you will often need assistance navigating the site and interpreting the data.

Some communities have private libraries that are open to the public—like the James J. Hill Library, a business library in St. Paul, Minnesota, or the Linda Hall Library, a science library in Kansas City, Missouri. These collections are often relatively small, and very specialized, but they often contain industry information specific to that region.

When you call one of these more specialized libraries, explain that you have been attempting to find resources on your topic and have called the public libraries and been told that information is unavailable there. Ask if this library has such information and what policies and rules they have about the general public using their reference facilities.

Libraries in a geographic region often join together into consortiums, agreeing to extend library privileges in various ways to people from other library systems. Interlibrary loan is one of these consortial services and allows you to request articles or books from other libraries. Libraries enforce each other's use policies in order to ensure good relations, so due dates for borrowed materials need to be respected.

Access to article databases at a particular library depends upon your affiliation with that library. Libraries may restrict access to their electronic databases; these restrictions are often not a library's decision but a result of the licensing agreement with the database provider. An activated barcode and PIN number for your library card is generally necessary for access to your library's databases from home or work. Check with the information desk or circulation department at the library for more details.

Preparing to Talk with a Reference Librarian

Regardless of the library that you use, determine when the reference librarians are on duty and whether you could make a 15-minute appointment with one of them. If this is not possible, ask if there is a day and time when the librarians are less busy. In any case, you should be prepared with your questions; treat this as you would any other information interview.

Sally has done a good job of listing questions to get you started; I will be using those questions to organize the rest of this appendix. Determine which questions are most crucial to you, and provide a little of the context of what you are trying to do in order to help the librarian understand the information you are trying to find.

If you start with "Hi, I'm looking for career information about XX," you are likely to be referred to primarily descriptive information designed mostly for people who are entering the labor market—pay scales and what skills sets are needed. People in mid-career—unless they are Changers—require a different type of information; they are looking for more detailed information because they are further into the working world.

Consequently, be more specific with your initial question. The librarian is likely to ask you additional questions to clarify what you are trying to do and to decide which resources are likely to be best suited for what you are interested in. This process is not meant in any way to make you feel stupid or uninformed but to elicit information about your needs—it even has a name, the "reference interview." Following are two very typical conversations:

You: I need information on _____ company.
Librarian: What kind of information are you interested in?
You: I'd like to know their current strategies for growth.
Librarian: Are they a publicly held company? Are they based locally?
You: I don't know.
Librarian: Well, let's find those things out first. Then, we'll know which databases to search.

***

You: I'm interested in finding information about competition in the construction industry.
Librarian: Is there a particular type of construction you're interested in—residential, commercial?
You: Commercial.
Librarian: Do you want local, regional, national, or international competitors?
You: Regional—will that include local firms?
Librarian: Yes. What kind of information are you looking for—a directory listing? Rankings? Current articles on trends in the industry?
You: All of it, but I could really use something that contrasts their strengths and weaknesses.
Librarian: Once we find the competitors in a directory, we can then try to find articles that profile each company or the local market. Maybe the Web site for the regional construction association would be useful as well. Let's see what we can find.

Public libraries are very busy places, and, while the librarians are generally very willing to help you find the resources that you need, they may not be able to spend a great deal of time helping you use the resources. Once you are on your own, whether at the library or at home, don't spend more than 15 minutes unsuccessfully looking for a particular type of information. At that point, return to the librarian, in person, by phone, or by email. Be prepared to explain briefly how you looked and to summarize what you did and did not find; also summarize exactly what you are trying to find out. This will show the librarian that you are a serious searcher and will lead to an exploration as to why that particular strategy didn't work. Next time, you'll be able to gather the information you want more quickly. This will be an ongoing process throughout your career, so recording in your career journal the names of resources that you have found that are particularly rich, as well as the key words that were successful, can be very helpful.

Successful Searching

Now that you're up to speed on libraries and how librarians can help you conceptualize your search strategy, let's get to work on the areas that Sally discussed. I have arranged the rest of this appendix to follow along with her chapters. For each topic, I'll suggest search strategies, resources, and key words and phrases you can use in searching article databases. It will be helpful to you to read through the entire guide to familiarize yourself with the topics I cover, so that you can then focus on what you want to learn about.

Looking for Work That Interests You—Articulating Your Personalized Work Focus

Sally suggests that if you are having trouble articulating your personalized work focus, you might look at the most recent year or two of a professional, industry, or special-interest publication. Identifying those publications can be accomplished in several ways:

- Libraries subscribe to directories (*Ulrich's, Serials Directory, Standard Rate and Data Service*) that list magazine titles by topic/industry.
- The industry overview source, *Industry Surveys,* provides a list of newsletters and magazines for each industry sector it covers.
- Industry and professional Web sites will often provide links to Web-based publications used by those in the industry.
- Some libraries do not allow checkout of magazines, so plan to spend a few hours browsing the publications. Browse each entire issue, not just the table of contents—even the advertisements can tell you things

about what Sally calls the *work arena* by helping you identify equipment and services necessary for the work. Be aware that the Web-based version of a publication is browsed differently than a print version; when using the Web version, make sure to click on the links for features such as news, features, and editorials.

Looking for Changes, Challenges, and Controversies—Finding Hot Topics for Multiple Employers

Why Use Article Databases First?

The free Web is for amateurs. You need to start with resources that reflect your experience and expertise. You need to start with resources that you can use without concern for wasting your most valuable asset—your time.

Article databases provide you with *authoritative* information on a topic. In order for articles to be published, they first need to be reviewed—this review can include fact-checking, review by an editor, and, for more scholarly articles, review by experts in the field. The article may be biased, but it should not deliberately contain false information.

There is a great deal of information on the free Web that has not gone through any sort of review process. Consequently, unlike the use of article databases, using the free Web requires knowing how to vet this information yourself. Should you start a conversation with a potential employer based on information provided at a particular free Web site? Here are some criteria to consider:

- Coverage: What is the primary focus of the site? Who is the intended audience?
- Accuracy: Are the sources of information provided? Are these sources reliable? Can you find this information elsewhere?
- Objectivity: Are biases clearly stated? Are affiliations clear? Is there a statement of purpose for the site?
- Authority: Who is responsible for the site? What are his/her qualifications? Can you vet them beyond these pages? What is the domain designation for this site (.gov, .com, .edu)?
- Currency: Are dates clear as to when the Web site was first created and last edited? Is there evidence that the site is actively updated, such as current news items or recent postings to discussions?

Article databases use a specialized set of words to index all the articles by subject. These are what Sally and I have called key terms. The articles in the database can be searched by any words but using the special set of terms used to index the database can often produce better results. Databases can also be searched by author name, publication name, dates, and a host of other identifying characteristics. While this sounds fairly complicated to do, it is really not that hard but explains why librarians who know some of these terms and use the databases regularly can be such a help. You can choose between a wide variety of article databases, choosing one that covers *just the type of information that you are looking for.* For example, *Business Source Premier* and *ABI Inform* are aimed at business professionals, and *Medline* and *CINHAL* are aimed at medical professionals. In contrast, to achieve such precision on the Web you need the help of an expert searcher (such as a librarian).

Many article databases contain not only a summary of each article but the *entire article* as well. On the Web, information created by an organization is often viewed as commercial property, and you must pay to get past a summary of it and access the full text. Can you get a full article from the *Wall Street Journal* without paying for it first?

Sally and I are *not* condemning the Web as a place to find information. Throughout this appendix, I will be referring you to particular sites or advising you on useful Web search strategies. I assure you, though, that searching article databases as one of your first information-seeking activities will reap benefits compared to Web-searching that you can't comprehend until you have seen the difference.

Searching Tips for Finding Hot Topics

Each database has a different look and a different way to search. The look, feel, and content of a Web-based database can also change overnight; content is added continuously, and changes to user interfaces are to be expected on an annual basis. Although any database that you use is unique in regard to the terms used to classify the articles it contains, I will suggest some key terms for use in starting your searches. A librarian who regularly uses a particular database will be able to suggest key words that work well in that particular source. Using the right terms will make your first round of searching much more successful, so seeking out a librarian early in the process can be a great help.

Sally suggests using the terms *changes, challenges,* and *controversies* when looking for hot topics, but these terms may not be the key words used in a particular database. Some of the other words that I use when searching for hot topics include the following:

trends	industry wide conditions
case studies	industry overview
success	failures

Such words are used in conjunction with a term describing your job function or work arena, such as "accounting" or "Web development."

If you are not getting the results that you need, click on the Help feature in the database to check for searching tips. Different databases (like different Web search engines) use different symbols to represent different search intents. Here are three common examples of different search intents:

- When searching for a phrase that is a multiple-word term (e.g., Web design), variations on signaling that intent include: "Web design"; Web+design; or a pull-down menu next to the search box that gives you options for search intent.
- When searching for a single word (e.g., account) that might also appear in the database as a plural or with a different word ending, variations on signaling that intent include: account?; account+; account+4.
- When searching for combinations of words, or when searching for one concept but *not* another, variations on signaling those intents include: accounting and trends; accounting+trends; accountants OR accounting.

Once you've found a useful article, check its subject headings and article summary for the classification terms that it was filed under and note any that you might not have thought of. You can also search for the magazine titles and the authors of the articles that appear in your searches. For example, if the same authors and magazines continue to appear in the results for your searches, you can look for additional articles by that author or in that publication. Every database allows you to narrow your search to a particular field in the database's records (author, title of article, publication title).

Currency

Watch the publication dates on the articles—you do not want to focus on old, resolved challenges and controversies! Articles in databases are often listed in reverse chronological order with the most recent article first. But since databases often provide the option of displaying the articles in another order, check to make sure the proper date order has been chosen. If it isn't, look for a dropdown box or ask the librarian for assistance in order to change the sort order.

Database Searching: A Good First Step

Database searching serves as a springboard to other sources. I make it a habit to note the names of pertinent experts, associations, and companies when they show up in a useful article. Later, I go to the Web in search of that expert ("Jim Brown" "web design"), association ("American Bankers

Association"), or company (www.target.com) for additional information—and that information often leads me right back into an article database or another Web search!

Building Your General Knowledge of Your Work and Its Near Future

If you are a Builder or a Maintainer, you know something about your work. Because of this commitment to individual career development that you are taking on, you are going to need to reference that information regularly to help you learn more about your hot topics and about potential employers. If you are a Changer, you need to develop your knowledge of your new work focus quickly.

This section provides an overview of information sources about work. It has been divided into approaches based on four of the five aspects of work that were introduced in chapter 3. That way you can focus in on the aspect you find most interesting. Each aspect is defined as a Personalized Work Focus (PWF). Included in this section—under each aspect—is an overview of the information sources that are most useful for that aspect. The "contribution" aspect is not covered, as it is not easily uncovered through library resources.

Sally and I think that this approach will make your information gathering easier and more immediately relevant. This can be important as you build your knowledge of the larger context of your work over time, and it will help you to nurture your network. For Changers, who need to develop knowledge of a new work focus, this library work can be particularly helpful.

If Your PWF Centers on a Work Function or an Occupation

Where can I find an overview of a function or occupation?

Career counselors and librarians refer people with general questions about occupations to the *Occupational Outlook Handbook* (http://stats.bls.gov/oco/home.htm). The U.S. Bureau of Labor Statistics creates this source, and its primary purpose is to classify jobs into categories for statistical purposes. This is not what you are looking for, unless you are a Changer who needs basic orientation to the occupation. People in mid-career usually want information on specialties within a work area, like accounting or nursing, which is beyond the scope of the *Occupational Outlook Handbook*.

One resource that may be useful at the Bureau of Labor Statistics site is the *Career Guide to Industries* (http://stats.bls.gov/oco/cg/home.htm).

This includes information on available careers by function and industry, including the nature of the industry, working conditions, employment, occupations in the industry, training and advancement, earnings and benefits, employment outlook, and lists of organizations that can provide additional information. The industry listings use traditional categories; more specialized and newer functions (for example, information management and many service areas) will not be listed.

Vault (http://www.vault.com/) is a superb value-added job search site. Use the Research link to access industry, company, and occupational profiles. The"electronic water cooler" is a message board full of questions and opinions on careers and companies.

Are there professional associations for this specialty?

Professional associations provide resources and networking opportunities for people interested in the field. Many associations publish journals and/or newsletters and also offer job postings, host discussion groups, and provide links to other related organizations and resources at the association's Web site. The organizational structure of the profession as a whole will be revealed through the Web site's structure—specialties and operational entities within the profession will have their own areas within the site. Anyone can query an association directly by email or phone—the Contact Us section of the Web site should provide the necessary information.

Looking through the pages of an association site will uncover some of the broadly applicable changes, challenges, and controversies for an occupation/function (look for sections on legislation, news, and continuing education) and may also reveal its criteria for excellent performance. The site can also provide useful information for further searches, including key terms and people's names.

Don't rely on your general knowledge about whether a function has a professional association or not. There are thousands of professional organizations. The resources listed below are some places to look for information about associations.

- The *Encyclopedia of Associations* (print version) or *Associations Unlimited* (online version) at the library: These contain information about thousands of associations, including the Elvis Presley Fan Clubs, the Leisure and Outdoor Furniture Association, and the Association of Collection and Credit Professionals.
- The American Society of Association Executives (www.asaenet.org) provides a directory of associations. Go to the Directories section and look for the "Gateway to Associations." This service allows you to search for an association by name, interest area, or geographic location. You also can search using a combination of fields.

- If you already know the name of an association and wish to find its Web site, type the name of the association, enclosed in quotation marks, into a good search engine, such as Google.

How do I discover if there is a local chapter of an association, in order to find out about local issues and connections?

- Check the association Web site for a link to regional/state/local chapters.
- Type in your state's name and the name of the association into a search engine. For example: "public relations" "Kansas City." (The quotation marks indicate to the search engine that the words are a phrase and should be searched together, not separately.)
- Your local library or Chamber of Commerce may have knowledge of regional and local associations.
- If your preferred locale is not where you currently live, use the techniques suggested above and search the local newspapers of the locale for articles about the industry or profession. (Some library databases have access to regional papers.) Such articles should have references to pertinent individuals and groups for you to contact.

If Your PWF Centers on an Industry or Business Type

Some people see a particular industry or business, such as the automotive industry or retailing, as the primary focus of their work. Sometimes individuals specialize in an organizational function within an industry (e.g., human resources in banking), and sometimes they are fascinated by the industry (e.g. airlines) itself and will do a variety of functions within it. Also, when gathering information about the critical path of an organization, you can expand your understanding of that path by comparing it to the critical paths being used by others in the industry. This is done by comparing strategy descriptions and by reading industry analyses of competitive differences.

Sometimes the most difficult task in industry research is to come up with terms that effectively identify it, without being too broad or too narrow. Industry terms—which often simply define the product or service provided—are developed in two ways. There are the terms that the industry and news communities use; you can discover these terms in articles, in association information, or in places like the Yellow Pages. The other is that governments use classification systems based on products and services to collect statistics, such as production and employment data, by industry. There is more on the U.S. classification system in the section covering the questions related to PWFs centered on products and services.

If the industry breakdown is not specific enough to include what you consider your industry, you will need to think about alternative ways of describing your industry and the competition. A fellow librarian recently had someone looking for information on the "saltshaker industry" in order to assess the competition for a new type of shaker. After some discussion between the searcher and the librarian, they concluded that the search terms to be used should focus on either the tableware industry (which according to industry overviews includes salt and pepper shakers) or the salt industry (to uncover consumer preferences in table and cooking salt). Librarians do this sort of thinking all of the time—so ask one for some ideas!

Where can I find an overview of the industry?

When you are looking at industry sources you want to focus on factors that are particularly important to the industry, such as phases of the business cycle, availability of raw materials, regulatory limitations, and product/service trends. These sources will also identify who the major competitors are and the strategies that major players in the industry are using to distinguish themselves.

- Standard & Poor's *Industry Surveys*: This full-text resource provides overviews of major U.S. industries; it covers trends and forecasts, major players and market-share data, key ratios and statistics, comparative analysis, and other information. Most large libraries have this resource available either in print or online (as part of *S&P Net Advantage*).
- The International Trade Administration's *Trade Development Industry Summaries* (http://www.ita.doc.gov/td/td_home/tdhome.html) covers key industrial and service clusters.
- *Encyclopedia of Business Information Sources*. A referral guide to associations, statistical sources, journals, and government agencies related to particular industries.

What trade or industry associations are involved with this industry?

Trade associations provide their members and the public with a broad range of information regarding the industry and its membership, including data and regulatory updates. Many associations publish journals and/or newsletters that can keep interested people up-to-date on news and trends. Trade association Web sites can often be found through the sources listed above in the section on questions related to the PWF centered on function/occupation.

If Your PWF Centers on a Particular Customer Group or Type of Clientele

Some people want to focus on serving or working with people or organizations with particular characteristics (such as entrepreneurs or senior citizens). The resources listed here will help you better define the group, understand key characteristics of the group, and inform you about current issues and needs for the group. Once you have a concrete idea of these factors, you can then work toward the names of products, services, and organizations that focus on those groups.

How do I find out the size of a particular consumer market?

- Government data: Much of the information found at government web sites will be in the form of data, with very little interpretation. Librarians can help you interpret this data. Libraries also have reference books, such as the New Strategist series, that put this data into easy-to-understand tables, with explanations, charts, and indexing.
  - National and regional data: *The U.S. Census Bureau Population Characteristics Study* (http://www.census.gov/population/www/index.html) contains links to data by topic, such as education and Hispanic origin. *The Consumer Expenditure Survey* (http://www.bls.gov/cex/home.htm) provides information on the buying habits of American consumers (individually and by households).
  - State and local data: Each U.S. state also has an agency that collects and interprets data about its citizens. This office is often called the State Data Center, and the officer in charge is called the State Demographer. Check your state government's Web site for this agency, and you'll be able to retrieve data on the state, county, and local levels. Again, your librarian can help with this.
  - International data: These statistics vary in how current and how detailed they are, depending upon the country collecting them. The United Nations *Demographic and Social Indicators* site (http://unstats.un.org/unsd/demographic/products/default.htm) publishes comprehensive basic data from all countries, while *Offstats: Official Statistics on the Web* (http://www.library.auckland.ac.nz/subjects/stats/ocountffstats) provides links to pertinent sites in each country.
- Articles: When searching article databases, form queries using your topic in combination with qualifying terms such as demographics, users, target market, or customers. You can also focus the search on a particular customer type combining terms such as "seniors," "aged," or "retired" with terms such as "needs," "products," or "services."
- Other sources: Niche marketing is a very hot topic, so you may be able to find books on your specific customers or clients of interest. Amazon.com is a great place to start looking for current books—just type terms into their search engine, such as "seniors" and "marketing." If any of the search results look promising, you can then check with your librarian to see if the local library has the book or items similar to it. If

not, you can always request the books from another library through interlibrary loan.

What if my "customers" are businesses?

Several U.S. government agencies collect data on businesses:

- Census Department (http://www.census.gov/econ/www/index.html)
- Department of Labor (www.dol.gov)
- Bureau of Labor Statistics (www.bls.gov)
- Department of Commerce (www.commerce.gov)

Each of these sites will have a search box you can use to pinpoint information within the site. Beyond these sites, you can use the resources suggested in "Learning about Potential Employers" below.

If Your PWF Centers on a Particular Product or Service

Some people's work focus is on a product or service or a group of products or services. To learn more about products and services, you want to look into how they are developing and the range of variations among them. Once you determine the skills and knowledge needed to keep a product competitive, you can then decide what you want and need to learn in order to contribute to that process.

As mentioned previously, governments identify industries using classification systems based on products and services. Governments create and use these codes to collect statistics, such as production and employment data, and commercial producers of directories and financial data also use these codes as a convenient way to identify competitors in a field. The U.S. government currently uses a seven-digit system called the North American Industrial Classification System (NAICS); until 1997, the U.S. government used a four-digit system called the Standard Industrial Classification system (SIC). You will often find NAICS and SIC codes used in databases as key terms as a means of organizing the data. You can consult the NAICS (http://www.census.gov/epcd/www/naics.html) or SIC (http://www.osha.gov/pls/imis/sicsearch.html) Web sites for further information, and your librarian should be able to help you interpret the information that you find.

Some databases will allow you to use these codes to narrow your searches; for example, in a search you might be able to put an NAICS or SIC code together with phrases like "new product development," "research and development," "trends," or "industry forecasts." As suggested before, take note of pertinent names, companies, associations, agencies, and alternate key terms as you proceed in order to help expand your searching.

Learning about Potential Employers

Your PWF, along with the hot topics that you are interested in, will determine your potential employers. In this section I will describe how to identify specific potential employers based on type of employer, locale, or strategic aim.

Who are the companies involved in a particular kind of work?

Once you've determined the type of work a potential employer is in, you can identify others in the same type of work. While you'll be able to ask those in the know who some of these other companies may be, the reference librarian has access to a wide variety of sources that can broaden that list. Information provided about companies will differ from resource to resource in the detail of coverage provided, as well as in the types of companies included (public/private, domestic/global, branch/headquarters). In order to get all of the information that you can, you should look at all of the sources that include the focus of your work interest.

- *General directories* list companies of all sorts. Always start with the indexes or search features that allow you to specify your search by industry/product name or by industry code (see discussion above), company, or geography. *Hoovers* and *Reference USA* are good starting places. *Hoovers* (www.hoovers.com) provides good basic information on prominent and emerging companies worldwide. The company provides free access to most of its materials; the information that requires payment, however, can often be found at your library for free. *Reference USA* can be found at most public libraries; use its Custom Search to locate U.S. businesses in a particular industry, location, or size range. You can also access a basic version of this database at www.infousa.com. Its Yellow Pages section will allow you to search for free, but will require payment for detailed directory listings. Remember that once you have a list of names, you can use the free Web or the library to find additional information about the companies.
- *Specialty directories* focus on the customers and suppliers of particular businesses. For example, in health care, you can find directories of hospitals nationwide, Catholic hospitals worldwide, and managed-care organizations in your state. *Kompass* and *Thomas Register* are both directories of manufacturing companies, but *Kompass* has global scope while *Thomas Register* concentrates on U.S. companies. Both have free online access with registration, but many large libraries also subscribe to print or electronic versions with more detailed entries for each company.
- *Association Web sites* often include a membership directory, a directory of suppliers or allied industries, and a list of exhibitors at the latest

annual conference. While some of these lists are accessible only by members, many are not, so always click on the link. I have found that the more local the association, the more likely that these links will be accessible. For more information on finding association Web sites, see above.

- *Industry magazines* often publish annual "suppliers guide" issues, which have ads or listings by suppliers who are interested in promoting themselves to the industry. This can help you look at the larger work arena for organizations that might need your skills, knowledge, and experience. My all-time favorites were those put out by *Milling and Baking News* (tortilla bakeries), *Aviation Week and Space Technology* (aircraft seat manufacturers in China), and *Personnel Journal* (time-clock software designers). Many of these annual guides end up on the magazine's Web site as a suppliers directory. You need to understand that these suppliers directories, like those on the association sites, are not usually comprehensive—companies may need to pay to be included or may nominate themselves for inclusion in some way. This method does, however, give you names of the most market-savvy companies and can help expand your thinking about employer types.
- *Industry articles found in databases* will mention companies in that industry. The more specialized the focus of the database (by industry or geography), the more specific the list of companies. The best database for you may depend upon the type of company, industry, and products you are looking at. A librarian will be able to recommend the most appropriate available database for your needs.

How can I find employer information for my local area?

Use the local news, business, and professional publications; check to see if archives are accessible online for any of them. Even if the full text of the articles is not available, take note of the title and date of promising search results so that you can check for them at the local library or historical society. There are also article databases at the library that allow you to search for articles in regional publications around the country and the world. These are particularly useful if the company that you are interested in is headquartered elsewhere.

What if I'm looking for organizations with a particular strategic aim, with a particular business challenge, or that are very progressive in a particular business practice?

In these cases, you will want to consult with a librarian to determine the best search strategy. Here are some suggestions:

- Search in an article database using terms describing the behavior/challenge (such as *Six Sigma* or *cost-cutting*) combined with terms such as *case study, benchmark,* or *success.* These articles will often identify or profile organizations.
- Look for rankings of organizations based on similar topics, such as the annual "Top 100 Best Corporate Citizens" (http://www.business-ethics.com/100best.htm) or "Top 100 Family-Friendliest Companies to Work For" (http://www.workingmother.com/100best.shtml). The librarian has access to lists of lists or could help with an article database search on the topic and rankings or awards.
- Identify organizations that do the research on this topic through Web searching, consulting article databases, and soliciting recommendations from known companies and individuals. These sources may be willing to identify local or regional companies that are known for their activities/interests in this arena.

Targeted Networking

Besides learning about your work at the library, you can also gather information to jumpstart your networking effort in other ways. As you read articles and view websites, keep two lists:

- *Organizations* that are profiled in the business press as doing or having interest in the kinds of work you are focused on. These could be companies or associations. The companies could be potential employers—either organizations that are actually profiled, or organizations similar to them in your preferred locale. Professional associations could be places to network. Suggestions for how to find information on pertinent companies or associations have been presented earlier in this appendix.
- *People* who are highlighted or interviewed in sources dealing with issues and challenges, or who are describing excellent performance in your chosen work focus. Get all the information about their position and organization that the source provides and make a note of what expertise they have and what source they were featured in. These people might help you if you have questions about their field of expertise. They can also help you decide whether to pursue a given issue or challenge and perhaps even provide opportunities for you to do so. They can become part of your network of resources on the work, even though you may never meet them face-to-face.

When you have a question that only an expert whom you have read about can answer, you will need to find a way to contact them and introduce yourself. You can send them an email or phone them; the way to warm up such an approach is to explain how you found their name and your interest in the topic of their expertise. If you call and get an assistant or their voicemail, make sure to leave this information in your initial message. Then be prepared to ask your question. Asking about something that the person is an expert in allows them to shine and shows your interest. At the point of that first interaction, you should also be thinking about the future. Thank them and ask if you can contact them again with similar questions or ask them if they know of others who could help you with your question/interest or of a professional group that is dealing with this issue/challenge.

Local Resources for Developing Skills and Knowledge

How do I find out which institutions offer courses or certifications that I need?

- Using a search engine, type in your interest and either "business education," "professional education," or "continuing education." Adding your state or city name to the search will further narrow the results.
- Go to *Peterson's Guide to Colleges* (in print or at www.petersons.com) and search for pertinent programs offered in your region.
- Go to Yahoo and click from Education to Colleges to your state. Click on each institution to go to their Web site and enter your desired area of interest into the search box on the front page of the site, or go to Academics and look through the departmental listing. Contact the appropriate department using the email or phone information provided.
- Attend a local College Expo event or visit the college booths at a county or state fair. Ask the people staffing the booths for suggestions and recommendations.
- Contact the agency in your state that deals with job training and employment issues. Inquire as to opportunities for continuing education that focus on your work or hot topic.

Remember when you are talking to representatives from these institutions to ask if they have non-credit courses or certifications for working professionals as well as whether they have a way that individuals can take one or two for-credit courses without enrolling for a degree. While a certification can be helpful proof of knowledge on a resume, you may only need the information in a course or two to pursue your work focus or hot topic interest. These courses can be added to your resume as an indication of your commitment.

Aspiring Business Owners

Start-up Advice

- The Small Business Administration has a great section entitled "Starting Your Business" on its Web site (http://www.sbaonline.sba.gov/). In addition, the site lists its offices and partners in every state. In many cases, larger public libraries often serve as a partner to the SBA and will be able to assist you with its resources as well.
- *Small Business Notes* (www.smallbusinessnotes.com) has a very clean design, so it is easy to find the types of resources that you are looking for. Resources are arranged in the following categories: Need (financing, marketing), Resources (books, agencies), and Interest (women, minority, rural).
- The *Small Business Sourcebook* and *Business Plans Handbook* can be found at many libraries and are organized by type of business (nursery, coffee shop, software design). The *Sourcebook* lists useful how-to books, associations, educational opportunities, magazines, and newsletters, while the *Business Plans Handbook* series reproduces actual business plans for many small businesses.

Support Organizations

- International Franchise Association (www.franchise.org)
- InventNet Forum (www.inventnet.com)
- National Congress of Inventor Organizations (www.invention convention.com)
- United Inventors Association of the USA (www.uiausa.org)—includes a directory of state, regional, and local inventors' groups
- National Federation of Independent Businesses (www.nfibonline.com)
- National Association for the Self-Employed (www.nase.org)
- Fellowship of Companies for Christ International (www.fcci.org). Great support network, self-study courses, and guidelines for leadership, ethics, and vision.
- World Trade Associations (www.wtca.org). Assists small businesses to start import or export operations; local organizations have libraries and offer networking events and courses.

Solo Professionals

Many professional associations have a solo practitioners' section with its own Web pages and newsletter. Look at your professional association's

Web site for menu options such as "divisions," "sections," "interest areas," or "special interest groups" ("SIGs").

- American Psychological Association, Division of Counseling Psychology, Section for the Independent Practice of Counseling Psychology.
- Special Libraries Association. Solo Librarians Division.
- American Bar Association. General Practice, Solo, and Small Firm Division.

Interestingly enough, CPAs are often solo practitioners, but the AICPA does not host a section for them.

Looking for Help and Support

This is definitely one arena where you do not want to start with an Internet search engine because what you will get is a list of coaches and counselors who want your business. You need to start with a referral source, one that certifies counselors and coaches. National organizations are a good place to start, and their Web sites will often offer the ability to do a search of members by geographic location. Certifying organizations in the area of career development include the following:

- *National Career Development Association* (www.ncda.org). Many career counselors are members of the NCDA. The NCDA offers membership categories to recognize those who have reached certain professional levels of achievement. You can access membership lists on the national NCDA Web site; some statewide websites (accessible from the national site) allow access to their lists as well.
- *International Coach Federation* (http://www.coachfederation.org/ICF/). This nonprofit organization supports and credentials business and personal coaches. The site hosts a wonderful "Find a Coach" section that allows you to select a coach based on specialization, location, method of coaching, and fees.
- *The Global Career Development Facilitator* credential can be granted to people providing career advice who are not professional career counselors. More information about this credential can be found at the Web site for the Center for Credentialing and Education (www.cdf-global.org), which provides standards, training specifications, and credentialing for those who provide these services.

Suggested Reading

Chapter 1 is essentially an overview of why managers/employers made the change they made in the psychological contract between employers and employees, and of the impact it appears to have had on white-collar workers. Most of the statistics and statistical studies are based on government figures, because that is the only entity that can gather such wide-ranging data. The best single source for people who want to read more about these things is *The State of Working America,* which is published every two years by Cornell University Press and put together by the Economic Policy Institute (EPI).[1] While the EPI is considered to be a liberal think tank, they are also considered to be very able analysts, and most of the academic world uses their analyses of the statistics on labor from various government agencies as their prime resource for such data.

You may not find these statistical reports totally satisfying because they do not report information about many of the new categories related to work (e.g., how many contingent workers there are and what the subgroups within that designation are). This is because government statistics are based on traditional category systems so that they can be easily compared across the years; most of these categories were set up during the Depression.[2] The EPI statistics and analyses are different from what you often read in the newspapers and the business press, because rather than looking at the statistics from the perspective of business, they look at the statistics in terms of their impact on living standards.[3] This is very much in line with my focus on individuals and their well-being.

Another stream in Chapter 1 is an overview of management thinking and how it has changed over the last thirty years, presented in terms of my subject.

I have tried to rely on major resources which include those by Henry Mintz-berg, Peter Drucker, Lester Thurow, and Peter Cappelli. Cappelli is particularly pertinent to this work because he has spent a good portion of his research life studying human resource management in the larger managerial context. His book *The New Deal at Work* was very influential on my thinking.[4] His writing would be of particular interest to those wanting to follow up on how business management is changing.

I have decided to use the word "downsizing" throughout the book when referring to the main impacts that the turbulence in the economy has on employees. Some of the time employers add jobs at the same time that they downsize—the last staffing survey of the American Management Association in 2001 reported that 69 percent of the companies reported that they would be adding employees and 36 percent of the companies were both downsizing and adding jobs, which has been termed "rightsizing" or "churning."[5] I have chosen to emphasize downsizing because, from the employees' perspective, that is the important event in this process. Many observers take the employers' perspective that often views the churning process as a healthy sign of change and call it "rightsizing."

Chapter 2 is an introduction to the Employability Plus model for mid-career management that is the focus of this book and connects it to the needs and challenges described in Chapter 1. This model is an extension and practical application of the work of many others. In the career management field two major concepts have dominated the thinking about careers of the future. One is that of the "boundaryless career," which focuses on the idea that many of the boundaries of careers in the past are now being erased. Six were defined in the book, the most obvious being the boundaries imposed by an employee working long-term for a single employer.[6] The other popular new concept among people who study careers is that of the "protean career," which focuses on the idea that the career should be self-managed in the pursuit of psychological success.[7] Both of these concepts continue to be studied, and you can find academic articles on them by using these terms as key words in a database search (see Chapter 4 and the appendix for more information about how to do that).

My model builds on these concepts by fleshing out how they might actually be implemented by individuals in mid-career. This requires a more pragmatic, how-to approach and involves work from a number of disciplines including education, psychology, management, and library science. I provide primary sources for the four success strategies in the chapters dealing with each of them, although the endnotes in this chapter provide more source material for learning on the job. In this chapter I highlight a number of calls for a model for the new type of career management needed now (see note 11 for Chapter 2) and claim that this book meets that call. The foundation for this book is an article I wrote with a coauthor in 2003.[8] To my knowledge there is no other model of this type currently offered, with the exception of a model described in a British academic journal which is more focused on the self-management of careers inside an organization.[9]

Chapter 3 focuses on the first success strategy of identifying your personalized work focus (PWF). There are, of course, many definitions of *work*—ranging from definitions that see work as something that must be endured to those that see work as a means of self-actualization, and from those that focus on work that is done in return for income to those that comprehend work as related to our religious beliefs. My approach focuses on work in the earning context and defines it as the ways of contributing to the operations and success of multiple earning organizations. This definition allows people to think more easily about their careers in a multiple-employer environment rather than being stuck in the job-centric and employer-centric perspectives of the last era of employment dynamics. The first time I read about the idea of dividing work from the job was in the work of William Bridges,[10] although he did not develop the idea in the same way I have here. Chapters 3 through 6 include some career management ideas for aspiring business owners. I have grouped all small-business efforts together, which include owning a small business, having a solo practice, and starting an entrepreneurial venture. There is very little known about career development or management for these kinds of goals and the majority of material available focuses on the challenges of running such ventures.[11] In order to harmonize with the rest of the book, I have expressed my ideas about career development for this group using the terms and concepts developed here.

Chapter 4 focuses on the second success strategy in the Employability Plus model—learning about the near future of your work. The approach to "futuring" used here is quite conservative. It only tries to extrapolate what is likely to happen among employers who use this work in their organizations based on what is currently under discussion by those involved in the work. My approach is based on what is termed scanning the environment. The classic source for this is a book written by Francis Aguilar in 1967,[12] but the best two articles for additional reading that I have found concentrate on how to think about the information you obtain.[13]

Chapter 5 is about taking action by building a targeted network and finding ways to get the skills, knowledge, and experience to prepare for the kind of work you are interested in doing. I want to provide additional resources for reading, thinking about, and using three concepts highlighted in this chapter: the need for additional skills and experience to develop a hiring edge, understanding an organization's critical path to aid in personal time management, and communities of practice, which is the academic name for groups of individuals who are focused on learning about a particular type of work.

There has been much discussion about the possibility that American workers need more and better skills. A review of the research that has been done on this subject has recently been completed.[14] The conclusions of this study are that there is little evidence for the argument that our level of skill is declining or that it is relatively poor when compared to other countries. The study also points out the difficulties of doing research on relative skill levels over time because there are not good benchmark studies that establish what skill levels were in the past; also, there are many, many definitions of "skills," confusion in the literature between skills and work attitudes, and different skills are assumed "basic" at different skill levels. This comprehensive study supports my contention that it is not "new" basic skills that people need to develop in mid-career, particularly white-collar workers who are among our most skilled workers generally. What white-collar workers need is to identify and take action to develop the constellations of skills, knowledge, and experience needed to deal with the issues in their work which employers currently perceive as important. For more information on the upsurge in the creation of such jobs, see a study sponsored by the McKinsey consulting firm.[15]

The second topic about which I want to provide some additional resources is my use of the concept of the employer's "critical path." This is the concept that I suggest you use to help manage your time working on your job responsibilities. This term is not often used in the way that I have used it here, although I believe that this is how Richard Kelley also uses the term in his book, *How to Be a Star at Work.*[16] Originally, the term came from operations management and defined the most efficient path from beginning to end of a project.[17] Rather than applying the concept to a single project, both Kelley and I use it to refer to the decisions that management makes about how to achieve the organization's strategic goals. Also, the concept includes how the organization currently makes its profits (or surplus in a nonprofit organization) because of the importance to the organization to keep its profits/surplus growing. I like this concept because it emphasizes the connections between the whole organization's goals and any one unit's goals. People may have trouble imagining what their organization's critical path might be, and that would cause them difficulty in recognizing it or asking questions about it. A number of sources provide excellent examples.[18] For those who want to read even more, there are also many sources about strategic approaches.[19]

The third concept in Chapter 5 that I want to expand on is using the network that you develop of other individuals, who are interested in your work and/or hot topic, as a group of colleagues to learn with. These are very similar to the "communities of practice" that are being studied as a way of creating and building corporate knowledge inside large organizations. For more information on how to nurture your own informal community of practice, you might get ideas from two books.[20] Nurturing the health and learning of these groups would be the same although the focus of organizationally sponsored groups would be more towards contributing to the critical path of the specific organization rather than building knowledge of a particular kind of work.

Chapters 4 through 6 describe an ongoing, iterative process. It involves learning more about the earning world in terms of your work, doing experiments to test your interest in various aspects of that world, working with others to build the skills, knowledge, and experience, and redirecting your career management based on your preferences and what you are learning. This iterative approach to career management is relatively new, but one person who has spent a good deal of time thinking through the details of this more iterative process of managing careers from the perspective of the individual is H. B. Gelatt, and reading his work may be helpful.[21]

Chapter 6 briefly discusses the ongoing need in mid-career for job-search skills, and I write that there are many sources of that information. I also at various times in the book talk about the large amount of work that has been done on networking generally, on performing well inside an organization, and on time management. Resources on these topics are so wide-ranging that I will not attempt to list them here with the exception of time management, where I have found what I consider some particularly good sources. What I suggest to individuals who want to brush up on one or more of these topics is to go to a book site that will give them an indication of what books are currently most popular with people using the site. You can also go to the library and check out their resources as well. I would certainly try to preview the book at the library or a book store or on line before investing as there are so many with so many different perspectives and, of course, a wide range of information quality as well.

Time management is a major issue for people using the Employability Plus model. For those who have not read in this area or want to remind themselves of some useful ways of approaching the task, I think that chapters of Steven Covey's classic, *The Seven Habits of Effective People,* can be very helpful. His focus on managing by identifying purpose and of looking at your activities in terms of urgency and importance are both helpful.[22] Also, there is a recent article from *Business Week* and a book by Leslie Perlow that are very pragmatically focused and may give you other, important ideas.[23] Finally, I found *The Power of Full Engagement* by Jim Loehr and Tony Schwartz a fresh new approach that was very helpful not just in managing time but also in making personal changes.[24]

Chapter 7 focuses on the idea that negotiations will become increasingly important because employees will more frequently change employers and renegotiate their employment deals. This can be positive if people have capabilities that are highly valued by their prospective employers, or it can be negative if they don't. Another factor that will influence the outcome of these negotiations is the individual's ability to negotiate. In the last era of employment dynamics, negotiation skills were not as important. Not only did people not change employers as often as they do now but also the general range of benefits was more homogeneous across employers, and there was less pressure to cut labor costs. To brush up on your negotiation skills, I advise that you get the classic text on win-win negotiations *Getting to Yes*.[25] This approach to negotiations is perfect for building a partnership, which is exactly what you want to do with an employer. Another book that may be of interest is a follow up book entitled *Win-Win Career Negotiations*.[26]

Notes

Preface

1. Phyllis Moen with Donna Dempster-McClain, Joyce Altobelli, Wipas Wimonsate, Lisa Dahl, Patricia Roehling and Stephen Sweet, *The New "Middle" Work Force,* (Ithica, NY: Bronfenbrenner Life Course Center, Cornell University, 2004) Available at www.human.cornell.edu/she/BLCC/index.cgm on 4/3/06.
2. Nancey Green Leigh, *Stemming Middle-Class Decline* (New Brunswick, NJ: Center for Urban Policy Research, 1994).
3. Herrminia Ibarra, *Working Identity, Unconventional Strategies for Reinventing Your Career* (Boston, Harvard Business School Press, 2003) xiii.
4. Donald E. Super, "A Life-Span, Life-Space Approach to Career Development," in *Career Choice and Development, Applying Contemplorary Theories to Practice,* 2nd edition, ed. Dwane Brown, Linda Brooks and Associates (San Francisco: Jossey-Bass, 1990).

1 Introduction: How the Career Landscape Has Changed

1. Tom Brazaitis, "Career Paths Are Gone," *The Plain Dealer,* March 10, 1996, final, B3. Available at http://www.lexisnexis.com/.
2. Conference Board, *HR Executive Review: Implementing the New Employment Compact* (New York: Author, 1997).

3. The phrase "golden age" was used in Lawrence R. Mishel, Jared Bernstein, and John Schmitt, *The State of Working America, 1998–99* (Ithaca, NY: ILS Press, 1999), 355, and "wonder years" in Stephen A. Herzenberg, John A. Alic, and Howard Wial, *New Rules for a New Economy, Employment and Opportunity in Postindustrial America* (Ithaca, NY: Cornell University Press, 1998), 1.

4. Peter Cappelli, "Assessing the Decline of Internal Labor Markets," in *Sourcebook of Labor Markets: Evolving Structures and Processes,* eds. Ivar Berg and Arne L. Kalleberg (New York: Plenum Publishing, 2001), 208.

5. Paul Osterman, *Broken Ladders, Managerial Careers in the New Economy* (New York: Oxford University Press, 1996). Peter B. Doeringer and Michael J. Piore, *Internal Labor Markets and Manpower Analysis* (Lexington, MA: Health Lexington Books, 1971), 17–23.

6. Thomas T. Gutteridge, "Organizational Career Development Systems: The State of the Practice," in *Career Development in Organizations,* ed. Douglas T. Hall and Associates (San Francisco: Jossey-Bass, 1986), 50–94.

7. Harold L. Wilensky, "Work, Careers, and Social Integration," *International Social Science Journal* 12 (1960), 543–574.

8. Cappelli, "Assessing the Decline of Internal Labor Markets," 2001, 220.

9. Peter Cappelli, *The New Deal at Work, Managing the Market Driven Workforce* (Boston: Harvard Business School Press, 1999), 25. Another reference for this common understanding about the earning world is Douglas T. Hall, *Careers In and Out of the Organizations* (Thousand Oaks, CA: Sage Publications, 2002), 19–21.

10. Spencer G. Niles, Edwin L. Herr, and Paul J. Hartung, "Adult Career Concerns in Contemporary Society," in *Adult Career Development: Concepts, Issues, and Practices,* 3rd edn., ed. Spencer G. Niles, 2–18 (Tulsa, OK: National Career Development Association, 2002), 3.

11. Lawrence M. Fisher, "The Paradox of Charles Handy," *Strategy + Business* (Fall 2003). Accessed at http://strategy-business.com/search/archieves/?issue=23667&x=79&y=6 on 3/25/06.

12. Lester C. Thurow, *The Future of Capitalism, How Today's Economic Forces Shape Tomorrow's World* (New York: Penguin Books, 1996), 22–35, was the first place where I read about how the economic situation of many employees in the United States had been changing since the 1970s. To see the actual figures, look in an edition of *The State of Working America* at a graph of family incomes during this time period. This book is published every two years, but virtually every edition has such a graph.

13. Michael E. Porter, *On Competition* (Boston: Harvard Business School Press, 1998).

14. James Brian Quinn, *Intelligent Enterprise, A Knowledge and Service Based Paradigm for Industry* (New York: MacMillan, 1992), 3–30.

15. Grace Toto and George Monahan (eds.), *Securities Industry Association Fact Book* (New York: Securities Industry Association, 2002), 66. Accessed at http://www.sia.com/research/pdf/2002Fact_Book.pdf on 4/1/06.

16. Henry Mintzberg, Robert Simons, and Kunal Basu, "Beyond Selfishness," *MIT Sloan Management Review* 44, no. 1 (Fall 2002); html full text available at http://www.ebsco.com/. Peter F. Drucker, "Reckoning with the Pension Fund Revolution," *Harvard Business Review* 69, no. 2 (March/April 1991), 106–114; available at http://www.ebsco.com/.

17. Richard Judy and Carol D'Amico, *Workforce 2020: Work and Workers in the 21st Century* (Indianapolis, IN: Hudson Institute, 1997), 35.

18. William J. Baumol, Alan S. Blinder, and Edward N. Wolff, *Downsizing in America, Reality, Causes, and Consequences* (New York: Russell Sage Foundation, 2003). A major finding in this book which is an exhaustive economic analysis of the downsizing phenomenon is that one of the major results of downsizing is labor cost reduction.

19. Louis Uchitelle, "Renewed Corporate Wanderlust Puts a Quite Brake on Salaries," *New York Times,* July 24, 2000, national edition, A1 and A20.

20. Donald D. Davis, "Form, Function, and Strategy in Boundaryless Organizations," in *The Changing Nature of Work,* ed. Anne Howard, (San Francisco: Jossey-Bass, 1995), 112–138.

21. Sarah L. Rynes, Marc O. Orlitzky, and Robert D. Bretz, Jr., "Experienced Hiring Versus College Recruiting: Practices and Emerging Trends," *Personnel Psychology* 50, no. 2 (1997), 309–339.

22. Diane E. Lewis, "Shift of Tech Jobs Abroad Speeding Up, Report Says," *Boston Globe,* December 25, 2002, E1. Available at http://proquest.umi.com/.

23. Thomas L. Friedman, *The World Is Flat: A Brief History of the Twenty-First Century* (New York: Farrar, Straus and Giroux, 2005).

24. Kenneth Labich, "The New Unemployed," *Fortune,* March 8, 1993, 47–48.

25. Matt Richtel and Laurie J. Flynn, "Getting a Job in the Valley Is Easy, If You're Perfect," *New York Times,* November 19, 2003, national edition, 1 and 8.

26. Diane E. Lewis, "Out in the Field: Survey Finds Many Can Relate to Job Loss," *Boston Globe,* August 10, 2003, G2. Available at http://proquest.umi.com/.

27. Cappelli, "Assessing the Decline of Internal Labor Markets," 2001, 212.

28. Henry S. Farber, "What Do We Know About Job Loss in the United States? Evidence from the Displaced Workers Survey, 1984–2004," Working Paper #498, Princeton University Industrial Relations Section, January 5, 2005 version. Available at http://www.irs.princeton.edu/pubs/working_papers.html.

29. Lawrence Mishel, Jared Bernstein, and Heather Boushey, *The State of Working America, 2002/2003* (Ithaca, NY: Cornell University Press, 2003), 5.

30. Lawrence Mishel, Jared Bernstein, and Sylvia Allegretto, *The State of Working America, 2004/2005* (Ithaca, NY: Cornell University Press, 2005), 102.

31. Mishel, Bernstein, and Boushey, *The State of Working America 2002/2003,* 2003, 10.

32. Bruce Nussbaum (with bureau reports), "A Career Survival Kit," *Business Week,* no. 3234 (October 7, 1991). Available at http://www.lexisnexis.com/.

33. National Research Council, *The Changing Nature of Work, Implications for Occupational Analysis* (Washington D.C.: National Academy Press, 1999), 46–47.

34. Patrick P. Murphy and Harman D. Burck, "Career Development of Men at Midlife." *Journal of Vocational Behavior,* 9 (1976), 337–343. Rimantas Vaitenas and Yoash Wiener. "Development, Emotional, and Interest Factors in Voluntary Mid-Career Change." *Journal of Vocational Behavior* 11 (1977), 291–304. Donna V. Bejan and Paul R. Salamone, "Understanding Midlife Renewal: Implications for Counseling," *Career Development Quarterly* 44 (1995), 52–63.

35. While I have made a logical, non-gender-specific argument here, there is also a much richer explanation based on developmental psychology. For an excellent discussion of the developmental psychology of being mid-career and how men and women arrive at the desire for change well into their careers but via very different psychological, social, and biological paths, see: Mainiero, Lisa A. and Sherry E. Sullivan, *The Opt-Out Revolt, Why People Are Leaving Companies to Create Kaleidoscope Careers* (Mountain View, CA: Davies-Black, 2006), 49–51.

36. Quinn, *Intelligent Enterprise,* 1992, 3–30.

37. Stephen R. Barley, *The New World of Work* (London: North American Research, 1996), 11.

38. National Research Council, *The Changing Nature of Work, Implications for Occupational Analysis* (Washington D.C.: National Academy Press, 1999), 4.

2   Four New Strategies for Career Management: The "Employability Plus" Model

1. Eleanor Roosevelt, United Nations diplomat and First Lady (1933–45). This quotation was found at http://en.thinkexist.com/ on 3/21/2006.

2. Peter Cappelli, The *New Deal at Work, Managing the Market-Driven Workforce* (Boston: Harvard Business School Publishing, 1999), 29–30. The term employability was first used with this definition by Rosabeth Moss Kanter in her book *When Giants Learn to Dance, Mastering the Challenges of*

Strategy, Management, and Careers in the 1990s (New York: Simon & Schuster, 1989), 321–26.

3. Ibid.

4. Yehuda Baruch, "Employability: A Substitute for Loyalty?" *Human Resource Development International* 4, no. 4 (2001), 543–66.

5. Throughout this book I will use real life examples of mid-career people whom I have worked with in my part-time MBA classes or other venues and who have taken part in various research studies. The names have always been changed, sometimes gender has been changed, and any details that would identify them have also been disguised to maintain confidentiality.

6. Sharan B. Merriam and Rosemary S. Caffarella, *Learning in Adulthood, A Comprehensive Guide,* 2nd ed. (San Francisco: Jossey-Bass Publishers, 1999), 32.

7. Amy Wrzesniewsky and Janet E. Dutton, "Crafting a Job: Revisioning Employees as Active Crafters of the Work," *Academy of Management Review* 26, no. 2 (2001), 179–201.

8. I have developed my own approach to independent learning and refer to it as "chunking." I got this term from the classic article on human information processing by George A. Miller, "The Magical Number Seven, Plus or Minus Two: Some Limits on Our Capacity for Processing Information," *The Psychological Review* 63 (1956), 81–97. This article argues that during decision making we can "receive, process, and remember" very limited amounts of information. We can handle more information, Miller writes, if we divide or "chunk" large amounts into subunits. For example, we can remember a long string of numbers— 20516701529159—more easily by dividing it into chunks: 205, 167, 01, 529, and 159. Similarly, my approach to long-term or continuous learning is to divide it into smaller chunks. There are a few articles and books in the educational literature on independent learning on the part of adults. For example, Alan Clardy uses the idea of learning projects, which is somewhat similar to my "chunking" concept, in his article, "Learning on Their Own: Vocationally Oriented Self-Directed Learning Projects," *Human Resource Development Quarterly* 11, no. 2 (Summer 2000), 105–25.

9. H. B. Gelatt, "Chaos and Compassion," *Counseling and Values* 39 (1995), 108–16.

10. Herminia Ibarra, *Working Identity, Unconventional Strategies for Reinventing Your Career* (Boston: Harvard Business School Press, 2003) 16.

11. Wayne Casio, "New Workplaces," in Jean M. Kummerow (ed.), *New Directions in Career Planning and the Workplace*, 2nd edn. (Palo Alto, CA: Davies-Black, 2000), 3–32. Edwin Herr, "Toward the Convergence of Career Theory and Practice," in Mark L. Savickas and Bruce W. Walsh

(eds.), *Handbook of Career Counseling Theory and Practice* (Palo Alto, CA: Davies-Black, 1996), 13–36. Lawrence K. Jones, "A Harsh and Challenging World of Work: Implications for Counselors," *Journal of Counseling and Development* 74 (May/June 1996), 453–59. Sherry E. Sullivan, "The Changing Nature of Careers: A Review and Research Agenda," *Journal of Management* 25 (1999), 457–84. A.G. Watts, "Toward a Policy for Lifelong Career Development: A Transatlantic Perspective," *The Career Development Quarterly* 45 (September 1996), 41–53.

3 Success Strategy #1: Articulating a Personalized Work Focus

1. Confucius (551–479 BC) is China's most famous ancient teacher, philosopher, and political theorist. This quotation was found at http://en.thinkexist.com/ on 2/3/2006.
2. Raymond E. Miles and Charles C. Snow, "Twenty-First-Century Careers," in *The Boundaryless Career, A New Employment Principle for a New Organizational Era*, ed. Michael B. Arthur and Denise M. Rousseau (Oxford: Oxford University Press, 1996), 97–115.
3. National Research Council, *The Changing Nature of Work, Implications for Occupational Analysis* (Washington D.C.: National Academy Press, 1999), 4.
4. Michael B. Arthur, Kerr Inkson, and Judith K. Pringle *The New Careers, Individual Action and Economic Change* (London: Sage Publications, 1999). One of the major findings of this major interview study done in the late 1990s was that people "enact" their career, that is, they give their careers their own meaning rather than following the paths specified by organizations or professions. Counseling is also studying this phenomenon; see, for example, Mark L. Savickas, "Career Counseling in the Postmodern Era," *Journal of Cognitive Psychotherapy: An International Quarterly* 7, no. 3 (1993), 205–215.
5. The definition I am using of a career is how an individual perceives the series of jobs or work experiences he or she has. This is very similar to recent definitions of careers by very well known career scholars, Tim Hall and Edgar Schein. Hall, Douglas T., *Careers In and Out of the Organization* (Thousand Oaks, CA: Sage Publications, 2002), 12. Edgar H. Schein, *Career Anchors, Discovering Your Real Values,* revised ed. (San Diego, CA: Pfeiffer, Inc., 1993), 11.
6. The Employability Plus model of career management can be adapted to individuals from various cultures and with varying attitudes about careers and work. This is possible because the model relies so heavily on individuals' personalized decisions about what is interesting or engaging (and why) about their work and their priorities for their larger lives. I am aware of the important work that researchers are doing to increase our

understanding of how cultural differences affect earning careers. Some summary articles on this important topic are: Louise F. Fitzgerald and Nancy E. Betz, "Career Development in Cultural Context: The Role of Gender, Race, Class and Sexual Orientation," in *Convergence in Career Development Theories: Implications for Science and Practice*, ed. Mark L. Savickas and Robert W. Lent (Palo Alto, CA: CPP Books, 1994), 103–117. Nadya A. Fouad and Angela M. Byars-Winston, "Cultural Context of Career Choice: A MetaAnalysis of Race and Ethnic Differences," *Career Development Quarterly* 53, no. 3 (March 2005), 223–233.

7. This is known as being in the "flow." Mihaly Csikszentmihalyi, *Flow: The Psychology of Optimal Experience* (New York: Harper Perennial, 1991).

8. Direct Marketing Association Web site for consumers, http://www.dma consumers.org/, accessed on 6/28/05.

9. *Business Wire: New York*, "The New Retirement Survey from Merrill Lynch Reveals How Baby Boomers Will Transform Retirement," February 22, 2005. Available at http://proquest.com/, accessed on 7/1/05.

10. S. Kathi Brown, Staying Ahead of the Curve 2003, The AARP Working in Retirement Study (Washington, DC: AARP Knowledge Management, 2003) 7, Available at http://research.aarp.org/, accessed on 4/19/06.

11. Po Bronson, *What Should I Do with My Life?* (New York: Random House, 2002).

12. David Whyte, *Crossing the Unknown Sea, Work as a Pilgrimage of Identity* (New York: Riverhead Books, 2001).

13. Frieda Reitman and Joy A. Schneer, "The Promised Path; A Longitudinal Study of Managerial Careers," *Journal of Managerial Psychology* 18, no. 1 (2003), 60–75.

14. Stephen R. Barley, *The New World of Work* (London: North American Research, 1996), 11.

4 Success Strategy #2: Learning about the Near Future of Your Work in the Multiple-Employer Environment

1. Lester C. Thurow, *The Future of Capitalism: How Today's Economic Forces Shape Tomorrow's World* (New York: Penguin Books, 1997), 68.

2. There have been many articles listing erroneous predictions about the future—for example, the famous, although arguably true, statement by Thomas Watson, Sr., considered the founder of IBM, in the 1950s: "I think there will be a world market for about five computers." Here is an example of one of the most recent such articles: Lev Grossman, "Forward Thinking," *Time*, October 11, 2004, 50–58. Available at http://search.epnet.com/.

3. Peter F. Drucker, Esther Dyson, Charles Handy, Paul Saffo, and Peter M. Senge, "Looking Ahead: Implications of the Present," *Harvard Business Review* 75, no. 5 (September-October, 1997), 20–32. Also see Peter F. Drucker, "The Future That Has Already Happened," *Futurist* 32, no. 8 (November 1998), 16–19. Available at http://ebsconet.org.

4. In the academic world, the study of how changes are adopted is known as the study of "the diffusion of innovations" and the best single book on the process is: Everett M. Rogers, *The Diffusion of Innovation,* 4th edn. (New York: Free Press, 1995).

5. Janice Kragness, "Revitalizing the Mid-Career Client's Career Focus: Case Studies." Handout distributed at the Minnesota Career Development Conference, Stillwater, MN, April, 2003.

6. CBS Broadcasting, "Inside the Wide World of Google." Accessed at http://www.cbsnews.com/stories/2004/03/25/sunday/main608672.shtml on 3/31/06.

7. John Schwartz, "E-Signatures Become Valid For Business," *New York Times,* October 2, 2000, national edition, C1 and C6. While I do not know if this is the article that John saw, it was a similar article—perhaps in his local newspaper—in this time period.

5 Success Strategy #3: Taking Action to Shape Your Career

1. Peter F. Drucker, *Management: Tasks, Responsibilities, Practices* (New York: Harper & Row, 1993), 122.

2. Michael M. Lombardo and Robert W. Eichinger, *Eighty-eight Assignments for Development in Place: Enhancing the Developmental Change in Existing Jobs* (Greensboro, NC: Center for Creative Leadership, 1989).

3. Jorgen Sandberg, "Understanding Human Competence at Work: An Interpretative Approach," *Academy of Management Journal* 43, no. 1 (2000), 9–25.

4. David J. Garrow, "Images of a Growing Nation, From Census to Census," *New York Times,* October 13, 2004, Books of the Times series.

5. Robert E. Kelley, *How to Be a Star at Work, Nine Breakthrough Strategies You Need to Succeed* (New York: Times Business, 1999).

6. Ibid, 74–97. This book is very good in its description of the skills and knowledge needed to do well as an organizational employee. What I have done is take the internal skill of networking as described by Kelley and apply it in the multiple-employer, work-oriented career-management context.

7. Lonnie Golden and Deborah Figart, "Doing Something about Long Hours," *Challenge* 43, no. 6 (November/December, 2000), 15–38. Barry Bluestone and Stephen Rose, "The Macroeconomics of Work Time," *Review of Social Economy* 56, no. 4 (Winter 1998), 425–41.

8. Juliet B. Schor, *The Overworked American: The Unexpected Decline of Leisure* (New York: Basic Books, 1991). Leslie A. Perlow, *Finding Time: How Corporations, Individuals, and Families Can Benefit from New Work Practices* (Ithaca, NY: ILR Press, 1997). Jerry A Jacobs and Kathleen Gerson, "Who are the Overworked Americans?" in *Working Time: International Trends, Theory, and Policy Perspectives*, eds. Lonnie Golden and Deborah M. Figart (London: Routledge, 2001), 89–105.

9. "Stalled Hiring and Sustained Overwork Cause Employee Stress Levels to Mushroom," at http://www.compsych.com/jsp/en_US/core/home/pressReleasesList2004.jsp?cid=420#, accessed on 2/1/06.

10. Brent B. Allred, Charles C. Snow, and Raymond E. Miles, "Characteristics of Managerial Careers in the 21st Century," *Academy of Management Executive* 10, no. 4 (1996), 17–27.

11. Michael Treacy and Fred Wiersema, *The Discipline of Market Leaders: Choose Your Customers, Narrow Your Focus, Dominate Your Market* (New York: Perseus Books, 1997). I use this model's three-pronged approach because it is easy to remember and captures three major groupings of organizational business strategies. Note that many organizations have much more detailed strategic approaches, for example, specifying how they are innovative or what about their customer service is important.

12. Amy Wrzesniewski and Jane E. Dutton, "Crafting the Job, Revisioning Employees as Active Crafters of their Work," *Academy of Management Review* 27, no. 2 (April 2001) 179–202.

13. Denise M. Rousseau, *I-Deals: Idiosyncratic Deals Employees Bargain for Themselves*, (New York: M.E. Sharpe, 2005).

14. Peter Cappelli, "Assessing the Decline of the Internal Labor Markets," in *Sourcebook of Labor Markets: Evolving Structures and Processes,* eds. Ivar Berg and Arne L. Kalleberg, (New York: Plenum Publishing, 2001) 230–31.

15. A discussion of managing your finances is beyond the scope of this book, but you need startup costs plus enough money to live on during the startup phase, when it is unlikely that you will be able to draw a salary. Also, you need to guard against risking the financial resources your family needs to live.

16. Herminia Ibarra, *Working Identity, Unconventional Strategies for Reinventing Your Career* (Boston: Harvard Business School Press, 2003), 14–18.

17. National Research Council, *The Changing Nature of Work, Implications for Occupational Analysis* (Washington D.C.: National Academy Press, 1999), 4.

6 Success Strategy #4: Managing Your Career Cycle

1. Michael B. Arthur, Kerr Inkson, and Judith K. Pringle, *The New Careers* (Thousand Oaks, CA: Sage, 1999), 1–2.

2. Career paths have long been recognized as cyclic: Danielle Riverin-Simard, *Phases of Work Life* (Montreal: Meridian Press, 1988). Rene V. Dawis, "The Theory of Work Adjustment and Person-Environment Correspondence in Counseling," in *Career Choice and Development*, 3rd ed., eds. Donald Brown and L. Brooks (San Francisco: Jossey-Bass, 1996), 75–120. Donald E. Super, Mark L. Savickas, and C.M. Super, "The Life-span, Life-space Approach to Careers," in *Career Choice and Development*, 3rd ed., eds. Donald Brown and L. Brooks (San Francisco: Jossey-Bass, 1996), 121–78. Judith Marshall, "Re-visioning Career Concepts: A Feminist Invitation" in *Handbook of Career Theory*, eds. Michael B. Arthur, Douglas T. Hall, and Barbara S. Lawrence (Cambridge: Cambridge University Press, 1989), 275–91.

3. Robert Presthus, *The Organizational Society*, 2nd edn. (New York: St. Martin's Press, 1978).

4. Kerr Inkson in a 2005 featured speech to the National Career Development Association pointed out how at least one human resources textbook had changed its prescription about how individuals and their employers should relate to each other with respect to their careers over the last decade. In the 1995 edition of the text, an individual's career should be "managed by the organization to ensure the efficient allocation of human and capital resources" (p. 310). In the 1998 edition of the same text, the relationship was described differently "the company and the employee are partners in career development" (p. 308). And in 2003 edition of the same text the author wrote: "a career . . . should be shaped and managed more by the individual than by the organization" (p. 373). This is a great example of how the relationship between employers and employees concerning career management has quickly evolved. Wayne F. Cascio, *Managing Human Resources: Productivity, Quality of Life, Profits*, 4th, 5th, and 6th ed. (Boston: McGraw Hill, 1995, 1998, and 2003).

5. Denise Rousseau, *I-Deals: Idiosyncratic Deals Employees Bargain for Themselves* (New York: M. E. Sharpe, 2005).

6. William J. Baumol, Alan S. Blinder, and Edward N. Wolff, *Downsizing in America, Reality, Causes, and Consequences* (New York: Russell Sage Foundation, 2003), 34.

7. Henry S. Farber, "What Do We Know about Job Loss in the United States? Evidence from the Displaced Workers Survey, 1984–2004," Working Paper #498, Princeton University Industrial Relations Section (January 5, 2005), 3. Available at http://www.irs.princeton.edu/pubs/working_papers.html. Of course, it should also be noted that less skilled workers always fare worse in terms of raw numbers; they also make up a much greater portion of the workforce.

8. Douglas Stone, Bruce Patton, Sheila Heen, and Roger Fisher, *Difficult Conversations: How to Discuss What Matters Most* (New York: Penguin,

2000). This is one of many books on the market that help you think through this skill.

9. American Management Association, "AMA Survey on Corporate Downsizing, Job Elimination, and Job Creation: Summary of Key Findings" (New York: American Management Association, 1996). This summary first reported that organizational restructuring in which management simply decides to reorganize was the reason for the majority of downsizings that year. This trend continued into 2001.

10. This is an application of a traditional SWOT (strengths, weaknesses, opportunities, and threats) analysis which is often used by managers. To read more about how that is done, usually with a focus on organizational management, see "SWOT Analysis: Discover New Opportunities and Manage and Eliminate Threats" at http://www.mindtools.com/swot.html.

11. William Safire, "Never Retire," *New York Times*, January 24, 2005, national edition, editorial page.

12. Baumol, Blinder, and Wolff, *Downsizing in America*, 2003.

13. Lawrence Mishel, Jared Bernstein, and Sylvia Allegretto, *The State of Working America, 2004/2005* (Ithaca, NY: Cornell University Press, 2005), 242.

14. Jeffrey Selingo, "The Bell Is Tolling for the Beeper," *New York Times*, April 11, 2002, east coast late edition, G1.

15. William S. Bridges, *Jobshift: How to Prosper in a Workplace without Jobs* (Reading, MA: Addison-Wesley Publishing Company, 1994).

16. Henry Mintzberg, *The Nature of Managerial Work* (New York: Harper & Row, 1973).

7   Epilogue: Changing the Deal

1. *Bartlett's Familiar Quotations,* ed. Justin Kaplan (Boston: Little, Brown & Company, 2002), 783.

2. Peter Cappelli, *The New Deal at Work, Managing the Market Driven Workforce* (Boston: Harvard Business School Press, 1999), 31.

3. Daniel H. Pink, *Free Agent Nation, How America's New Independent Workers Are Transforming the Way We Live* (New York: Warner Business Books, 2001) and Daniel H. Pink, *Free Agent Nation, The Future of Working for Yourself* (New York: Warner Business Books, 2002).

4. Sharon S. McGowan, "The Lure of Autonomy: A Global Study of Professional Workers," sponsored by Hudson Highland Group, 2005, available at http://us.hudson.com/documents/us-hudson-index-autonomy.pdf, accessed on 4/4/06. This study gives a profile of the opinions and challenges of the most successful (as measured primarily by income) independent professionals.

5. This discussion will not go into developing actual negotiation skills, although many may need a brush up on them as well. In the Suggested Readings section of this book, I suggest some resources for those who are interested in this subtopic.

6. Cappelli, *The New Deal at Work*, 232–34. Also see Denise M. Rousseau, *I-Deals: Idiosyncratic Deals Employees Bargain for Themselves* (New York: M.E. Sharp, 2005).

7. Bradford C. Johnson, James M. Manyika, and Lareina A. Yee, "The Next Revolution in Interactions," *The McKinsey Quarterly*, no. 4 (2005), available at http://www.mckinseyquarterly.com, accessed on 4/3/2006. This article highlights the growth in positions with these characteristics throughout developed economies.

Suggested Reading

1. A number of editions of the *The State of Working America* have already been cited. EPI's Web site is a great source for regular information on the economy and jobs: http://www.epinet.org.

2. John W. Duncan and A. C. Gross, *Statistics for the 21st Century: Proposals for Improving Statistics for Better Decision Making* (Chicago: Irwin Professional Publishing, 1995).

3. Lawrence Mishel, "The Economy, the War and Choosing Our Future." Keynote address to the Society of American Business Editors and Writers, Royal Sonesta Hotel, Cambridge, MA (April 27, 2003). Available from the Communications Director of the Economic Policy Institute.

4. Peter Cappelli, *The New Deal at Work, Managing the Market Driven Workforce* (Boston: Harvard School of Business Press, 1999).

5. From approximately the mid-1980s until 2001, the American Management Association (AMA) did an annual staffing survey that was a good general measurement of how the job market was changing. They were available at the association's Web site (http://www.amanet.org). Unfortunately they seem to have discontinued this series of studies after 2001. These reports are no longer available on the Web site, but you could contact the AMA directly. For a comprehensive overview of downsizing in the United States, which includes the AMA data, see William J. Baumol, Alan S. Blinder, and Edward N. Wolff, *Downsizing in America: Reality, Causes, and Consequences* (New York: Russell Sage Foundation, 2003), 1–62.

6. Michael B. Arthur and Denise M. Rousseau (eds.), *The Boundaryless Career, A New Employment Principle for a New Organizational Era* (Oxford: Oxford University Press, 1996), 6.

7. Douglas T. Hall, *The Career Is Dead, Long Live the Career: A Relational Approach to Careers* (San Francisco: Jossey-Bass, 1996) was focused on the subject, but Hall's 2002 book *Careers In and Out of the Organization*

(Thousand Oaks, CA: Sage Publications, 2002) has a particularly clear description of it on pages 23–24.

8. Sally J. Power and Teresa J. Rothausen, "A Work-Oriented Midcareer Development Model: An Extension of Super's Maintenance Stage," *The Counseling Psychologist* 31, no. 2 (March 2003), 157–97.

9. Zella King, "Career Self-Management: A Framework for Guidance of Employed Adults," *British Journal of Guidance and Counseling* 29, no. 1 (2001).

10. William Bridges, *Jobshift: How to Prosper in a Workplace without Jobs* (Reading, MA: Addison-Wesley Publishing Company, 1994).

11. Primary articles that individuals seeking more information on this subject should consult are as follows: Nancy M. Carter, William B. Gartner, Kelly G. Shaver, and Elizabeth J. Gatewood, "The Career Reasons of Nascent Entrepreneurs," *Journal of Business Venturing* 18, no. 1 (January 2003),13–30. Gideon D. Markman, David B. Balkin, and Robert A. Barox, "Inventors and New Venture Formation: The Effects of General Self-Efficacy and Regretful Thinking," *Entrepreneurship: Theory and Practice* 27, no. 2 (Winter 2002), 149–66. Michele O'Dwyer and Ryan Eamon, "Management Development Issues for Owners/Managers of Micro-Enterprises," *Journal of European Industrial Training* 24, no. 6/7 (2000), 345–54. David A. Baucus and Sherrie E. Human, "Second-Career Entrepreneurs: A Multiple Case Study Analysis of Entrepreneurial Processes and Antecedent Variables," *Entrepreneurship: Theory and Practice* 19, no. 2 (Winter 1994), 41–71.

12. Francis J. Aguilar, *Scanning the Business Environment* (New York: McMillan Publishing, 1967).

13. Denis E. Waitley and Robert B. Tucker, "How to Think like an Innovator," *Futurist* 21, no. 2 (May/June 1987), 9–15; available at http://ebsconet.org. Hemant C. Sashittal and Avan R. Jassawalla, "Fast Forwarding Time as the Essence of Managers' Strategic Effectiveness: Learning from Wayne Gretzky," *Organizational Dynamics* 30, no. 4 (2002), 341–55.

14. Michael J. Handel, *Worker Skills and Job Requirements, Is There a Mismatch?* (Washington, D.C.: Economic Policy Institute, 2005).

15. Bradford C. Johnson, James M. Manyika, and Lareina A. Yee, "The Next Revolution in Interactions," *The McKinsey Quarterly, 2005, no. 4*, available at www.mckinseyquarterly.com, accessed on 4/3/2006.

16. Robert E. Kelley, *How to Be a Star at Work, Nine Breakthrough Strategies You Need to Succeed*, (New York: Three Rivers Press, 1999), 67–79.

17. Mind Tools, "Critical Path Analysis and PERT Charts, Planning and Scheduling More Complex Projects," available at http://www.mind tools.com/critpath.html, accessed on 4/1/06.

18. Michael Treacy and Fred Wiersema, *The Discipline of Market Leaders, Choose Your Customers, Narrow Your Focus, Dominate Your Market* (Reading,

MA: Addison-Wesley, 1995). Don Debelak, *Successful Business Models* (Irvine, CA: Entrepreneur Press, 2003). James Bryan Quinn, *Intelligent Enterprise, a Knowledge and Service Based Paradigm for Industry* (New York: Macmillan, Inc., 1992). *Intelligent Enterprise* is also an excellent resource for understanding how companies are supposed to look at the idea of contracting out their work.

19. I will only list a few here to get you started. Michael E. Porter, "What is Strategy?" *Harvard Business Review* 74, no. 6 (November/December 1996) 61–78, available at www.ebsco.com. Kathleen M. Eisenhardt, "Has Strategy Changed?" *MIT Sloan Management Review* 43, no. 2 (Winter, 2002), 88–91. Michael E. Porter, *Competitive Strategy, Techniques for Analyzing Industries and Competitors* (New York: Free Press, 1998).

20. Etienne Wenger, Richard McDermott, and William M. Snyder, *Cultivating Communities of Practice,* (Boston: Harvard Business School Press, 2002). Jean Lave and Etienne Wenger, *Situated Learning: Legitimate Peripheral Participation (New York: Cambridge University Press, 1991).*

21. H. B. Gelatt and Carol Gelatt, *Creative Decision Making, Using Positive Uncertainty,* revised edn. (Boston: Thomson Course Technology, 2003).

22. Stephen R. Covey, *The Seven Habits of Effective People* (New York: Simon and Schuster, 1989), 145–82.

23. Michael Mendel, Steve Hamm, Carol Matlack, Christopher Farrell, and Ann Therese Palmer, "The Real Reasons You're Working So Hard," *Business Week,* No. 3953, October 3, 2005, 60–67. Leslie Perlow, *Finding Time: How Corporations, Individuals, and Families Can Benefit from New Work Practices* (Ithaca, NY: ILR Press, 1997).

24. Jim Loehr and Tony Schwartz, *The Power of Full Engagement, Managing Energy, Not Time, Is the Key to High Performance and Personal Renewal* (New York: Simon and Schuster, (New York: Simon and Schuster, 2003).

25. Roger Fisher and William Ury with Bruce Patton (eds.), *Getting to Yes, Negotiating Agreement Without Giving In* (Boston: Houghton Mifflin Company, 1981).

26. Peter J. Goodman, *Win-Win Career Negotiations: Proven Strategies for Getting What You Want from Your Employer* (New York: Penguin Books, 2002).

Index

References found only in tables, figures, or quotations on a page are indicated by "t," "f," and "q" respectively.

Adoption of changes by employers, 55–56
Analysis paralysis, 82
Aspiring business owners
  career development, 112–113
  competitive edge and career preparation, 77–79
  cycles, 139–140
  library resources, 171–172
  unique challenges, 44–45
Assessment tools, 47

Bridging, xii, 42–43, 71
Builders, xiii, 50–51
  information gathering at the library, 162
  learning about the near future, 61–62, 69, 71
  managing your career cycles, 125, 131, 134
  negotiating employment deals, 149

  taking action to shape your career, 85–86, 95, 102, 107, 115–116
Burnt out individuals, 48
Business executives, 48
Business plan, writing, 113

Cappelli, Peter, 7, 13, 145, 147
Career advice, traditional, 20–21
Career counselors, 45, 47, 138f, 173
Career cycle, 21–23, 118–120, 121f, 129f
Career, definitions of, xi, 3, 47. *See also* Organizational career
Career development: building momentum during, 25, 114
  employees responsibility, 120
  examples, 114–115
  for Maintainers, 133–134
  gathering information for in job interviews, 116

new needs for, 83–86, 99–100
Career management
    evolution of skills needed for,
        21–23
    and identity, 114
    questions about, 143t
    strategies for, 83, 100
    surprises in, 134–137
    techniques for, 142t. *See also*
        Independent career
        management
Career management, levels of
        intensity, 25, 50–52, 118. *See
        also* Builders; Changers;
        Maintainers
Career paths, 1, 3, 6, 10, 115
Career success, xi, 3, 151
Change, pace of, 55–56
    risk related to, 111
Changers, xiii, 51–52
    information gathering at the
        library, 157, 162
    learning about the near future of
        your work, 62, 69, 71
    managing your career cycles,
        125, 126, 131, 134
    negotiating employment deals,
        149
    taking action to shape your
        career, 85, 95, 102, 107–108,
        109, 116. *See also* Bridging
Changes, challenges, and
        controversies, 57, 160
Changing employers
    not encouraged, 111
    questions to guide decision
        about, 133–134. *See also*
        Changing jobs
Changing jobs
    employers' view of, 127
    more frequent, 6. *See also*
        Changing employers
Chunking, xiv, 100–102

connection to planning, 21
    management of, 103–104t
Chunks, 57, 81
    components of, 101t
    example of, 62–69
    experimental nature of, 113
Client/Customer, personalized
        work focus (PWF) centered
        on, information resources
        165–67. *See also* Five aspects
        exercise
Coaches, 138f
    finding, 173
Competition for jobs, 19
    effect on career development, 83
Competitive pressure on
        organizations, 26
Contribution of your work to
        employers, 30–31. *See also* Five
        aspects exercise
Conversation, careers as, 47, 57,
        83–84, 90. *See also* Feedback
Courses and seminars: finding, 171
    and investing in self, 110
    role in mid-career development,
        84
    and win-win opportunities with
        employer, 108
Crafting your job, 20, 109
Criteria for employment rising, 6
Critical path, xiv, 24, 93, 102–106,
        110, 125, 164

Databases, 11, 19, 56, 144, 159–162
    key words for, 60, 63, 160
    using to identify hot topics, 60
Deals. *See* Employment deals;
        Idiosyncratic deals; New deal;
        Psychological contract
Debt, household, 7–8
Denial of employment changes,
        146–147
Difficult people and groups, 126

Disloyalty to employers, 3, 110
Downsizing, 5–6, 7, 22–23
   as career management surprise,
      135–136
   examples of proactive responses
      to, 61–62
   relationship to job performance,
      130
Drucker, Peter F., 55

Education, 11, 95, 149
Emotional challenges, 137–138
Employability, definition of, xii,
   13–14
Employability Plus, definition of,
   xii, 14
Employers
   identifying high potential, 62, 122
   information resources about,
      168–170
   and locale, 72–76
   of choice, 151
   variety of, 40
Employment deal, 145–146. *See also*
      New deal; Psychological
      contract
Employment dynamics, 2–3, 6–8, 18
Entrepreneurs. *See* Aspiring
      business owners
Experience
   connection to resume, 95–99
   crafting the job for, 109
   employer expectations, 43
   role in development, 84

Feedback, 105, 114–115, 126, 128t.
      See also Conversation
Finances, personal, 113, 136. *See also*
      Investing in yourself
Five aspects exercise, 34–38
   to aid in refocusing personalized
      work focus (PWF), 136
Flexibility in careers, 8

Free agents, 146
Function, personalized work focus
      (PWF) centered on, 162–164.
      See also Five aspects exercise

Going back to school. *See* Education
Google, 59

Handy, Charles, 3
Hiring edge, 54, 55, 70, 77, 95
Hot topics, xiii, 60–62, 95, 124
   example of finding, 62–69
   information resources on, 160–161
   and innovations, 112
   networking to learn about, 90–91
   questions about, 74t
   selecting among, 69–71
How to Be a Star at Work, 90
Human potential movement, 9

Identity, personal, 21, 114
Independent career management
   challenges to, 49–50
   and expanded career cycle, 129–31.
      See also Career management
Idiosyncratic deals, 84, 109
Industry, personalized work focus
      (PWF) centered on, 164–165.
      See also Five aspects exercise
Information
   about work at other employers,
      56
   accessibility, 11, 19
   need for more sophistication in
      mid-career, 60
Information gathering
   to combat risk 111
   choosing information sources,
      57–58
   global and local needs, 88
   limits to, 81–82
   maintaining your skills at, 81
   multiple employer focus, 55

on near future of work, 18–20, 54
Innovations in work, 111–112. *See also* Hot topics
Interesting and engaging work, 30, 33–34, 36, 114, 118. *See also* Personalized work focus (PWF)
Interviewing, 121
Investing in yourself, 109–110

Job interviews
    to gather information, 116
    questions for, 123–124
Job loss, individual, 141
Job offers, surprise, 135–136
Job performance
    impact of Employability Plus model on, 124–128
    managing time commitment to, 102–106.
Job redesign, 24
Job search skills, 22–23t, 120–123
Job search time frame, 123–124
Job search websites, 59
Job variety, 30. *See also* Work specialties increasing; Employers, variety of
Jobs vs. work, 30–31
Journaling, 49–50, 76, 130. *See also* Notes, taking

Kelley, Robert R., 90, 92
Key words (for databases), 60, 63, 160

Labor costs, 4
Learning groups, informal, 91–92
Librarians
    questions for, 60, 63, 68, 73–74
    questions from, 157
Librarians, reference, 138t, 154–155
Libraries
    changes in, 11, 19, 56

and networking, 90
    overview of, 154–157
Library vs. Web, 58–59
Life span, increase in, 8–9
Lifetime learning, 137
Locale, 72–73
Loyalty to employers, 3, 110

Maintainers, xiii, 50
    gathering library information, 162
    learning about the near future of the work, 62, 69, 71
    managing your career cycle, 131, 133–134
    negotiating employment deals, 149
    taking action to shape your career, 85–86, 95, 102, 106–107
Mentors, 92
Mid-Career, definition of, viii, xi
Midcourse corrections, 111, 112. *See also* Modifying career aspirations
Midlife crisis, 9
Modifying career aspirations, 89. *See also* Midcourse corrections
Mintzberg, Henry, 137

Near experience, 92, 112
Near future, 18–20
Negotiating employment deals, 109, 124, 135, 146–151
Networking, targeted, 89–94
    aid on the job, 125
    gathering library information for, 170
    helping combat risk, 111–114
    intensive, 122–123
    limitations of old, 58, 60
New deal, 13, 145. *See also* Employment deal; Psychological contract

Newsletter articles, writing, 92, 98t
Norms, 3, 130, 145, 151
Notes, taking, 69, 76, 101t. *See also*
    Journaling

On-the-job learning, description of
    the past, 20
Organizational career, 119
Organizational culture, 126
Organizational success, 126
Overwork, 90–91, 131

Personalized work focus (PWF)
    definition of, xii, 17–18
    developing options for, 38–42
    differences from a job, 30–32
    difficulties with articulating, 45–49
    and intensity levels, 50–52
    personalization of, 33–34
    questions about, 35
    refocusing your, 76, 124, 131–132,
        141–142
    shaping to employers needs, 53
    threshold criteria, 32
Personal management, 97, 99–110
    support for, 137–139. *See also*
        Independent career
        management; Time
        management
Personal time, loss of, 115
Planning, 21, 83–84
Post-World War II, 2–6, 13, 22, 121
Predicting the future, 55
Product development, 83–84
Product/service personalized work
    focus (PWF) centered on, 167.
    See also Five aspects exercise
Psychological contract, 2–3, 6, 13,
    145–146
PWF. *See* Personalized work focus

Quality improvement systems, 5
Questions

connection to chunks, 69
importance of, 57
inexact answers for, 88

Rayonier Inc., 4–5
Reflection, personal
    importance to independent
    career management, 49,
    100–101, 112
    in relation to chunking, 68
    with respect to entire career,
        131–132
Reputation
    in the work, 92, 97, 102,
        106
    on-the-job, 121, 125–126, 128t
Resume, 27, 86, 96–99, 121, 128
Rewards from work, xi, 149
Risks, 7–8, 83q, 109, 110–113
Rousseau, Denise, 109
Rural locale, 72. *See also* Locale

Safire, William, 132
Silverstein, Craig, 59
Skills, knowledge, and experience,
    xiii
    connection to work, 29, 31, 54
    development of, 84, 86, 94
    relation to hot topics, 76–77
Specialization, 39–40, 43
Starter personalized work focus
    (PWF), 30, 31, 32, 47
Success strategies, 12–23
Support, 102, 137–139, 172–173
Surveys, personally conducting,
    122

Tests, 47
Time, loss of personal, 115
Time management, 23–25, 100–106,
    114
Training by employer, 19, 20, 22,
    109

Transitions, career, 118–119, 132
True calling, 47

Value of work. *See* Contribution
Volunteering, 98–99t, 107, 109–111,
    114

Want ads, 121
White-collar workers, why focus on,
    ix
Win-win opportunities for career
    development, 106–109
Website, for the Employability Plus
    model, 27, 139
Web vs. library, 58–59

Web, World Wide
    criteria for assessing quality,
        159–160
    limitations 153
Work, 29–30
    as contribution to employers,
        32–33
    changes, challenges, and
        controversies about, 57
    and identity, 21
    skills and knowledge about, 53q,
        84, 86, 111, 149, 171
Work arena, xii, 40–42, 159
Work specialties increasing, 9–10,
    112

About The Author

SALLY J. POWER is Professor of Management, College of Business, University of St. Thomas, in Minneapolis, where she teaches courses in organizational theory and behavior, business ethics, and career development. She has published many articles in such journals as *The Counseling Psychologist*, *Global Economics Quarterly*, *Teaching Business Ethics*, the *Journal of Business Ethics*, and the *Journal of Psychological Type*, and presents frequently at the conferences of the Academy of Management and National Career Development Association.